Teacher Development

Teacher Development:
A Model from Science Education

Beverley Bell
and
John Gilbert

 Falmer Press

(A member of the Taylor & Francis Group)
London • Washington, D.C.

UK   The Falmer Press, 4 John Street, London WC1N 2ET
USA The Falmer Press, Taylor & Francis Inc., 1900 Frost Road, Suite 101,
Bristol, PA 19007

First published in 1996

**A catalogue record for this book is available from the British
Library**

**Library of Congress Cataloging-in-Publication Data are available on
request**

ISBN 0 7507 0 426 8 cased
ISBN 0 7507 0 427 6 paper

Jacket design by Caroline Archer

Typeset in 10/12 pt Times by
Graphicraft Typesetters Ltd., Hong Kong.

*Printed in Great Britain by Biddles Ltd., Guildford and King's Lynn on
paper which has a specified pH value on final paper manufacture of not
less than 7.5 and is therefore 'acid free'.*

Contents

Acknowledgments

We wish to acknowledge and thank the following people for their help and support in the writing of this book:

- The teachers who were involved in the Learning in Science Project (Teacher Development) who took the risk to change their teaching and to talk so openly and honestly about it.
- The New Zealand Ministry of Education for funding the Learning in Science Project (Teacher Development) and the other Learning in Science Projects over the previous ten years, thus enabling a sustained research programme.
- The Centre for Science, Mathematics and Technology Education Research staff, associate staff and students who have discussed the research findings with us. In particular, we would like to thank Andy Begg, Fred Biddulph, Malcolm Carr, Margaret Carr, Chu Meiying, Wendy Drewery, Mike Forret, Jane Gilbert, Allan Harvey, Hassan Hameed, Alister Jones, Elizabeth McKinley, Vicki Mather, Abdul Muhsin Mohamed, and Pauline Waiti.
- The British Council, and in particular Francis King, for funding our travel so we could meet to work together on the book and the University of Waikato Research Committee for funding the research equipment.

1   Teachers Seeking Teacher Development

Teachers want the best for their students. In particular, they want their students to have the best possible learning opportunities and outcomes. Often in their own time, teachers seek new teaching ideas, new resources and equipment to improve the learning of their students. They seek to improve their teaching skills, their knowledge about the subjects they are teaching, their relationships with the students and their management of the schools in which they work. After completing the initial teacher education required in most societies, teachers continue to learn about teaching and learning throughout their professional lives.

Learning is at the heart of teacher development. This book is about teachers' learning and about responding to the challenges that face the provision of teacher development in today's and tomorrow's world. Teacher development, including the ongoing learning about how to teach and to support student learning, is seen as the key to being a successful teacher.

Whilst different teachers seek different kinds of teacher development within science education today, the professional growth they seek includes responses to such concerns as continuity, progression, differentiation, the inclusive curriculum, assessment, teaching and learning activities, curriculum science that is relevant, meaningful, and useful to the students, and resources to support teaching and learning. All these concerns are united by the teachers' agenda of improving the learning of students. Those concerns, which are related centrally to this book, are now discussed.

Concerns of Teachers

'Continuity' of learning as students move between the different structural sectors of schooling has been an ongoing concern for many teachers. It requires the systematic coordination of the professional activities of the teachers on both sides of the (often) four structural divides: kindergarten–primary, primary–compulsory secondary, compulsory secondary–optional (senior) secondary, and senior secondary–tertiary. It involves the implementation of the official curriculum written for students of 5–17 years in education systems divided on the basis of age. Whilst such a curriculum is a simple concept, at a practical level its implementation is difficult because of the different priorities and tasks of the teachers involved. There are subtle but real differences between many teachers in the various sectors in terms of their professional commitment with respect to the status of the subject-matter taught, the purposes of education, and the natures of teaching and learning.

Such differences may make effective communication awkward initially but teachers are working to enhance continuity. In in-service contexts, some teachers are seeking help with curriculum planning across sectors, visiting each other's classrooms, and sharing professional knowledge in groups representing more than one sector. For example, in-service courses attended by both primary and secondary teachers of science may help primary teachers to learn some science from the secondary teachers and the secondary teachers to learn about teaching and learning approaches from the primary teachers. Likewise, university staff may seek information and assistance from senior secondary teachers of science about what first-year university students have been taught.

'Progression' is another concern for some teachers seeking professional development. Progression with respect to a curriculum is that characteristic which makes steadily greater demands on students and which entails the continuous raising of the requirements laid on students over the duration of their schooling (Department of Education and Science, 1985). It is an issue because of the need to sequence and segment the curriculum in order to manage teaching and learning in current education systems and because of the concern in the community for accountability of teachers. For example, parents may seek evidence that their child is learning more each year and is making progress. Teachers' concerns are focused on what to teach when and on responding to accountability measures of their teaching. Progression is essentially a requirement of a curriculum in response to governments', teachers' and parents' concerns to account for progress in teaching and learning.

Despite the use of the terms such as 'learning objectives', progression in many curricula is more about a progression of teaching than a progression of learning, since the progression usually prescribes what a teacher must teach (in an attempt to achieve the desired learning outcomes). This is because most curricula today are based on a view of learning as transmission of knowledge.

Most approaches to progression involve students learning an increased number of facts or concepts in each year of schooling, adding to those already learnt. The progression indicated in the science curriculum is therefore based on writing a progression of simple to more complex science (for example, learning about the characteristics of living things before learning about the notions of food chains). The assumption is that the simpler concepts are more suitable for learning by younger students. Another approach to progression in science education is based on a kind of historical recapitulation of the sequence of the invention of concepts in a field. Assessment-driven models of progression, such as that one used in the United Kingdom, have a basis in language ('a little' leads to 'some', to 'more' and to 'a lot') rather than in any psychology of learning, and are probably of little practical utility to teachers.

Teachers and curriculum developers with a constructivist view of learning have had difficulty in responding to the perceived need for progression to be articulated in the curriculum (Bell, 1990). Consequently, recent research has begun to explore how children's alternative ideas develop towards the currently accepted scientific ones within conceptual themes (Simon, Black, Brown and Blondel, 1994).

The issue of progression has sharpened for teachers recently with the development of curricula for students aged 5–17, rather than for students of a narrower age groups, say 5–12 or 13–15 years, as was the situation previously (Fensham, 1994). Fensham (1994) suggests that a basis for progression relating to learning outcomes over such a wide age range of students is problematic. He proposes that a more appropriate basis might be the purposes and aims of science education. In other words, the purposes for science education would from the basis and rationale for a progression. Thus, the purpose for learning science for a 5-year-old starting school would be different to that of a student who had been studying science for ten years.

Another concern for which some teachers seek professional development is 'differentiation', or ensuring that the learning expected of a student at a given time is closely geared to the current learning skills and attainment status of that student, and that the prior experiences, knowledge, interests, concerns and values of the student are taken into account in teaching. It includes concerns about students reaching their full potential and concerns about individual differences. The concern to improve differentiation, and hence learning, has arisen for three reasons. First, the 'science for all' basis of many science-education systems requires that all students, including the high and low achievers and students of different genders and cultures, engage and learn in science lessons and that their needs are met. Secondly, teachers have been concerned to find ways to retain students' interest in the study of science. Thirdly, the research into the conceptions that students bring to science lessons has challenged teachers to take students' existing ideas into account in their teaching. The current curriculum statements of many governments seem to assume that differentiation is based only on the pace of learning: alternative goals and routes are poorly recognized.

Postlethwaite (1993) discusses differentiation in terms of students' different educational, psychological, physical, social, socio-economic and cultural circumstances. Educational differences refer to the range of previously acquired knowledge and skills which are relevant to a particular learning task, while psychological differences refer to a collection of traits of varying degrees of plasticity, such as cognitive skills, attitudes to a school subject, students' attitudes to themselves as learners, and their preferred learning styles. Physical differences encompass such physical capabilities as dexterity, mobility, stamina, and the functioning of the senses. For many, these will arise from the different extents of development of students of the same age. For some, differences will be due to long-term physical or sensory handicaps. Social differences in the classroom, although perhaps related to the above categories, are manifest by variations in willingness and capability to interact with the teacher and with other students. Socio-economic and cultural differences refer to the varied expectations that students have of themselves, or which others have of them, which arise from their socio-economic and ethnic background, and their gender.

Research and development in science education over the last decade or so have enabled considerable progress in helping teachers address differentiation in their classrooms. Much of this progress stems from the emergence of a group of science-education researchers with an interest in the study of 'students of science as thinkers', and their findings have been a major reason for teachers seeking professional development. Their research will be examined in greater detail here because it was central to the teacher development work documented in this book.

Of the whole range of students' educational differences, the one which has received the most detailed attention over the last fifteen years or so has concerned the nature of their prior understanding of the concepts which they are being taught in science classes (see Gilbert and Watts, 1983, for a review of the field; and Pfundt and Duit, 1994, for a recent bibliography of research papers), and the consequences of their understanding for teaching and learning. White (1991), in one of the more recent overviews of this field of inquiry, has summed up the general conclusions of the research so far, including:

- people construct their own interpretations of communications and experiences;
- personal interpretation is determined largely by existing beliefs, which are prior constructions;
- interpretation is often influenced, although not necessarily determined, by the interpretations expressed by others — parents, teachers, peers, texts, and other media;
- students at all levels enter the classroom already holding beliefs relevant to the topic to be studied;
- the extent of beliefs and the intensity with which they are held varies from topic to topic;
- in any given class, there will be a range of beliefs among the students;
- students' beliefs about scientific principles and natural phenomena often differ from the scientists' established beliefs;
- where students' views differ from those of the scientists, they are less economical in interpreting or predicting outcomes of an extended range of events;
- a person can hold beliefs that contradict each other, applying one belief in one context, another belief in another context;
- people often interpret events in a manner that supports a belief, and so avoid confronting discomforting instances. That is, they see what they believe;
- people might alter their memory of an event that contradicts a belief so that their recollection is consistent with what they believe;
- beliefs resist change but students can exchange an alternative conception for the scientists' conception;
- changes of belief, or resolution of contradictions, are usually slow and require repeated experiences that favour the final accepted interpretation; and
- teaching that encourages resolution of (the contradiction between) alternative conceptions with the scientists' view will include elucidation of the students' beliefs, discussion of the beliefs and their implications, and the design and execution of events that test the accuracy of the beliefs.

Through research and development, there has been wide exploration of teaching strategies to bring about conceptual development in science at school level, given the differentiation in students' cognition. Scott, Asoko and Driver (1991) distinguish between those teaching strategies which are based on cognitive conflict and those that are based on the development of the students' existing ideas. An essential characteristic of the conflict approaches is the replacement of the alternative, prior understanding with the scientific conception. A four-stage model incorporating the broad notion of cognitive conflict was proposed by Posner, Strike, Hewson and Gertzog (1982) and has been widely adopted. They argue that concepts are changed or replaced only if a student of science, to some extent in sequence:

- becomes dissatisfied with an existing concept. This arises when it is used to make a prediction which is either incompatible with other existing evidence or which proves unsatisfactory when tested;
- understands another concept, which is therefore available for use;
- finds the new concept plausible, in that it seems to present an opportunity to propose more acceptable predictions and to explain events when they are tested;
- finds the new concept fruitful, in that it can explain a range of analogous or otherwise similar events.

Further teaching approaches and sequences of teaching and learning activities based on a conflict notion are documented in Nussbaum and Novick (1982), Stavy and Berkovitz (1980) and Cosgrove, Osborne and Forret (1989).

Teaching approaches based on conceptual development are characterized by the development of the scientific concept in relation to the alternative conception. This approach recognizes that many alternative conceptions are also everyday concepts and understandings which the students may still have to use in some contexts. Examples of teaching approaches which have a developmental basis are Biddulph and Osborne (1984), Solomon (1983), Driver (1988) and Bell (1993c, 1994a). All the teaching approaches, whether their focus is conceptual replacement or development, require the teachers to differentiate between their students on the basis of conceptual understanding and the intervention required for learning.

Another aspect of some teachers' and science educators' concerns regarding differentiation is addressing the learning and educational needs of both girls and boys, and all ethnic groups to ensure their continued participation and success in learning science. Also of concern to many teachers now is that New Right governments, such as those in power in New Zealand and the United Kingdom, are attempting to move discussion and action in respect of such matters from the public to the private domain. If this shift is legitimated, gender and ethnic concerns would be deemed to be outside the professional duties of teachers (Epstein, 1993).

Gender differences in science education were highlighted by research and development in the 1980s (Kelly, 1981; Harding, 1983; Smail, 1984; Whyte, 1985). The case was made for considering girls as a group distinct from boys to highlight the under-representation of girls and women in science and science education.

Teacher development during that time consisted largely of implementing a 'girl friendly' curriculum in the classroom, in which the prior experiences, interests and concerns of girls were the focus of teaching and learning activities. As a political strategy for change, this approach highlighted concerns to be attended to as an area for research and development. Jane Gilbert (1994a) points out, in a discussion of the treatment of gender issues in the New Zealand science curriculum, that differentiation in this context is problematic and in need of further theorizing:

> The strategy of establishing a specific identity for girls has only been partially successful in creating a political space within which claims to equality can be made. Part of the establishment of an identity involves, on the one hand, the selection of certain features which are defined as being part of the essence of 'girlness'. Immediately the identity 'girl' is created, it begins to solidify, allowing the attributes that define it to begin to adhere permanently in a way that starts to seem 'natural'. On the other hand, the establishment of an identity also involves the suppression of features that are *not* defined as essential to 'girlness', thus leaving no basis for claims to the human rights of equality, justice, and so on. (Gilbert, 1994a pp. 35–6)

The influence that a student's culture and language has on learning, over the last decade or so, has been increasingly recognized in science education, with debates arising on indigenous science education, multicultural and bicultural science education and anti-racist science education. Thus, the scope of the issue has been spelt out (Atwater and Riley, 1993), past and future research and development in the area discussed (McKinley, McPherson Waiti and Bell, 1992) and specific case studies produced (for example, Rakow and Bermudez, 1993). Prescriptions for action, both in outline (Hodson, 1993) and in more detail (Reiss, 1993), have appeared, as have handbooks for teachers (e.g., Thorp, Deshpande, and Edwards, 1994). As with gender, teachers are distinguishing between students to take into account cultural differences while also treating the students as having similar educational needs to implement an inclusive and 'science for all' curriculum.

In addition to the areas of continuity, progression and differentiation, another area of interest for some teachers seeking professional development is increasing and updating *subject knowledge*, and preparing the subject knowledge for teaching and learning activities. Shulman (1987) has identified seven knowledge bases from which teachers draw during their teaching:

- **Content knowledge**. This is the teacher's understanding of the substantive structure of the subject, that is, of the basic concepts which delineate the subject, and the ways in which they are related. It is also the teacher's understanding of the syntactical structure of the subject, that is, of the ways in which its truths are established through the inter-relationships within that structure.
- **General pedagogical knowledge**. This encompasses the broad principles

on which the conduct of teaching is based, for example, approaches to classroom management.

- **Curriculum knowledge**. This is a knowledge of the official curriculum, the particular examination prescriptions, the school curriculum, and the materials, for example, textbooks, which are used in teaching.
- **Pedagogical-content knowledge**. This is the form that content knowledge takes in order that it can be effectively taught; for example, explanations that can be legitimately given, examples and illustrations that can be used to good effect.
- **Knowledge of the characteristics of the learners**. Of particular importance are what Postlethwaite (1993) calls the educational differences between the learners as outlined above with reference to differentiation.
- **Knowledge of educational contexts**. This broad category includes knowledge about the potential of different forms of classroom management, knowledge about the school as an institution, and an appreciation of the culture of community from which students are drawn; and
- **Knowledge of educational goals and values** and of the philosophies and historical precedents on which they draw.

For Shulman (1987), any act of teaching is cyclic. To start with, a teacher must comprehend the material to be taught, that is, grasp the relevant content knowledge. This must then be transformed, by the use of pedagogical-content knowledge, into a form in which it can be taught. The actual teaching, what Shulman (1987) calls instruction, then takes place, accompanied and followed by an evaluation of the effectiveness of that instruction in fostering student learning. The teacher then reflects on the significance of that evaluation for teaching when the particular cycle is entered again.

In recent years, the crucial importance of the comprehension and transformation elements of this cycle has been recognized in science education, as it has elsewhere in the school curriculum. The substantial inclusion of science in the primary-school curriculum and the increasing emphasis on science as a whole, rather than on the separate sciences of biology, chemistry and physics, in secondary schools, have shown up the weaknesses in pre- and in-service teacher development programmes in these regards. For example, Kruger, Summers and Palacio (1990) have shown that primary teachers' comprehension of key science concepts is often inadequate. This conclusion is reinforced by Carré (1993), who also drew attention to accompanying weaknesses in the grasp of the philosophy and methodology of science. The comprehension of content demanded as a precursor to teaching any age group is substantial. Anderson (1989) has shown that it consists not only of the structure of the knowledge (the concepts and their inter-relationships), but also its functions (what questions it enables to be answered), and its development (how that knowledge developed both historically and in learners). The transformation of a particular section of content knowledge requires, in addition, preparation (the selection of materials for use in instruction), representation (the consideration of how key ideas might best be presented), instructional selection (the use of an appropriate teaching method) and adaptation (the provision of appropriate differentiation) (Shulman, 1987).

Teachers themselves, then, have developed and sustained their own agendas for professional development, which emphasize a range of concerns including the ability to provide for continuity, progression, differentiation, an inclusive curriculum and different subject-knowledge bases. The teachers' agendas may be a part of, or in addition to, the agenda which governments have for teacher development, for example, the implementation of new summative assessment and reporting.

Concerns about Teacher Development

Teacher development (and teaching) faces a daunting array of challenges. As already mentioned, some of the challenges stem from the teachers themselves, who are concerned to provide a more effective education for all that is currently available. They seek professional development in order to help all their students, and particularly those from social groups who currently seem to be underachieving, to make more progress in students' learning over the years of compulsory schooling and to persist with education and training into adulthood. Other challenges derive from the parents and guardians, who are concerned that the young people in their families are prepared more effectively for adult life, in a world of increasing social turbulence, particularly in terms of being able to get, hold, and exchange waged employment. Further challenges arise from people in government who declare that they want to improve national economic performance by increasing overall educational achievement. No doubt students themselves would wish to assert their own agendas: unfortunately few societies afford them any significant formal voice. There are thus many demands on teachers to 'improve' their teaching.

These challenges for teachers, teaching and teacher development, which are publicly declared from at least three different sources, seem compatible in theory. Yet it has become very evident that they are not compatible in practice in many countries. Governments, having control of law and resources, are taking greater control of the detail of education. Teachers are consequently expected to follow avenues of activity which they cannot reconcile with their own everyday experience of teaching, their projections of the future of education, or with the increasingly incisive findings of research.

To varying degrees, governments provide funding for teacher development to implement new government policies, such as new curricula, new directions arising from recent government-funded research findings and new developments in classroom activities, for example, in the assessment of learning. But many in the bureaucracy and government see teacher development as problematic, with respect to the time taken to bring about change, the low proportion of teachers who engage with the requested changes, the funding implications of universal teacher development, the failure to effect discernible change in learning outcomes, and the lack of career incentives to entice change. One of the most educationally damaging aspects of the changes currently being pushed through in the United Kingdom is the Government's assumption that their legislation is coterminous with its imple-mentation. Resources for curriculum development are being progressively with-drawn in many countries (notably the United Kingdom) and teachers are thrown back on their own resources, to be deployed in 'after-school hours' for in-service work. The likelihood of real, sustained development can seem remote.

School management also express concerns about teacher development. It may be seen as problematic in terms of: dealing with parental concern over the disruption to teaching provision caused when teachers are away during school time; finding quality replacement teachers; focusing on specific areas for teacher development, for example, new teaching approaches, without considering the implications for the other aspects of their professional work, such as assessment; the need for integ-rated programmes of development rather than matching staff to courses on offer; the resource implications of requests for change that may result from teacher devel-opment; those teachers who are non-attenders and the non-engaged in teacher-development activities; and the disruption caused by career movements through promotion.

Teachers themselves, as a group, also have concerns about their professional development. Often on their own initiative, in their own time, at their own expense and with a commitment to professional development (Wylie, 1992, p. 128), they attend teacher-only days, subject association meetings, conferences, and in-service courses, study for university qualifications, talk with other teachers or read profes-sional articles to get new ideas for teaching science to students. But many teachers, even after attending an in-service course, for example, feel unable to use the new teaching activities, curriculum materials or content knowledge to improve the learning of their students. Unfortunately, it is common for teachers to find themselves teach-ing in the same way they always have, perhaps utilizing some of the new materials but adapting them to fit traditional patterns (Briscoe, 1991). Many teachers are aware of this pattern and feel frustrated in their attempts to change. This frustration may lead some teachers to develop a cynical view of new initiatives and to hold back from further professional development. They may even leave the teaching profes-sion. Teachers also express concerns about: feelings of powerlessness of being told what to do (for example, some curricula are prescribed to a high level of detail, with no room being left for professional decision making); the demands made on their 'own' time to undertake the development activities, which may imply that such activities are not valued by the school; perceived lack of resources to support the change; the fatigue from attending too many meetings; the lack of encouragement for and valuing of innovation in the classroom; and not seeing how an innovation can be actually implemented in the classroom, that is, what they have to do differently.

These experiences and concerns lead many associated with education to ask the questions:

- What is the nature of teacher development?
- What factors help and hinder teacher development?
- What model of teacher development can be used to plan teacher develop-ment programmes and activities?

9

- What teacher development activities promote growth?
- Why are some teacher development experiences so frustrating for teachers who want to change?
- Why does the change process occur over a longer rather than shorter time span?
- Why do some innovative teachers want to move away from classroom teaching?

Learning in Science Project (Teacher Development)

This book addresses these questions and reports the findings of a research project which focused on the teacher development process and, in particular, those factors that help or hinder teacher development. The Learning in Science Project (Teacher Development) was a three-year research project carried out at the University of Waikato, funded by the New Zealand Ministry of Education. It investigated the development of some New Zealand teachers of science as they learnt new teaching activities that enabled them to take into account students' thinking (Bell, 1993a, b) as researched by the previous Learning in Science Projects (Tasker, Freyberg and Osborne, 1982; Osborne and Biddulph, 1985; and Kirkwood and Carr, 1988). Over the last fifteen years, much of the international research into students' learning in science has been based around the notions of children's science, constructivist views of learning and conceptual development (Osborne and Wittrock, 1985). This research has been summarized and reviewed extensively (Gilbert and Watts, 1983; Osborne and Freyberg, 1985; White, 1988; Driver, 1989; Northfield and Symington, 1991); and critiqued by Millar (1989), Osborne (1993), and Solomon (1994).

One of the main implications of this large body of research is the changed roles and activities of the teacher in the science classroom (Osborne, Bell and Gilbert, 1983; Biddulph and Osborne, 1984; Cosgrove and Osborne, 1985; Hewson and Hewson, 1988; Scott, Asoko, and Driver, 1991; Fensham, Gunstone and White, 1994). Essentially, the teacher of science is challenged to change her or his teaching from being predominantly a process of transmitting a body of scientific knowledge to being a process of helping the students to develop the currently scientifically accepted concepts, taking into account the students' existing ideas. Rather than regarding the students as empty vessels waiting to be filled up with the scientific knowledge, the teachers are challenged to consider the students' thinking and to facilitate the students' conceptual development.

The teachers who took part in this project, in accepting the invitation to be involved in the research, also accepted that they were expected to use new teaching activities based on this research and on a constructivist view of learning. Teaching based on a constructivist view of learning, is defined here as teaching that takes into account students' thinking and in particular involves:

- finding out the ideas, opinions, interests, concerns, and experiences that students bring to a lesson;

- encouraging the students to think about their own prior ideas and (new) scientific ideas;
- finding out what meanings the students are constructing during the lesson;
- presenting and explaining the scientific ideas using a variety of resources (including the teacher);
- responding to, and interacting with, the students' thinking;
- helping students ask questions, find answers to their questions and to investigate and test out their own ideas;
- initially teaching science in contexts that are familiar and of interest to students;
- helping the students to reflect on their own learning, in terms of both the degree of understanding of the content and ways of thinking and learning; and
- assessing the change and growth in students' ideas, as well as the extent to which they had learnt the scientific ideas.

This list does not cover exhaustively teachers' activities but is given to convey a sense of the emphasis of teaching based on a constructivist view of learning. Essentially, the teachers are first creating the opportunities to enter into a meaningful dialogue with the students and then making use of those opportunities to interact with the students' thinking. The teachers in this research changed their teaching activities and roles to achieve the first step but found it harder to change to implement the second (Pearson and Bell, 1993).

The forty-eight teachers, who volunteered to take part in the teacher development programmes run as part of the research were primary and secondary teachers, women and men, assistant teachers and heads of departments, and beginning and experienced teachers. Four teacher development programmes were run as part of the research project. In 1990, two programmes were run — a school-based and a locally-based one. In 1991, the teachers from both programmes run in the previous year were involved in another locally based programme. In 1992, a new group of teachers was invited to be involved in the research and a second school-based programme was run.

The programmes consisted of two-hour weekly meetings, in after-school time, over one or two school terms. Involvement in the programmes did not give the participants any credit towards a qualification. The meetings were made up of sharing sessions — in which the teachers shared, through the use of anecdotes, the new teaching activities they had been trying out in their classrooms — and workshop activities on various aspects of science and science education. These aspects covered, for example, views of teaching and learning, teaching approaches based on a constructivist view of learning — the interactive teaching approach and the generative teaching approach, gender issues in learning science, current assessment debates, and the then newly proposed changes to the national curriculum. The workshop activities themselves included keeping a journal, modelling the suggested classroom teaching activities, discussion activities to clarify and share thinking on issues in science education and readings on aspects of science education. The programmes also consisted of a small number of classroom visits made by the teachers to the classrooms of other teachers — the facilitator made no classroom visits due to time constraints. Using a constructivist view of students' learning, a constructivist view of teachers' learning was developed to underpin the programmes. The final programme developed over the three years of the research can be found in Bell (1993b).

The research was mainly qualitative, interpretive collaborative, reciprocal, and guided by the ethics of care. Multiple data-collection techniques were used, including interviews, surveys and classroom observations (Bell, 1993a, p. 41). The teacher-development activities were largely separate from the research activities of the date collection and discussions of the draft research reports. However, it is acknowledged that the research activities did promote reflection by the teachers over and above that which was facilitated in the programme. The data reported in this book are illustrative rather than representative given the constraints it space. Readers are referred to Bell (1993a) for a fuller documentation of data.

The teacher development programme run as part of the research was developed over the three years of the research in response to data collected. The aims of the 1992 and final programme conveyed to the participants as follows:

1   Develop your ideas of what teacher development is and to adopt roles for the teacher of:
    • teacher as learner;
    • teacher as researcher;
    • teaching as reflecting; and
    • teaching as supporting.
2   Develop your classroom practice to take into account students' thinking and in particular, to adopt the roles for the teacher in the classroom:
    • teaching as finding out what the students are thinking;
    • teaching as getting the students thinking;
    • teaching as responding to, and interacting with, students' thinking;
    • teaching as managing for learning;
    • teaching as assessing; and
    • teaching as power on, off, with, for.
3   Learn about the research findings as to how students learn science.
4   Develop a constructivist view of learning, and consider its implications for teaching.
5   Attend to and manage the feelings associated with being a teacher of science and with the process of change.
6   Work with other teachers in collaborative and collegial ways. (Bell, 1993b, p. 9).

While the research was conducted in the context of science education, the findings and the discussion of them in this book will be of interest to educators working in other subject areas and in primary schools. We therefore, discuss teacher development in general — it being very clear that these insights were derived from the context of science education alone. The book is addressed to those involved in teacher development activities, whether as policy makers, managers, teacher developers, or as participants. The focus of the book is on teaching, teachers and teacher education in state-school systems; that is, on the teaching provided for the great majority of students. Teachers, in a modern society, are those who spend much or all of their time, often for the whole of their working lives, on the complex activity of teaching.

The Theme of the Book

The theme of the book and our main argument is that teaching, while supposedly an individual activity, is practised in a public arena and is a social activity governed by rules and norms, however tightly or loosely defined. We argue that teachers' learning and teacher development is also a social activity and may be theorized in terms of social cognition and the social construction of knowledge. Teachers' learning may be seen from a social constructivist perspective. Social interactions are a key part of the learning process:

> Social exchanges are continuous and essential bases for advances in individuals' ways of thinking and acting. Communication and shared problem solving inherently bridge the gaps between old and new knowledge, and between partners' differing understanding of the values and tools of the culture, which itself is revised and recreated as they seek a common ground of shared understanding. (Hennessy, 1993, p. 15)

Hence, we argue that teacher development can be seen as a form of human development, involving social as well as the professional and personal development which has been previously documented in the literature. Social development as part of teacher development involves the renegotiation and reconstruction of what it means to be a teacher (of science, for example). It also involves the development of ways of working with others that will enable the kinds of social interaction necessary for renegotiating and reconstructing what it means to be a teacher of science. Personal development as part of teacher development involves each individual teacher constructing, evaluating and accepting or rejecting for herself or himself the new socially constructed knowledge about what it means to be a teacher (of science, for example), and managing the feelings associated with changing their activities and beliefs about science education, particularly when they go 'against the grain' (Cochran-Smith, 1991) of the current or proposed socially constructed and accepted knowledge. Professional development as a part of teacher development involves not only the use of different teaching activities but also the development of the beliefs and conceptions underlying the activities. It may also involve learning some science.

We argue that teacher-development programmes and activities must address and support all three aspects of development for change to occur. Moreover, the social development is crucial if personal and professional development are to happen. Hence, teacher development can only be effective if several roles entailed in being a teacher are addressed; for example, teacher as a facilitator of learning in the classroom, as member of a school staff, as a member of a professional community and as an employee. Most importantly of all, because teachers bear the ultimate responsibility for teaching, their centrality in the social construction of knowledge about teaching must be recognized.

This theme and main argument is developed in the book in the following way. In this chapter, the concerns of teachers seeking professional development have been outlined, as have their frustrations over wanting to change but not always achieving it. It is argued in the remainder of the book that this frustration occurs because the social dimension of teachers' learning is overlooked in policy makers' and educators' views of teacher development. It is not just an individual teacher who must achieve that change; the social construction of what it means to be a teacher of science must be reconstructed and renegotiated as well, with teachers having the central role in the process and outcome.

In Chapter 2 the descriptive model of teacher development arising from the three-year research project is outlined. The key aspects of professional, personal and social development are elaborated. In Chapter 3, we propose our own view of learning, a social constructivist view, as it relates to teacher development. Chapters 4 to 7 document, with the aid of illustrative data, the factors that helped the development of the teachers in the research project: 'feeling better about myself as a teacher', 'better learning', support, feedback and reflection, knowing about the change process and the use of anecdotes. In Chapter 8, we discuss the wider social influences on teaching and teacher development today: the New Right political movement and the post-modern world. These two major social frameworks may make reconstructing what it means to be a teacher of science problematic for teachers. The challenges of the educational contexts of teacher development are also discussed. The final chapter provides the challenges of the new model to policy makers, school management, teacher developers and teachers.

Lastly, we acknowledge that our voices as researchers are dominant in this book. The quotations in the book give samples of the teachers' voices we listened to and from which we have constructed our view of teacher development.

2 A Model for Achieving Teacher Development

The learning of the teachers involved in the research project, the Learning in Science Project (Teacher Development), is analysed in this chapter. The data were analysed to give an overview of the adult learning process as it relates to the teachers' learning or teacher development in the study. The model, based on an earlier version (Bell and Gilbert, 1994) has three central features. First, it is possible to describe three main types of development for the teachers involved in the research — social, personal and professional development. Social development as part of teacher development involves the renegotiation and reconstruction of what it means to be a teacher (of science, for example). It also involves the development of ways of working with others that will enable the kinds of social interaction necessary for renegotiating and reconstructing what it means to be a teacher of science. Personal development as part of teacher development involves each individual teacher constructing, evaluating and accepting or rejecting for himself or herself the new socially constructed knowledge about what it means to be a teacher (of science, for example), and managing the feelings associated with changing their activities and beliefs about science education, particularly when they go 'against the grain' (Cochran-Smith, 1991) of the current or proposed socially constructed and accepted knowledge. Professional development as a part of teacher development involves not only the use of different teaching activities but also the development of the beliefs and conceptions underlying the activities. It may also involve learning some science.

Secondly, the teachers' development was occurring within the context of the effective components of a teacher-development programme. These effective components were support, feedback, and reflection (see Chapter 5 for further details) and not an overall specified programme such as the particular in-service programme run in any one year of the research. The data are being reported to describe the learning process of the teachers, not a particular programme.

Thirdly, there is a loose and flexible sequence implied in the model which describes the main aspects of learning for each teacher with respect to time. Different situations (confirmation and desiring change, reconstruction and empowerment) are described only to highlight facets of the teacher development process. These situations are not intended to be discrete. There is much interaction between the learning tasks in each type and each situation, and the teachers' learning activities may not indicate a movement 'forward'. For example, the teachers throughout their learning continued to clarify the problematic nature of their teaching. It was not something carried out just at the beginning of the programme.

The Model

The model is described and explained with respect to the teacher development that occurred as part of the research. The quotations given are to illustrate the overview only. Full details of the data and data analysis are given in Bell (1993a). A diagrammatic representation of the model is given in Figure 2.1.

Initial Personal Development

As part of this initial personal development, a teacher was aware, however inchoately, and accepting of a professional dissatisfaction or problem. This aspect of

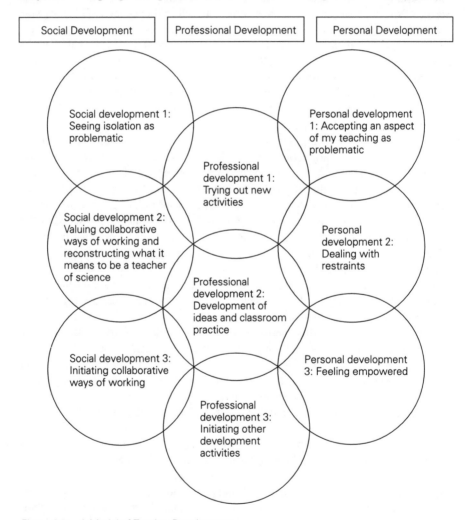

| Social Development | Professional Development | Personal Development |

Social development 1: Seeing isolation as problematic

Personal development 1: Accepting an aspect of my teaching as problematic

Professional development 1: Trying out new activities

Social development 2: Valuing collaborative ways of working and reconstructing what it means to be a teacher of science

Personal development 2: Dealing with restraints

Professional development 2: Development of ideas and classroom practice

Social development 3: Initiating collaborative ways of working

Personal development 3: Feeling empowered

Professional development 3: Initiating other development activities

Figure 2.1: A Model of Teacher Development

development was usually private, having been self-initiated and sustained before the teacher engaged with the teacher development on offer. For example, one teacher commented on her reasons for joining the programme:

> Because I wasn't happy with how I was presenting things. The kids were getting good marks. But I wasn't happy, I just didn't like it, I wasn't getting to every kid in the class, you could see their eyes glazing over . . . So I was looking for something new and I didn't really know what I was looking for. I wanted a new approach to the same stuff but I wanted to be able to present it in a different way that was going to break through those barriers. (11/I2/91)

Another teacher commented that her reasons for joining the programme were:

> . . . the kids were obviously not responding to what I was doing very much. They were sitting there being very lethargic and it was coming from me and not from them. And they were sort of sponges, I suppose, and really didn't see where they were going or any relevance. (1/I3/90)

> [The first part of the transcript code indicates the teacher who is quoted; the second part indicates the interview (I), survey (S), programme session (P) or meeting (M) in which that comment was made; and the last part indicates the year.]

Prior to the teacher development programme, the teachers had decided that the broad type of activity offered might help overcome the dissatisfaction or problem, and the risk of joining the group and the programme had been taken. The dissatisfaction may have been with the learning of students in the classroom, not feeling competent or confident to implement the new curriculum, or feeling stagnant with respect to their own growth and learning. Hence, the teachers saw the development activities as providing opportunities for their self-initiated growth, overcoming a professional problem, exploring an interesting avenue or helping implement new policy.

In deciding to take the risk of publicly acknowledging the need for improvement or help with changing, the teacher had considered the broad content of the activity, the credibility of the facilitator and, for some teachers who knew each other already, the other group members. The teachers entering the teacher development activities associated with the research project, were seeking new teaching suggestions that work, new theoretical perspectives with which to think about their teaching, to improve the learning in their classrooms, to feel better about themselves as a teacher, and to learn how to put new ideas into action. This personal development may have been as a result of school-development discussions and initiatives or as a result of the individual teacher's deliberations. It involved the clarification and awareness of the problem rather than an experience of being 'wound up' over possible problems.

A few of the teachers who joined the teacher development programme (as 'volunteers') had not undergone the personal development as described above. Therefore, whilst they attended the programme at the onset, they were not necessarily engaged in the learning, change and development initially. They may have been nominated for the programme by the school management, rather than the initiative coming from them; they may have gone along with peer pressure, for example when the rest of the science department volunteered and they didn't want to be on the outside of the group; or they may have joined the programme to enhance their CV for promotion rather than to improve learning in their classrooms.

In these instances the individual personal development had not occurred before the programme commenced and their personal development needs had to be addressed within the programme, by both the facilitator and the other teachers. This usually involved helping the teachers to value their overall teaching competence, and to view only one aspect, that which was the focus of the programme, as problematic. No progress was made until this personal development was undertaken.

Initial Social Development

Before joining a teacher development programme, the teachers were also aware that their isolation in the classroom was problematic. While being the only adult in a classroom can feel safe from negative criticisms and pressures to change, it does not provide the new ideas, support and feedback necessary for teacher development (Hargreaves, 1992). In addition, while joining a teacher development programme involved taking some risks, the expected benefits of working with other teachers to improve teaching and learning were perceived as greater. The teachers who engaged with the teacher development programme were to varying degrees seeking to work with other teachers:

> I didn't have another teacher in my school that was on the course which was perhaps a disadvantage, looking back on it, and so I tended to use other people at our weekly sessions in that respect to give me confidence because I found it was really quite scary to leave your textbooks behind, to leave your dictatorship from the front behind, to risk having chaos in your classroom, to try something new. So I found the weekly sessions really quite good and the discussions. (11/ M1/90)

> Certainly the big group situation, listening to other teachers, other practising teachers — that was a big plus, to hear how other teachers coped with certain circumstances, to hear that other teachers had the same sorts of difficulties and what they had tried and what successes and failures they have had. But they certainly had more credibility for me than reading it in a book. (7/I5/91)

The opportunities to discuss their teaching with other teachers and to collectively renegotiate what it means to be a teacher of science were seen positively and as helpful for change.

Initial Professional Development

The teachers appreciated clarifying the problematic aspect of their teaching. But while they appreciated clarifying an aspect that is problematic, they also needed to feel that their teaching overall was not problematic. The facilitator helped by communicating that they were perceived as competent teachers who were developing, rather than as teachers who were struggling. Valuing their ideas about teaching, by giving time in the sessions for them to talk about what they were doing in the classroom, was part of this communication. It would appear that aspects of the initial personal development still needed to be addressed in the programme sessions.

The teachers were also encouraged to adopt the role of teacher-as-researcher. They valued finding out more information from their students and about their teaching; for example, what views of floating and sinking the students had and how many times in a lesson they asked the girls and the boys to answer their questions. This additional information helped them to clarify the problem they may have perceived in their teaching.

The teachers were also asked to adopt the role of teacher-as-learner so that they viewed their professional development as learning rather than as a remedial process. A supportive atmosphere helped to ease the uncomfortable feelings associated with learning — feeling incompetent or inadequate — and the uncomfortableness of getting in touch with feelings associated with prior experiences and beliefs. Part of the programme was given to enabling the teachers to learn about the change process. Gaining this metacognition was supportive in that it helped the teachers to understand what was happening for them.

From the beginning of the programme, the teachers were given new teaching activities to use in the classroom, with the expectation that they would use the activities when they felt ready, and that they would have an opportunity to talk about their use of them in a sharing session. Using the new activities required prior planning, visualizing what it might be like to use the activity, preparation of new resources and being convinced that the new activity was needed and would work. The activities were small in scope — an activity not a unit of work or whole teaching sequence; were short in duration, for example, ten to thirty minutes in length; could be done with a wide range of students, for example, across age and attainment groups; were not part of the official teaching and therefore could be done with a small group of students, rather than the whole class; and involved a change of teacher and student performance.

Another important feature of the new teaching activities was that they were seen as likely to lead to better learning conditions, to better classroom management, to 'feeling better about myself as a teacher', and to better learning outcomes (Bell, 1993a, pp. 154–214). The new activities could be understood, talked about with colleagues, and reflected on. However, the activities were also able to be used by the teachers as technicians and as novices rather than experts. Examples of the activities used were an interview-about-instances on burning and a survey based on a piece of research on students' alternative conceptions of burning (Biddulph, 1991). These activities helped the teachers to find out more about their students' thinking.

In doing so, they were clarifying a problematic aspect of their teaching, adopting the role of teacher-as-researcher, and using a new teaching activity — one that can be used by a teacher who takes into account students' thinking.

The use of new teaching activities led to talking and thinking about the new teaching activities. The teachers wanted to talk about how the activities went for them. Initially, the discussions were about the concerns the teachers had with getting the activities to work with respect to classroom management and resource management. For example:

> As far as operating the interactive teaching within the school I think we may have to look at getting resource materials together to take some strain off staff and how we actually operate our lab technicians. (1/I5/90)

Later on, the discussions tended to be more about the educational issues involved in using the activities; for example, the issue of assessment:

> . . . I really think the assessment area is one that still needs work. How do we actually go about it and do something in a sort of objective assessment way. We have said we all feel that the kids are doing better, we feel that this is going on and that sort of thing. We have no real measure of it and that is a wee bit of a problem, I think, because there would be those who wouldn't accept that sort of analysis. (1/I12/91)

The other teachers valued listening to whether or not the activities worked in the classroom, and discussing concerns and problems arising from their use. For example:

> Well I think the camaraderie of that big group was a strong factor in all (our) development. The sharing of ideas, the realization that others had the same sorts of problems and also the chance to look at a problem from a different angle, to hear someone else's point of view on a particular problem, someone else's solution to a particular problem. (7/I1/90)

The talking went on in the sharing sessions through the telling of anecdotes (Bell, 1993a, pp. 279–319). The discussion arising helped the teachers to clarify their existing ideas on teaching, the role of the teacher, learning and learners. It also enabled new theoretical perspectives on science education to be introduced. For example, the findings of the interviews and surveys about burning (Biddulph, 1991) were shared with the rest of the group in the sharing sessions and the facilitator's questions helped the teachers to clarify their ideas about 'better' learning (Bell and Pearson, 1992). The notions of children's science and constructivist views of learning were also introduced and reflected on over many sessions. In addition, the discussions raised the problem of what to do next; for example, how does the teacher interact with a student who views burning as a process in which things disappear. Problematic aspects of teaching were able to be clarified.

A priority for the teachers was the development of a supportive atmosphere

— one in which they felt encouraged to use the new activities; felt that their knowledge and expertise were valued and were seen as useful contributions; felt that their concerns about the possibility of judgments and put-downs were allayed; perceived that the feedback given was supportive and helpful; were able to share their problems and concerns publicly; felt supported; and found that their feelings associated with change were attended to in a non-threatening way. For example:

> I found the discussion quite essential really because it is — you need a bit of raw courage to go out of the security of a textbook and go into something that is totally unknown and the first time I tried I really didn't have a good experience at all. But because of the encouragement of the group and you get various ideas from various people around the group, then you think well I will have another go. It really gave you the support that you needed. (11/M1/90)

The Second Personal Development

As the teacher development continued, the teachers developed further in a personal way. Each individual teacher had to construct and evaluate for himself or herself, an understanding of the socially reconstructed knowledge of what it means to be a teacher of science. This second phase of personal development also involved dealing with restraints; in particular, attending to the feelings and concerns of behaving differently in the classroom and changing their ideas about what it means to be a teacher of science. Their concerns included fear of losing control in the classroom; amount of teacher intervention; covering the curriculum; knowing the subject; meeting assessment requirements; relationships with students; and appraisal.

Fear of Losing Control in the Classroom

Many teachers get a sense of worth and competence from keeping control in the classroom and having a reputation amongst colleagues of being a teacher who has good classroom control. Using new activities made some teachers feel that they had little or no control. This was indicated in the classroom by an increased noise level; for example:

> The things that you notice initially, especially when you are starting things up, is the amount of noise level that you get and have to be tolerant of. Generally speaking it is constructive noise though. If you come from a situation where you have taught very much teacher dominated, you are very much in control. It is quite difficult to get over, first thing. (15/M2/91)

Other occurrences that may suggest less control were more movement around the room by students; students making decisions about curriculum content and activities within a broad framework; students challenging the teachers' ideas and being perceived as challenging their authority; and the teachers not being able to plan in the same way as before and feeling that they did not quite know where they were going and what to expect. The teachers were probably still in control but they did not feel like they were. Developing their notions of what it means to be in control in the classroom and attending to the associated feelings were important.

Amount of Teacher Intervention

In changing roles in the classroom, a teacher may feel uncertain and insecure about the new amount and kind of teacher involvement in giving students the information and the 'right' answers. A lesser amount of intervention resulted in some teachers feeling that they were irresponsible, not helping students and not doing their job — teaching — properly. Also, how to respond to students who have constructed the 'wrong' answer or are doing the 'wrong' things was of concern. These feelings associated with what it feels like to be helping or not helping students to learn, needed to be attended to.

Covering the Curriculum

Most teachers are rightly concerned about their responsibilities to students, parents, employers and the Government to ensure that the prescribed curriculum is covered. When using new teaching activities, the teachers had concerns and needed reassurance that the curriculum was being covered and that the students were not being disadvantaged; for example:

> It was more that their questions, what they were interested in, (were) not necessarily what the scheme said that we had to cover or the syllabus says we have to cover. It was more the fact that it is all very well answering questions, and I can see that they have learned, but if they still don't know, at the end of the year when they come to the common test and they go into the fourth form, all of the things that the syllabus says they should know, then I am not doing my job as a teacher according to the rules. (16/I2/91)

The teachers sought evidence and confirmation that the curriculum was being covered, or that an initially reduced 'pace of coverage' could be redressed later because the quality of learning was improved. Only then, did they feel that they were being responsible and able to be accountable.

Knowing the Subject

Many teachers (primary and secondary) feel insecure about their knowledge of the science content in the curriculum. In using a new teaching activity, the teachers had to learn new aspects of the topic or answer unexpected questions from the students. For example, a primary teacher commented:

> It (knowing the science) does, it affects it (my teaching of science) quite a bit. I avoid it if I can. Even the science unit I am doing now I had to go away and re-think. It was presented to me — why don't you try bubbles etc. The whole time it was going on I thought I don't even understand what I am really doing here. There were some great processes going on and the kids were experimenting with the sort of mixtures they should make and I understood the sorts of things that would make bubbles break, etc. But I didn't really understand the actual whole idea of the bubble and what formed it. And so I went away and read that water has a film and then it all fitted in. (3/I1/90)

Developing teaching strategies to address these incompetencies in the classroom and attending to the feelings of inadequacy associated with not always knowing the answer, needed to be given time in the teacher development programme.

Meeting Assessment Requirements

Teachers will not continue to develop and use new teaching activities if they feel that they are unable to meet requirements for assessment and reporting using these new teaching activities. These requirements may be school-based ones such as reporting to parents or using common science department tests. They may be national requirements such as the New Zealand national examination of the School Certificate, sat by students aged 15 years. Given that teacher performance may be judged on examination or test results, it was important that the teachers felt confident that this aspect of their responsibilities and duties was addressed. For example, one teacher commented:

> It is the same with School Certificate. We are going to get our exam marks for School Certificate (SC) looked at because at the moment we are doing a bit of a drive on trying to raise our expectations and improve our exam results. And there is one way in which I can do it, I can turn around and you can rote learn your information in SC. You can go through heaps of questions SC, we can lift those marks alright doing a very traditional method of teaching. And if that then raises our School Certificate marks then that is going to be looked at and say 'you have done a good job'. Hopefully we can also do it through an interactive or a constructivist teaching approach but. . . . (1/I11/91)

If this aspect was not addressed, the teachers felt insecure and unwilling to continue to use a new approach and they may have re-evaluated the facilitator's credibility. The teachers needed to feel confident about new learning outcomes, such as learning-to-learn skills and how to assess these skills. Not all teachers initially felt this was a worthwhile learning outcome, in comparison with content-learning outcomes, and needed time and support to develop their ideas about learning in science and to attend to the feelings associated with this.

Relationships with the Students

Of concern to most teachers is their relationship with their students. Most teachers want to be both personally liked and professionally respected by their students. A new teaching activity was evaluated in terms of its effect on the teacher–student relationships. In some cases the feelings associated with a change in the relationship were positive; for example, the students saying that the teacher is more on a par with them now. The changes could also invoke negative feelings, such as feeling not useful when the students were becoming more independent at answering their own questions using a variety of resources other than the teacher; or feeling negative in response to the students challenging the ideas of the teacher more or complaining about not getting so many notes. For example:

> My fifth form has been quite critical that I don't give them notes. One of the other teachers has got everything on OHPs (overhead projector transparencies) and he wanders in, plonks down the OHP, turns the thing on and there is all your notes and they feel very secure. They have got the notes, they are going to learn them in that note form and they are very secure. They don't like coming to me because I don't give them notes like that at all. They write up their experiments, and their conclusion to their experiments, formulate their notes but they don't like it like that because they have got to think and they would rather just turn the handle. So you have got to teach them to actually think . . . And that means there is more effort on their part and they don't like having to put the effort in. So I have had a certain amount of resistance, from the exam classes particularly. 'Just give me the answers'. 'No, you go and find them out'. And they don't like that. (11/13/91)

The feelings associated with the change in teacher–student relationships needed to be attended to by the teachers.

Appraisal

A new teaching activity may not produce the evidence required by the Government or the employers for the existing techniques of teacher appraisal. For example, members of the New Zealand Education Review Office or a principal may judge the performance of a teacher on the quality of the student workbooks or notebooks. These may be used to assess if the content of the curriculum has been covered and if the students have learnt the curriculum content. One secondary teacher commented:

(How would you feel if an Inspector had come in and looked at the books, what would have been your response?) Yes, I might have felt slightly uncomfortable. I actually was aware that a couple of times during each unit I would make sure that we did some very solid written book work, sort of intersperse it in there. Just tidy up what we have been doing and then we get something on paper. I think that was also to satisfy parents and students because they like, particularly this school, it is a working-class area and work is book work. Work is having a lot of tidy things on paper. So I do it, you balance it out. (8/13/91)

Using a new teaching activity therefore induced negative feelings in some teachers if the new teaching activity did not result in books full of student notes. These feelings needed to be attended to if further teacher development was to occur.

Addressing and resolving the above concerns had both a cognitive and an affective aspect. It appeared to the researchers that it was most crucial to address the affective dimensions if teacher development was to continue. Moreover, the development was both personal and social, in that the culture of what it means to be a teacher was being challenged and renegotiated by the group. Each individual teacher was having to position himself or herself with respect to the newly reconceptualized culture. The extent to which each teacher was able to do this determined their level of engagement in the change process.

In the programmes run as part of the research, these concerns or constraints were attended to in the sessions. First, the facilitator attempted to communicate that these restraints were concerns to be attended to and that teachers' expressions of concern were not being viewed as giving excuses for not changing. Secondly, the teachers received suggestions from the facilitator and the other teachers on ways to get around the restraints. For example, one teacher shared how she got the students to compare their before and after-concept maps with the learning objectives in the national curriculum for that topic. The students were able to give feedback to the teacher that they felt the curriculum content had been covered in their learning activities. At times, the concerns were addressed in a specific workshop activity. However, most of these concerns were addressed when they arose in the telling of anecdotes in the sharing sessions.

The Second Social Development

As the programme continued, the teachers' comments indicated that they were valuing collaborative ways of working. As the trust, support and credibility of the facilitator and other teachers became established, the teachers felt more able to contribute and more comfortable with contributing to the programme activities. They were more likely to share with the group anecdotes about what was happening in their classrooms, to give support and feedback to other teachers, to offer suggestions for new teaching activities, to suggest solutions to problems, and to voice their opinions and views. They were contributing to developing and sustaining collaborative relationships. The value the teachers placed on these relationships is evident in their comments on the sharing sessions and talking with other teachers; for example:

> Yes, I have been quite amazed at the techniques that various people have. I reckon discussion in a large group like that is really invaluable. Like last year we had two special science people telling us everything they knew and they were very experienced but they still didn't have all the answers as a group of twelve, fifteen would have, obviously. And also what you'll find, is what I have noticed, myself, personally, is with these teachers, they are really good teachers . . . , they were really top of their field. Most of them are authors of books and as a role model I found them really good but you didn't see the problems that you could have, whether they were hiding the problems or they just didn't come across the problems — even still you just weren't told about some problems that can happen . . . we had quite a bit of talk about problems in the classroom, and hitches and that is what I find, the hardest part for me is the trip-ups you have along the way and how do you deal with them. I think that is what teachers want to know. (4/I5/90)

> Well initially I was quite insecure. To try something new, when you have always got the idea at the end of the year with those magic marks, is quite a courageous thing, if you like and so the fact that we went back every week and could get support — being in a little school I don't get much support from other teachers. But to go back there and have a group of teachers accepting what I said was a big plus because being part time I wasn't — well I was here most of the time but I wasn't accepted totally as a real teacher. Whereas at the course I was. And when I said something people were interested to hear. So I think the fact that it ran over several weeks was quite important, that you got this reinforcement each week and you thought 'Oh well, that was a mess that first one but I will have another go.' (11/I2/91)

The collegial relationships were important as they provided opportunities for listening, contributing, discussing, supporting, giving feedback and reflecting on their teaching. In doing so, the teachers were renegotiating and reconstructing their shared knowledge about what it means to be a teacher of science.

The Second Professional Development

The teachers continued to develop their ideas about science, science education and professional development and to develop their classroom activities. They were engaging in cognitive development and the development of classroom practice. With respect to their cognitive development they were:

- clarifying their existing concepts and beliefs about science education — teaching, learning, the roles of the teacher, learners, the curriculum, the nature of science;
- obtaining an input of new information by listening and reading;
- constructing new understandings by linking the new information with existing ideas;
- considering, weighing up and evaluating the newly constructed understandings;
- accepting or rejecting the new constructions;
- using newly accepted understandings in a variety of contexts and with confidence; and
- reconstructing what it means to be a teacher of science.

With respect to the development of their classroom practice, they were:

- obtaining new suggestions for teaching activities;
- considering them, visualizing and planning for their use in the classroom;
- adapting and using the new activities;
- sharing their classroom experiences with others and obtaining feedback about the use of the activities;
- evaluating the new teaching activities;
- receiving support.

In particular, the teachers were more able to go beyond their classroom management of the new activities, and develop new ways of interacting with the students' thinking. The development of the teachers' classroom activities in this phase was usually to make use of the opportunities created by the use of the new activities to interact with the students' thinking.

The main characteristic of this phase of professional development was that the two aspects of professional development were more connected. The teachers were reflecting on their classroom actions, not just as to whether they worked in terms of classroom management and within school restraints, but as to whether the actions matched their new theoretical ideas. The teachers were also planning for new action in that they were able to initiate or generate new teaching activities by considering the theoretical ideas and by taking into account their students' thinking. They continued to seek new teaching suggestions from the other teachers. Their repertoire of strategies to use in response to students' thinking was growing and they were using the new teaching ideas in new contexts.

The reflection-in-action that the teachers did in the classroom was also changing. Their thinking about their teaching and their role in the classroom, and the thinking underlying their decisions and actions were more in line with a constructivist view of learning. For example, a teacher commented on something he was reflecting on:

> . . . I think the term science teacher is a misnomer for me. I am more of
> a science educator. There is a difference. I have many colleagues who are

good science teachers. They plan really good lessons, with lots of 'teachem workem' slots, have well presented materials, manage their students and resources well and get good test marks. But their students are asked to *remember* a whole lot of new stuff and not much effort is made to link the material being covered to *personal* experiences of the students. I feel I am more of an educator because I try to educate the student from where the student is at the moment in their thinking. (14/S3/91)

The teachers were changing from being techicians using new activities to teachers who had a constructivist view of learning and who took into account students' thinking. They were not only able to use the new activities from a classroom management point of view but were also able to respond to, and interact with, the students' thinking. Being a teacher who had a constructivist view of learning was becoming a way of thinking and behaving for the teachers, rather than the implementation of some new teaching activities. They were trialling activities and thinking in the classroom to reconstruct what it means to be a teacher of science.

The Third Personal Development

Towards the end of the programme, the teachers' comments indicated that they were feeling more empowered to be responsible for their own development.

Developing a sense of trust is part of this personal development. Developing a trust that things will balance out over a longer period of time (the teaching year, rather than in one lesson) was important. The teachers often expressed a concern that there was not enough time to use a new teaching activity all the time. The time spent on one topic might be more than with the former teaching activities and there was a concern that all topics in the curriculum might not be covered. Some teachers also felt that the time and energy they had to put into using a new teaching activity were too great, limiting their use of the activity to once or twice a week or to some topics only.

These concerns decreased as the teachers evaluated the new teaching over a period of time and learnt to trust the new teaching. Discussion of what more experienced teachers had found was helpful. For example, teachers who have a constructivist view of learning, in contrast to techicians who are just using teaching activities based on a constructivist view of learning, comment that although the time spent on one topic seems to be longer, they find, at the end of the year or in the following year, that the students have retained the new learning. There is less time spent on revision and revisiting previous learning, and the students appear to recall the new concepts more readily in their later learning activities. Although more time is spent during learning, time is saved in later learning. Also, as the teachers developed further they realized that being a teacher who has a constructivist view of learning, was about the way they think and the way they respond to students' thinking in the classroom, not just about the overt activities they do in the classroom. When the teachers moved from being a technician using specific activities to being a teacher responding to and interacting with students' thinking, they commented that they gained rather than expended energy.

It appeared that to continue to develop professionally, the teachers also had to develop their trust in the students — to be more trusting that the students would have ideas on the topic being taught in science, that they would contribute to the discussions in the lesson, that they would learn the content of the curriculum, and that they would continue to take responsibility for their own learning. For example, a secondary teacher commented on students' contributions to the lesson:

> Well just the expectations of the pupils now that when they come into the room I will expect contributions from them. (8/I5/91)

The teachers had to develop personally to be able to stand back and let go. There was personal development in attending to the feelings of apparent loss of control and not being centre stage. Some of the teachers had to consider other kinds of feedback, such as indicators of learning, to maintain their sense of self-worth as a teacher.

Some of the teachers commented that they felt that they were relying more on the students in their teaching. Now that they were acknowledging and valuing the students' knowledge and expertise, they sought their ideas out more and they felt they needed to consult with students more. They no longer felt that they could teach without knowing what the students were thinking. For example:

> It is neat to see the kids actually respond. You sometimes don't acknow-ledge that they — well I guess lots of teachers don't acknowledge that they actually have some knowledge already and they have experiences and they are involved with people who have had experiences, especially in this (unit on) health and disease. It was interesting the depth of know-ledge that collectively the class had. (5/I3/91)

Their personal development involved not only this greater respect for what the students brought to the lesson, but also attending to feelings associated with this — feelings that they were still competent teachers even if they felt they had to consult and rely on the students more.

They also commented that the experience of contributing in the programme sessions was empowering for them as staff members. They had felt empowered by having the opportunity to contribute to the group discussions, as well as having others listen to, and respond to, their ideas and opinions, and felt that they could voice their ideas without having to always be 'right'. They did not feel so uncom-fortable if someone disagreed with their ideas. They were more able to acknow-ledge that different people could have different ideas from them and that this did not decrease their self-worth. This personal development had enabled them to con-tribute more to staff debates. Many had become more involved in school manage-ment, such as being on working parties formulating new school policies and in local and national debates, for example, over bulk funding and draft curricula. A beginning teacher commented:

The deputy principal is really keen on getting the whole school working on mixed ability teaching, so in fact, I have been roped in as an expert, a local expert on mixed ability teaching because of the work that we have been doing and 'constructivist' teaching. (14/I4/91)

The sense of empowerment was accompanied by a greater congruence between their personally constructed knowledge and the socially constructed knowledge of what it means to be a teacher of science.

The Third Social Development

As the teachers developed more, they began to actively seek and initiate the activities and relationships with other teachers which they felt fostered their own development. The activities were initiated in the sessions and outside the programme time. For example, one teacher asked for specific help when she felt a new teaching activity had not worked. She was asking her colleagues to work collaboratively with her on the problem. Other teachers commented on conversations they had had with colleagues in the gym, over the telephone, in the staffroom, in the car travelling to and from the programme sessions, and in planning a conference presentation together on the new teaching activities. For example:

I have got to know three or four other teachers, women teachers very well, so a network has been set up. We frequently ring one another on the phone. We wouldn't have known one another as well and we are a support network. There are various problems that we have that I know now there is somebody I can talk to of a like mind. It has been personal contacts with other teachers. (7/I2/91)

Subsequent Professional Development

Some of the teachers took initiatives to continue their development after the end of the programme run as part of the research project, by doing some form of curriculum development or facilitating teacher development programmes themselves. For example, some became involved in writing a unit of work for the school scheme or a teacher's guide on one topic. Others introduced a colleague to the new teaching activities and facilitated the use of activities by the colleague in his or her classroom. Some applied for contract jobs to facilitate regional teacher development programmes for the Ministry of Education. They viewed writing and facilitating as additional ways to receive new theoretical and teaching ideas, support, feedback and further opportunities for talking with other teachers and for reflection. While they were giving, the teachers valued what they were receiving from the teachers with whom they were working. They were using the reconstructed knowledge about being a teacher of science.

Progression in the Teacher Development

There was a loose and flexible sequence implied in the model which describes the main aspects of learning for each teacher with respect to time. This progression is reported here to help raise the metacognitive awareness of the teachers about their own learning, and to guide the planning and actions of facilitators. The progression is here described as three situations:

Situation 1: Confirmation and Desiring Change

In this first situation, the teachers to varying degrees shared a dissatisfaction with an aspect of the current culture of science teaching. They also had to establish themselves and feel valued and accepted within the group. A component of this involved a checking that their teaching and views of teaching were at least partly within the collectively agreed to knowledge of what it means to be a teacher of science. Receiving validation of themselves as competent professional teachers was an aspect of the confirmation.

The key aspects of the first situation were joining the group and using new and small teaching activities in their classrooms. Teachers undertook these two key activities so long as their respect from their colleagues (in the programme and in the schools) was not endangered. A part of engaging in the change process was the group and the programme activities confirming and affirming them. The teachers had to establish or reinforce their self-esteem at the personal level. The changes therefore focused on an aspect of themselves, their teaching, and their position and standing with their peers.

In teacher-development programmes where this confirmation does not occur, the teachers are likely to feel excluded from the group, unvalidated as a teacher, and a threat to their self-esteem. They are also likely to be unaccepting of any reconstruction of what it means to be a teacher of science. Disengagement is highly likely. Given the short duration of most in-service programmes, many teachers in in-service programmes do not get the opportunity to progress beyond the confirmation stage. That is, they join the group, learn about some new teaching suggestions and begin trialling them.

Situation 2: Reconstruction

In the reconstruction situation, the teachers were considering and reflecting on new teaching activities and new theoretical ideas; experimenting in the classroom with new teaching, learning and assessment activities; and taking initiatives to adapt materials for their own use. As a consequence, they were also having to deal with the feelings associated with the change process and with being different to the commonly accepted culture of teaching. They were reconceptualizing and renegotiating what it means to be a teacher of science within the group. They were using the support and feedback of the group and confirming the trust in the group.

Situation 3: Empowerment

In the empowerment situation, the teachers were accepting of the changes that they had explored and the reconstructed social knowledge of what it means to be a teacher of science. In accepting the changes, the teachers had a new platform of beliefs from which to operate and maybe to change their world. This platform was empowering in that it gave a basis for making decisions about what to do and not to do. The new socially constructed knowledge about what it means to be a teacher of science had been largely accepted by the teachers.

With respect to the personal dimension, the teachers were gaining strength in knowing who they were as teachers, and from having a trust, conviction, and faith in, and an ownership of, their ideas and beliefs. There was a match between their own views of themselves as teachers of science and the newly socially constructed view. At the social level, they were setting up new situations and seeking out new groupings, to support and continue their development. With respect to professional development, they were showing competency in the classroom with the new strategies, being realistic, and establishing the limitations and strengths of their new activities.

Not a Stage Model of Teacher Development

The progression outlined above is a development of the purposes for which the teachers are seeking support from teacher development programmes. The progression in our model does *not* mean that a stage model of teacher development is being advocated, even though one of the major approaches to the description of teacher development relies on the notion of 'stages'. For example, Leithwood (1992) has summarized three stage models which appear relevant to teacher learning: the development of professional expertise; psychological development; and career-cycle development. According to Kohlberg (1970), stages imply a number of distinct, qualitatively different structures that perform the same function at various points in the development of an individual. The different structures for a given function form an invariant sequence of development, which can be accelerated or retarded, but not changed. Each structure is a whole, with the sequence being an hierarchical integration: higher stages incorporate the structures which characterize the lower stages.

Burden (1990) has summarized some of the weaknesses in all stage models. The stages are often too imprecisely defined to be readily reconcilable with behaviour, so they cannot be empirically tested. Individuals can be found who develop in a way which is not predicted by the model, for example, by omitting (or 'jumping') stages. Such models often do not describe what is actually involved as an individual moves 'upwards' to the next stage, so that support for that transition cannot be given readily. Given the small groups who are surveyed in the production (as opposed to the confirmation) of stage models, it may well be that they are artefacts of sampling. As very few longitudinal studies on individuals are carried out, it may also be that the 'stages' are just a categorization scheme rather than implying actual progression by an individual. Arguably the greatest weakness in the use of stage models to describe teacher development is that they are insensitive to the circumstances of the life of the individual teacher.

In our view, the nature of the learning that any individual achieves is influenced by their perception of the circumstances of their life: their personal history, their present activities, and their more realistic hopes for the future. To be effective, any teaching that is provided must recognize these influences. The greatest influence on the learning of teachers (as a special group of learners) is the 'school climate' or 'school ethos' in which they work. Although this metaphor has been criticized for its width and imprecision (Finlayson, 1987), it is generally used. The pattern perceived by an individual teacher in a given school — of opportunities. expectations and inhibitions, rewards and punishments — both moulds and shapes what is done and not done, and when, how and why professional decisions are taken (for example, Zeichner, Tabachnick, and Densmore, 1987; Sikes, 1985; Tickle, 1989). Accordingly, we are not promoting the given model as a stage model of teacher development; rather, we see it as loosely describing a progression to aid teachers and facilitators in monitoring change.

Discussion

Our analysis of the descriptive data reported in this chapter highlights certain aspects of teacher development:

Learning

Teacher development can be viewed as teachers learning, rather than as others getting teachers to change. In learning, the teachers were developing their personally and socially constructed beliefs and ideas about science education and about what it means to be a teacher of science, developing their classroom practice and attending to their feelings associated with changing. Another aspect of the teacher development was learning about professional development and change processes, and how they themselves learn. Metacognition was thus a part of the teacher development process, as was reconceptualizing what teacher development is.

Learning in the teacher-development process can be viewed as a purposeful inquiry. The teachers were inquiring into, or investigating, an aspect of their teaching — an aspect that they saw as problematic and wished to change.

Social, Personal and Professional Development

The teacher development of the teachers in the research project can be described as social, personal and professional development. Social development involved working with, and relating to, other teachers and students to reconstruct the socially agreed knowledge about being a teacher of science. Personal development involved attending to feelings about the change process, about being a teacher and about science education, and reconstructing one's own knowledge about being a teacher of science. Professional development involved changing concepts and beliefs about science education and changing classroom activities. These three aspects were interactive and interdependent. The process of teacher development can be seen as one in which social, personal, and professional development is occurring, and one in which development in one aspect cannot proceed unless the other aspects develop also.

Professional development included the teachers using new teaching activities in the classroom. The contributions from the teachers and the facilitator about new teaching activities initially needed to be ideas for new teaching strategies rather than written resources, such as teachers' guides. For example, initially the teachers found it more helpful to learn about a new way to find out what their students were thinking, such as brainstorming, than to receive a teacher's guide on the teaching of 'energy'. The teacher development programmes had a focus on new teaching activities and on being a teacher. Aspects related to learning, science and the curriculum arose from these two foci.

Teacher development programmes can be seen as having two components. One is the input of new theoretical ideas and new teaching suggestions. This tends to be present in current teacher-development programmes and is usually done in more formal situations, such as seminars and lectures. The second component is trying out, evaluating and practising these new theoretical and teaching ideas over an extended period, and in a collaborative situation where the teachers are able to receive support and feedback, critically reflect, and renegotiate and reconstruct what it means to be a teacher of science. In our experience, this second component tends to be underplayed in many in-service programmes and tends to occur through more informal modes such as telephone conversations, conversations in the staff-room, sharing anecdotes and visiting each other's classrooms. Both components are important if all three aspects of teacher development — social, personal, and professional — are to occur.

Professional development also involved the teachers developing their personally and socially constructed beliefs and ideas about science education, the teaching and learning process and teacher development. The teachers brought to the teacher development programmes different ideas, beliefs, experiences, concerns, interests and feelings. They had different starting points in the development process and achieved different outcomes, within the broad goals of the programme, even though they had attended the same programme. The teacher development programmes had both anticipated and unanticipated outcomes, and the facilitators needed to be prepared for both. Therefore, the teacher development activities were designed so as to acknowledge, incorporate, and address (rather than ignore) the teachers' prior ideas, beliefs, experiences, concerns, interests and feelings about science and science education.

Personal development was an essential aspect of the teacher development.

Learning experiences can be set up to help the teachers develop professionally but the personal development, which often occurs outside of a programme, cannot be so readily facilitated. The personal development appeared important in the process in that personal and social development were intertwined, personal development preceded the professional development, the pace of personal development influenced the pace of professional development, and the personal development was often influenced by factors outside the professional and teaching work of the teacher. The restraints mentioned in the second phase of personal development can be viewed as cultural constraints (Tobin, 1990), but dealing with the feelings of teaching 'against the grain' (Cochran-Smith, 1991) to go beyond the restraints was an individual and affective process, done with the support of colleagues. For many teachers, the social development enabled the personal development.

Taylor (1991, p. 21) suggested that 'radical pedagogical reform might require teachers to engage in the renegotiation of the culture of teaching, rather than going it alone'. The social development is seen as necessary for this renegotiation. Through talking with other teachers, the culture of teaching for the teachers in the study was being renegotiated (Tobin, 1993). The social communication and interaction among the teachers were important in the teacher-development process.

A part of the social development was working with other teachers in ways to provide a forum for discussing and reconstructing what it means to be a teacher of science. The teachers developed ways of working with, and relating to, other teachers and students from whom they trusted and received support and feedback. The isolation of the classroom was valued less, and collaborative ways of working were valued more for the support and feedback they gave. Social development can be facilitated to a certain extent by facilitating a contrived collegiality (Hargreaves, 1992), but true collaborative ways of working originate from the teachers valuing them as ways of fostering their own and others development.

Teacher development was helped when the teachers were able to talk with each other about what they were doing in the classroom, as an integral and key part of the programme. For example, the sharing sessions were structured around the use of anecdotes (Bell, 1993a, pp. 279–319). It was not something to be left to chance before or after any meetings. Thus, for instance, the discussion about classroom activities was focused around a task of using a new teaching activity in the classroom. During this talking, the teachers were able to decide what to talk about and not just be on-task in response to a facilitator-initiated activity.

However, the isolation in the classroom is not necessarily problematic. For women teachers working in a hostile environment, isolation may be a sane response to the stress resulting from their experienced powerlessness, disenfranchisement, and professional frustration in a male-orientated curriculum, administration and school environment (Robertson, 1992). A woman teacher joining a group of teachers who are insensitive to gender differences, may not feel supported, encouraged or in a situation of mutual trust. The feedback she would most likely receive may not be helpful in terms of professional, personal or social development.

The classroom can also be a source of teacher development (Thiessen, 1992) and the social development involves the changing of the relationships between the teachers and the students. Here, it is the students who are providing the source of feedback and support for the teacher. When a school culture does not encourage collegial relationships between teachers, a teacher may prefer to work with the students rather than a group of teachers. But in this situation, the teacher is not isolated in her or his development, just isolated from other teachers.

For this overview, the three aspects of teacher development — social, personal, and professional — and the three phases within each have been separated from each other to highlight the multi-faceted nature of teacher development. However, the data indicate that the three aspects and the three phases overlap considerably and it has to be acknowledged that the matrix of nine subsets of the process has its limitations.

Empowerment

The teacher development process can be viewed as one of empowerment for ongoing development, rather than one of continued dependency on a facilitator. The aims, activities and facilitation of a programme were planned for teachers to experience this empowerment. The programmes enabled teachers to feel included as part of the group; contribute to the programme and feel that their contributions were valuable to the programme, for example, feeling that their opinions, ideas, teaching activities, suggestions in decision-making, and initiatives were worthwhile; experience competency in teaching; develop a sense of ownership towards their own development; address their concerns and needs; volunteer for the programme or an aspect of the programme; negotiate the content and form of the programme; determine the pace and nature of the changes; reconceptualize their view of teacher development; view themselves as learners; innovate and be creative, rather than only implement given strategies; and feel that the changes are possible and beneficial in the current school and political situation.

At the outset of the teacher development programmes, the facilitator had a strong say regarding the programme sessions to meet the perceived expectations of the teachers. The teachers had been invited to participate in the research and the teacher development programme — it was not initiated by them. Also, other teacher development programmes at the time were very much directed by the person running them. Thus, initially, suggested teaching activities were given to the teachers according to what material was available to implement the findings of the previous research into students' learning. However, as indicated by the model, the facilitator did not maintain this directive position and the teachers increasingly determined the agenda of the meetings as the programme progressed.

The teachers appreciated being given space to decide, for themselves, the pace and nature of the changes they would make to their teaching in the classroom, within the broad framework of the programme. For example, the teachers felt their development was hindered if they were told by the facilitator to try a specific activity in the classroom before the next session. They felt their development was supported if the facilitator gave them a range of activities to try out over the time of several sessions. They were then able to select which activity they would try given the contexts in which they were teaching. Teachers appreciated the opportunity to manage the risk involved in changing what they did in the classroom.

The teachers were able to contribute to the programmes by talking about what they are doing in the classroom, providing their ideas and opinions for discussion, giving support and feedback, and negotiating the content and ways of doing the activities. The teachers gained as much from each other as they did from the facilitator. The act of contributing was seen as empowering by the teachers. Merely responding to the facilitator's questions or directions was seen as a contribution of lesser value. Once the teachers contributed, they were able to be given support and feedback, which are important to their development.

The desired teacher development was not achieved by trying to force the teachers to change. Although the facilitator was explicit about her expectation that the teachers would try out new activities in the classroom, and although the programme had a structure and goals, the precise direction of any change was not predetermined by the facilitator. The teachers needed to be convinced about the need for change, and to determine the direction of the change, before they would engage in development activity in such a way that they would learn.

Empowerment can also be viewed as the teachers being empowered to act on their world, to change or reconstruct the socially constructed knowledge about teaching science. In this emancipatory sense, teacher development is about helping teachers to critique beliefs underlying different educational policies and teaching approaches, to clarify their own beliefs and commitments in science education and to act in ways congruent with their own beliefs and commitments. In the teacher-development programmes run as part of the research project, the teachers were volunteers and there was no legal requirement for them to change, which is in contrast with teacher development programmes run to implement new policy or curricula. The teachers were able to choose whether to come on the programme or not, and whether to use the new teaching activities or not once they had learnt about them. However, the programme can be criticized in that only one view of learning (and teaching) — a constructivist view — was presented and focused on.

For teacher development to continue beyond a particular programme, the teachers had to have been supported to reach the third aspect of their personal and social development. This took time and could not be neatly orchestrated for within the tight timelines set by some administrators wanting to implement new policies.

In summary, the analysis of the research findings suggests that teacher development can be conceptualized as social, personal and professional development. When all three aspects are addressed, as in the teacher-development programmes run as part of the research project, teacher development is promoted (Pearson and Bell, 1993). In the following chapter, relevant literature on teacher development and human development is reviewed and critiqued with respect to the model.

3 Views of Learning to Underpin Teacher Development

The main reason why many teachers engage in teacher development is to be able to do a better job — to be a better teacher and to improve the learning of their students. The teachers in the research project commented that their main reasons for continuing to change, despite the uncomfortable feelings associated with changing, were that it led them to feel better about themselves as teachers, and to achieve better learning outcomes in the classroom (Bell, 1993a, pp. 84–161). While these professional concerns were foremost, they were also protecting their own sense of well-being, their sense of being in control, and their self-esteem, as well as ensuring that they as teachers were still viewed with respect by their students, colleagues and the community. Hence, teacher development involves not only the professional but the personal and social as well.

In the model presented in the previous chapter, the three aspects of teacher development — social, personal, and professional development — and the three phases within each, were separated from each other to highlight the multi-faceted nature of teacher development. This method of analysis should be helpful to teacher developers and teachers as they think about what to do to promote teacher development. However, while there is some value in focusing on each of the three, the three are inextricably linked. In this chapter, the interactive, interwoven and merged nature of the three aspects of teacher development will be discussed with reference to views of human development, learning and the reflective, inquiring teacher. The main focus will be on explanations of the learning of teachers.

Teacher Development as Human Development

Teacher development can be thought of as human development, a major aspect of which is the development of self-identity and Lave (1995) has suggested that the main task of learning is identity work. In a professional context, teachers as changing people are developing a sense of themselves as teachers. In western culture, the study of human development and the development of self-identity has focused on the individual (Forgas, 1981; Olssen, 1991). Behaviourist and cognitive development psychologists have tended to study the individual abstracted from culture, focusing on genetic, environmental, and inner mechanisms. Social influences have been downplayed and little recognition given to the impact of structural or collective aspects of culture or society on an individual's life. As such, this view of human development has difficulty conceptualizing the relationship between individuals and complex social structures. The interface between the personal and social is seen as problematic and, as in the model suggested in the previous chapter, the personal and social aspects of human development are linked but separated. For example, Claxton (1989) asserted that both a psychological and sociological perspective on teacher development is required. He stated that 'teachers must look inwards, to gain insight into the dynamic of their own stress; and they must look outwards, to understand better the social forces that surround them' (Claxton, 1989, p. 8).

This separation of the personal (individual) from the social (collective) in human development studies, stems from the dominant and powerful world view in western culture that is based on individualism — that is, the self as an individual is separate, unique and autonomous, possessing the capacity for self-direction, self-reliance and responsibility (Gergen, 1991, p. 11). Individualism is evident, for example, in our interest in the unique character or essence of individuals that makes them who they are; in the western legal and moral systems which give rights and responsibilities to individuals, not their families, friends or organizations; and in the different views of the State's responsibilities held by different political parties (for example, compare New Right governments and social democrat governments on their views of the individual). This individualism is supported in psychology by the notion that people have 'inner tendencies — personality traits, attitudes and values, moral principles, sense of self-worth — and that these inner tendencies determine their behaviour' (Gergen, 1991, p. 98). With respect to teacher development, the notion of individualism is also evident. Responsibility for change is given to individuals, as they are seen as self-determining and having agency to effect change. When no change occurs, the individual is held responsible. The terms 'the reluctant teacher', 'taking responsibility for one's own professional development', 'needs analysis', and 'coping with the feelings associated with changing' reflect this individualism in current teacher development discourse.

One notion arising from this 'individualism' is that individuals possess abilities for cognition, can think for themselves and can make rational choices. People are seen as having particular cognitive abilities of rationality and rational reasoning is viewed as the way that knowledge is created and established. Individuals can make informed choices and effect changes through rational thinking. This notion is most visible in psychology in Kelly's (1969) notion of 'man the scientist' and in science education in the notion of 'pupil as scientist' (Driver, 1983). However, it is acknowledged that this does not happen all the time and that non-rational behaviour does occur (Sutherland, 1992).

A social view of cognition and human development has been articulated within psychology in response to the focus on the individual. Forgas (1981, pp. 1–26), in an overview of social psychology, stated the view that cognition (that is, all the processes of knowing) is social and that knowledge is a social product; that social cognition cannot simply be reduced to information processing models since our knowledge and ideas about the social world are intrinsically normative, motivated and social; that social cognition recognizes the affective, motivational and social factors in cognition; and that cognition is not strictly an intra-individual process as societies, groups and collectives are also engaged in the creation, processing and definition of knowledge. O'Loughlin (1992a) added that the process of coming to know or learning may be conceptualized as a social process.

In the area of the development of identity and emotion, it is advocated in both social constructionism (Gergen, 1985) and social constitutionism (Greenwood, 1994) that identity and emotion are socially constructed (or, as Greenwood says, socially constituted) and are thus relational. They both reject the traditional positivist and empiricist account of science. But they differ by adopting a relativist and a realist position respectively and hence by holding contrasting positions with respect to objectivity. However, despite their differing ontological commitments, both support the social construction of knowledge.

Gergen (1985) described social constructionism as a meta-theory of knowledge:

> Social constructionism views discourse about the world not as a reflection or map of the world but as an artefact of communal interchange. (Gergen, 1985, p. 266)

Such a view is based on one or more of the following assumptions:

> What we take to be experience of the world does not in itself dictate the terms by which the world is understood. (ibid., p. 266)

> The terms in which the world is understood are social artefacts, products of historically situated interchanges amongst people. From the constructionist position the process of understanding is not automatically driven by the forces of nature, but is the result of an active, cooperative enterprise of persons in relationship. (ibid., p. 267)

> The degree to which a given form of understanding prevails or is sustained across time is not fundamentally dependent on the empirical validity of the perspectives in question, but on the vicissitudes of social processes (e.g., communication, negotiation, conflict and rhetoric). (ibid., p. 268)

> Forms of negotiated understanding are of critical significance in social life, as they are integrally connected with many other activities in which people engage. (ibid., p. 268)

These assumptions challenge the correspondence theory of truth and traditional empiricist notion of scientific inquiry; deny the notion of objectivity; and dismiss the perceived need for empirical theory adjudication. Thus, a social constructionist view of human development asserts that knowledge production is a social process, one aimed at constructing acceptable truths, and is seen as involving plays of power within a society. It is not seen as something abstract, corresponding to a reality which everyone could agree on, regardless of their particular culture or outlook. Social processes and practices, such as communication, negotiation, conflict and rhetoric, create particular views of reality and knowledge (Gergen, 1985).

Greenwood (1994) argues for social constitutionism, which includes a view of knowledge as socially created and constituted, but which adopts a scientific realist position:

> The realist can and does recognise that theoretical descriptions are socially constructed or created. Their meaning is not abstracted from observations of the phenomena to which they purport to refer, nor are they ostensively or operationally defined: their meaning is a product of conventions based upon theoretical modelling. For the realist, however, this poses no threat to their linguistic or epistemic objectivity. (Greenwood, 1994, p. 30)

Such a view enables a social psychologist to recognize the social dimensions of psychological phenomena without embracing the social constructionist denial of objectivity.

Emotions can also be viewed as socially constructed rather than biological givens or manifestations of an inner state (Gergen, 1991, p. 10). Teachers' feelings of anxiety, discomfort or lack of control when changing what they do in the classroom can be seen as social constructions. These feelings arise when teachers are going 'against the grain' of what is socially acceptable in terms of the socially constructed knowledge about what it means to be a teacher of science.

Individualism has been critiqued as a social construct of western culture. In some non-western cultures, the group has a higher importance and the individual is seen only as a member of a group (Gergen, 1991, p. 8). In these cultures, such as the Samoan culture, one's relationships with others are more important than one's status as an individual. Hence, individualism can be seen as a social construct of western culture, rather than as an essential characteristic of a person, and self-identity can be viewed as a social construction. The social constructionist movement (Gergen, 1985) asserts that our sense of self, who we are and where we see ourselves in relation to others, is socially constructed. It also asserts that there is no 'true self' inherent inside an individual but a self which is a product of language. The difference between people does not arise from essential differences within people, but from individuals experiencing differing interactions with the social world. Each culture determines 'what we are really like'. Our sense of self is part of our cultural heritage, it is constructed, and can be reconstructed.

To adopt a social view of cognition is to view cognition as not merely about causal models of reasoning but as concerning moral statements as well (Harré, 1981). While rational thinking is accepted as a valuable intellectual skill, it is acknowledged as only one aspect of cognition. Social aspects are accepted also. Thus thinking by adults in everyday and professional situations, in addition to rational cognitive activities, embodies aspects of cultural values, moral standards, 'rhetoric and ritual in which social actors seek to demonstrate their legitimacy and moral worth and not just their capability as rational information processors' (Forgas,

1981, p. 261). Hence, cognition has a normative aspect and does not occur in a moral vacuum. Norms, rules, roles and expectations regulate teachers' professional lives as much as they do their everyday lives. Gergen (1985, p. 273) commented that 'not anything goes' because knowledge systems have an inherent dependency on communities of shared intelligibility: activity (including scientific activity) will be always governed in large measure by normative rules.

Shotter (1984) acknowledged the social construction of knowledge:

> ... the inherently social nature of everyone's self-conscious activity (all the activities in which people themselves know what they are doing, even if the action is as trivial as raising an eyebrow or waving a hand). I can only be self-conscious in my actions — i.e., know who I am, by knowing how I am 'placed' or 'situated' — by acting in the knowledge of my relation to others. (Shotter, 1984, p. 38)

Shotter regarded human development as growth towards becoming an autonomous, responsible person, which may be viewed as about 'how we account for ourselves to ourselves in and against the background of our ordinary, everyday affairs' (Shotter, 1984, p. ix). He promoted a 'social accountability thesis' that our understanding and our experience of our reality are constituted for us very largely by the ways in which we talk in our attempts to account for the things and events within reality. An autonomous person acts in the knowledge of who and what one is, and what one is trying to do in relation to others with whom one is sharing one's life. A person is not just accounting for his or her behaviour so that others will recognize it but in order to recognize it himself or herself. Only if we make sense of things in certain approved ways can we be accounted for by others in our society as competent, responsible members of it. To account for one's own behaviour is not to merely illustrate, depict or represent it, but to communicate something about what one's behaviour was or might be. To preserve their autonomy, people must be able to account for their actions to others as well as to themselves, to communicate who and what they are. An autonomous person is not reliant like a child upon others to complete and give meanings to acts, having them decree what one is doing. An autonomous person is able to deliberate and clarify to self and others reasons for the actions — the rational connections between what is being done, its antecedents and where one hopes, it might lead (Shotter, 1984, p. 5).

Hence development is embedded in communications between those who are already autonomous. The communications are about more than giving information; communications involve instructing children (and novices) in how to be the kind of person required by society and a particular culture. The social order is thus self-producing. In accounting for themselves, people are required to make reference to the standards, values, and criteria of the society or culture if they wish to remain an intelligible, acceptable member of the group. 'As members of a "moral order", they have a duty to act in ways which are not only intelligible, but which make sense in other kinds of ways' (Shotter, 1984, p. 5). Giving accounts of one's behaviour in everyday social life, is therefore context-dependent, personal, and undertaken to make an event recognizable in terms of a society's ways of making sense.

Social psychology to date, however, has largely retained a view of the individual operating in a social world, given its links to cognitive science. Social psychologists, to varying degrees, make a distinction between the personal and social aspects of self. In contrast, a poststructural approach to the social construction of knowledge challenges the separation of the personal and the social (Gergen, 1985) in cognition and human development, including the development of a sense of self. In this approach it is argued that too much importance is placed on consciousness and human agency, and an individualistic view of human development is criticized as a voluntaristic perspective of social processes, exaggerating the ability of individuals to actively construct their own realities and downplaying the social, cultural and organizational factors (Davies, 1991).

Such a poststructural view of the social construction of knowledge proposes that humans are essentially social beings (Olssen, 1991). The mind is social and therefore human thought, perception and action must be approached in these terms. If the mind is social and public, the object of psychology is not the individuals as such but the spaces between them; that is, the cultural codes or meaning systems that structure action. The meaning of individual action is not something inherent in the behaviour (as it is for behaviourists) or something inherent in the mind (as it is for cognitivists); it is located in the public realm. What individuals think of as their attitudes, values and actions are public-rule systems or codes which define all possible modes of thought and action. The notion of the essential self is replaced by the notion of personal identity being created and recreated in relationships — the concept of relational self (Gergen, 1991, pp. 139–70). It is the relationships that construct and make possible the self. As Davies (1991) stated:

> In this [post-structuralist] model, our existence as persons has no fundamental essence, we can only ever speak ourselves or be spoken into existence within the terms of available discourses. We are thus multiple rather than unitary beings and our patterns of desire that we took to be fundamental indicators of our essential selves [such as the desire for freedom or autonomy or for moral rightness] signify little more than the discourses, and the subject positions made available within them, to which we may have access. (Davies, 1991, p. 42)

She proposed this view of agency:

> an agent could well be defined as someone who was able to speak with *authority*. That ability would not derive from their personal individual qualities, but would be a discursive positioning that they and others sometimes had access to. (ibid., p. 52)

To be positioned as one with agency, is to be heard as a legitimate speaker. The reader is referred to Harré and Gillett (1994) for further elaboration on a poststructural view of knowing, and human development.

In this book, we adopt the position that what it means to be a teacher of science (or of any other subject) is socially constructed and a part of a culture of (science) teaching. We position ourselves within a social psychology rather than a poststructuralist framework, given the theoretical underpinnings of the research questions, data collection and data analysis done from 1990 to 1993. We hold the view that socially constructed knowledge is powerful in determining the legitimate and illegitimate knowledge and ways of behaving, for teachers of science.

Most teachers operate within this socially constructed knowledge and it is the innovative teachers, researchers, and policy makers, who initiate change in the culture, perhaps in response to changes in the wider social, political and economic contexts in which we live. Hence, for teacher development to occur, the culture and socially constructed knowledge must be renegotiated and reconstructed by all those engaged in science education — students, teachers, teacher educators, researchers, parents, politicians and industrialists. We adopt the position that the individual has some degree of responsibility and agency in the change process, while at the same time accepting that an individual teacher has limited power to change the culture and socially constructed knowledge. Expecting individual teachers to change their classroom activities, values, and thinking, in a major way, on their own and against the norm, is unrealistic and undesirable.

Constructivist Views of Learning

Teacher development may also be viewed as learning by teachers; the research documented in this book was informed principally by social, conceptual development and constructivist views of learning. We will discuss a view of learning of teachers informed by the views of learning of science by students developed in science education over the last fifteen years. Over the last decade or so, constructivism has increasingly been adopted by researchers, curriculum developers and teachers in science education as a view of learning and knowing by students and teachers. This consensus has been reached, to some extent, by avoiding a debate about its central ideas (Suchting, 1992). Many of those who have contributed to the development of a constructivist approach to science education would agree with Solomon (1994) that there is a need '. . . to try to avert a long period of stalemate while an over-used theory slides into decline' (p. 17). The assertion made in this book is that constructivism has enabled a powerful and fruitful research programme in science education and is an important base for a coherent approach to teacher development in science education. The challenges to constructivism must therefore be addressed.

Taken in its most general form, constructivism asserts that all learning takes place when an individual constructs a mental representation of an object, event or idea. Mental representations are used as a basis for mental and physical action, and both enable and constrain an individual's process of meaning making (Resnick, 1991, p. 1). These mental representations may be referred to as knowledge or beliefs. While Gauld (1987) has distinguished between knowledge and belief on the basis of the criteria of justification, in this book we use the terms 'knowledge' and 'belief' interchangeably. Whilst such a definition of constructivism does enable a wide diversity of interpretations of learning to be gathered under one label, its looseness can inhibit theorizing on the learning process. We wish to distinguish five major sub-groupings within constructivism: Piaget's (1970) approach; Kelly's (1969) personal construct psychology approach; personal constructivism as exemplified by Osborne and Wittrock (1985); radical constructivism, promoted by von Glasersfeld (1984); and social constructivism (for example, Burger and Luckmann, 1966; Schutz and Luckmann, 1973) in its several forms. A brief exposition of each will be given so that, following a review of the criticisms levelled against constructivism in general, the interpretation that informs our view of teacher development is clarified.

Piaget's approach proposes that a person's mental representations are produced during progressively more complex interactions by that individual with the world of physical objects. Incoming information is initially assimilated by existing mental structures. If this assimilation proves inadequate — that is, the incoming material cannot be understood in terms of the existing mental structure — accommodation takes place; that is, a modified structure evolves. The interplay between assimilation and accommodation, known as equilibration, results in mental structures which are progressively more decentred; that is, are less and less concerned with the immediate, the concrete and the personal.

Whilst it is primarily concerned with the development of scientific rationality, and therefore perhaps of special significance to the learning of science teachers, it is a stage theory, and therefore subject to all the weaknesses outlined in Driver (1978) and Burden (1990). There are a number of other problems with Piaget's approach to constructivism (O'Loughlin, 1992a). First, Piaget's model assumes that an individual comes to understand the world as it is; that is, comes to know reality in order to adapt to it. This realist approach is conservative in outlook, in that individuals can only converge on one ultimate mental structure, that of so-called formal operations which operates on a world that cannot be changed. Secondly, construction for Piaget refers to 'the process of constructing abstract, decentred, content-free, representations that are universal enough to be modelled by mathematical formalisms' (O'Loughlin, 1992a, p. 795). Development is seen as the development of content-free logical structures and operations. This view of construction ignores the socially and historically situated nature of knowing. It gives 'primacy to abstract mental structures and rational thought processes at the expense of the historically and socially constituted subjectivity that learners bring to the reasoning process' (O'Loughlin, 1992a, p. 800). Thirdly, the model infers that communication is only possible between individuals within the limits set by the capabilities of the person at the lower stage of development. Lastly, the process of knowledge construction is seen as individual and personal, with no attention being given to the social. As O'Loughlin (1992a) puts it after reviewing a range of critics of Piaget's theory:

> . . . knowledge is socially constructed . . . we cannot talk of knowing without considering the historically and socially constituted self that engages

in the process of knowing . . . knowing is a dialectical process that takes place in specific economic, social, cultural, and historical contexts. Knowing is . . . a process of examining current reality critically and constructing critical visions of present reality and of other possible realities so that one can become empowered to envisage and enact social transformation. (p. 799)

Although Piaget has articulated a social dimension of learning (May, 1982; Chapman, 1986), this dimension is not as visible in accounts and critiques of his work as the individual dimension. The dissatisfaction with stage aspects of his work by the educational community has led to other views of conceptual development being explored.

Kelly's personal construct psychology (see Pope and Keen, 1981; Pope and Gilbert, 1983) leaves the issue of realism to one side: 'the open question for man [sic] is not whether reality exists or not but what he [sic] can make of it' (Kelly, 1969, p. 25). Kelly proposed that each person constructs a representational model of the world, composed of a series of interrelated personal constructs, or tentative hypotheses about the world, with which past experience is described and explained and future events are forecast. Communication is possible to the extent that one person can construe, or understand, another person's construct system; a similarity of construct systems is not strictly necessary. In this sense, Kelly's constructivism is also implicitly social in that as a clinical psychologist he was concerned with the relationships between people and especially how each individual construed them.

Kelly's great contribution to constructivism is his assertion that there are no pre-determined limits on constructs in terms of the nature and range of their application. The limit to their creation is only set by the imagination of the individual concerned and by the constructs being continually tested for their predictive and explanatory adequacy in physical and social contexts: those that prove successful will be retained, used again, and used in a wider range of contexts, whilst those that do not will be modified or abandoned. The apparent weakness of his theory is the lack of emphasis on the impact of others on the production, testing and modification of a person's constructs, that is, the sociocultural aspects of learning are little considered. Also, a very high level of autonomy of agency is assumed; that is, the person is able to make changes to herself or himself readily.

These first two sub-groups of constructivism, which were seen as focusing on the individual and on the personal construction of meaning, informed the research into children's learning in science internationally in the 1980s, including research in Australasia (Northfield and Symington, 1991) and Europe (Driver, Guesne and Tiberghien, 1985), and the Learning in Science projects in New Zealand (Osborne and Freyberg, 1985; Bell, 1993d). In particular, the role of prior knowledge in learning was considered as was the domain-specific nature of learning and the conceptual development view of learning (Gilbert, Osborne and Fensham, 1982; Osborne, Bell and Gilbert, 1983). In New Zealand, a personal constructivist view of learning (arising from cognitive psychology) was developed by the researchers at the University of Waikato to theorize on the research findings on alternative conceptions and 'children's science' and was best articulated in Osborne and Wittrock

(1985) and Osborne and Freyberg (1985). The key postulates on which this constructivist view of learning is based were given as:

(i)   The learners' existing ideas influence what use is made of the senses and in this way the brain can be said to actively select sensory input.
(ii)   The learner's existing ideas will influence what sensory input is attended to and what is ignored.
(iii)   The input selected or attended to by the learner, of itself, has no inherent meaning.
(iv)   The learner generates links between the input selected and attended to and parts of memory store.
(v)   The learner uses the links generated and the sensory input to actively construct meaning.
(vi)   The learner may test the constructed meaning against other aspects of memory store and against meanings constructed as a result of other sensory input.
(vii)   The learner may subsume constructions into memory store.
(viii) The need to generate links and to actively construct, test out and subsume meanings requires individuals to accept major responsibility for their own learning. (Osborne and Wittrock, 1985, p. 65–7)

The personal but not the social construction of meaning was considered and individuals were seen as being able to change their own thoughts and actions. There is no acknowledgment of the sociocultural perspectives of learning. This personal constructivist view of learning was to underpin the research and development at the University of Waikato for the rest of the decade (Northfield and Symington, 1991; Bell, 1993d). This view of students' learning was used as an analogy to theorize about teachers' learning when the research reported in this book commenced. It was felt useful to explore the extent of the model of learning science by students to learning by teachers of science.

Another kind of constructivism (which did not play a role in the theoretical underpinnings of the research documented in this book) is von Glasersfeld's (1984) perspective on learning, known as radical constructivism. The term 'radical' is used because of its vehement rejection of the concept of reality:

> . . . radical constructivism . . . is radical because it breaks with convention and develops a theory of knowledge in which knowledge does not reflect on an 'objective' ontological reality, but exclusively an ordering and organisation of a world constituted by our experience. The radical constructivist has relinquished 'metaphysical realism' once and for all. (p. 24)

Radical constructivism is based on four precepts (von Glasersfeld, 1991). First, the rejection of the notion that we can know reality in an absolute way (see above). Von Glaserfeld has pointed out that radical constructivism is ontologically neutral (1992a, p. 32) and is consistent with the idea of a real existing world outside — all it denies is the possibility of any certain knowledge of that reality. As Duit (1994) explains, the constructivist view does not necessarily lead to an idealist (or relativist) position — it is compatible also with a critical realist view. Secondly, the assertion that scientific knowledge can only be judged by its instrumental value in helping individuals manage their subjective, experiential reality. Thirdly, the notion that concepts are the outcomes of an individual's attempts to represent that subjective experience. Fourthly, the notion that concepts evolve until they provide a functionally effective presentation of subjective experience. This approach has been criticized in terms of utility (Ellerton and Clements, 1992) and its inability to address sociocultural contexts of learning (Confrey, 1993). A challenge to its intelligibility (Suchting, 1992) was responded to by von Glasersfeld (1992b) who mounted a strong defence of his views.

There is now, however, a growing recognition of the role of the social and cultural aspects in learning in science as well as the personal, constructivist aspects (Solomon, 1987; Tobin, 1990; Driver, Asoko, Leach, Mortimer and Scott, 1994) which parallels the recognition given in the literature on learning mathematics (Confrey, 1993), human development (Olssen, 1991), and learning (Resnick, 1991; Nuthall and Alton-Lee, 1993).

Berger and Luckmann (1966) argued that what passes for 'knowledge' in society is not just the theoretical knowledge of the kind that academics might concern themselves with, but also common-sense knowledge — that which guides people in everyday life, through routines, habits, and patterned behaviour. They stated that:

> The world of everyday life is not only taken for granted as reality by the ordinary members of society in the subjectively meaningful conduct of their lives. It is a world that originates in their thoughts and actions, and is maintained as real by these. (p. 33)

Their claim was that reality is socially constructed. They argued that common-sense knowledge is inter-subjective, shared with others, can be referred to as the 'social stock of knowledge' (p. 56), is able to be 'transmitted' from generation to generation, and which is available to the individual in everyday life. Berger and Luckmann asserted that society exists as both objective and subjective realities. The concept of society as objective reality was described in such terms as social order, the habitualization of human activity, and institutionalization of habits. The concept of society as subjective reality was described as the personally constructed reality of a person as a member of that society. The process by which a person achieves a degree of internalization of the objective reality was termed 'socialization':

> which may be thus be defined as the comprehensive and consistent induction of an individual into the objective world of a society or a sector of it. Primary socialization is the first socialization an individual undergoes in childhood, through which he [sic] becomes a member of society. Secondary socialization is any subsequent process that inducts an already socialized individual into new sectors of the objective world of his [sic] society. (p. 150)

Human development was said to occur through interactions of people with the natural and social environments which, for a child, are mediated by significant others. Moreover, the objective and subjective realities are interactive and mediate each other. They stated: 'Society is a human product . . . Man [sic] is a social product' (p. 79). Hence, Berger and Luckmann acknowledged both the personal and the social.

The social constructivist position with respect to education is of long standing. Schutz and Luckmann (1973) pointed out that the extensive socially mediated learning of young people, derived from interaction with their parents and peers as well as from watching television, can lead to a well-developed 'life-world' knowledge in any field which might conflict with what schools are trying to teach about the same field. This split between life-world knowledge and school knowledge is well documented in the field of science (see, for example, Bell, 1981; Solomon, 1983). However, social views of learning have recently gained general attention, perhaps influenced by the ideas of Vygotsky (1978).

The term 'social constructivism' is not well defined in the science education literature and is usually used to make a contrast with personal constructivism and to acknowledge the sociocultural aspects of learning. The definition given by Driver, Asoko, Leach, Mortimer and Scott (1994) is: 'a social constructivist perspective recognises that learning involves being introduced to a symbolic world' (p. 5). We see this as in need of elaboration. Other terms used to indicate the role of the social and cultural in learning include social cognition, everyday cognition, situated cognition and learning, cognitive apprenticeship, common-sense ways of knowing, learning in context and sociocultural views of learning. For example, situated cognition supports the view that:

> . . . learning is a process of enculturation or individual participation in socially organised practices, through which specialised local knowledge, rituals, practices, and vocabulary are developed. The foundation of actions in local interactions with the environment is no longer an extraneous problem but the essential resource that makes knowledge possible and actions meaningful. (Hennessy, 1993, p. 2)

Most of these terms relating to social perspectives of learning, imply that cognition is not bounded by the individual brain or mind. Cognition is seen as a social process, and not just cognition about social processes. The social and personal are intertwined, as the social context in which a cognitive activity takes place is an integral part of the activity, not simply its context (Resnick, 1991). Socially constructed knowledge is both the medium for and the outcome of human social interaction.

A criticism to date of social views of learning in science education is the underdeveloped and vague use of terms and concepts, for example, 'socially constructed knowledge'. This lack of definition gives rise to questions such as: Where is the socially constructed knowledge? What is the process(es) by which social beliefs and knowledge are constructed? With what criteria are socially constructed beliefs and knowledge in science education judged and evaluated by the group and by individuals? In what ways is the social construction of knowledge linked with rational and other ways of knowing, for example, intuition? What is the role of the affective aspects of learning in the social construction of knowledge? Are these fruitful questions to ask?

We argue that there are two important criteria with which to review these different social views of learning. The first is the extent to which a view considers not only the culture of the classroom, but also the wider sociocultural views of society. The second is the extent to which they give consideration to the reconstruction of the social as an individual interacts with it. Most accounts view the individual as changing in response to the social. For example, the terms 'enculturation', 'socialization', 'introduction to the culture', 'appropriate the cultural tools', and 'arriving on a foreign shore', emphasize that the individual's personal constructions develop during the learning process towards the socially shared and agreed to knowledge.

We support a view of learning in teacher development which considers both the development of the individual's construction of meaning towards the socially agreed to knowledge and the reconstruction and transformation of the culture and social knowledge itself. In other words, such a view of learning would acknowledge the partially determining and partially determined characteristic of human agency — the interaction of the individual with the social can change both. The personal construction of knowledge is mediated by socially constructed knowledge and the social construction of knowledge is mediated by personally constructed knowledge. Such a view could position teachers as agents, empowered and legitimate speakers, constrained by the social. The issue of power in social discourse is currently addressed in poststructuralist views of knowledge, knowing and development, and readers are referred to the writings of such authors as Bronwyn Davies (Davies, 1993) and Jay Lemke (Lemke, 1990) for further elaboration.

We support the view of Cobb (1994) that 'mathematical learning should be viewed as both a process of active individual construction and a process of enculturation into the mathematical practices of wider society' (p. 13) — the description could also be applied to learning science and to learning by teachers. Cobb views the two perspectives — constructivism and the sociocultural — as each telling half the story. Each perspective implies the other but foregrounds one aspect only. We advocate that a view of learning needs to address both the personal and the social.

We propose that a social constructivist view of learning in teacher development which recognizes these components:

- Knowledge is constructed by people.
- The construction and reconstruction of knowledge is both personal and social.
- Personal construction of knowledge is socially mediated. Social construction of knowledge is personally mediated.
- Socially constructed knowledge is both the context for and the outcome of human social interaction. The social context is an integral part of the learning activity.

- Social interaction with others is a part of personal and social construction and reconstruction of knowledge.

Constructivism has provided a powerful and fruitful research programme in learning in science education (Duit, 1994). However, the plethora of interpretations of constructivism, and the foundation of much of the work in the field on an amlagam of them which has not been defined expressly, have led to the emergence of a number of criticisms of constructivism *per se* (see above, and also Millar, 1989; Osborne, 1993, Duit, 1994). Criticisms have come from both those within and those outside the broad field of constructivism. If constructivism is to have an assured future, it must address all the doubts that have been raised. The main criticisms concern the loosely defined terms, ontological issues of realism and relativism, making sense, theory adjudication, science curricula, progression in the curriculum, the capabilities and learning styles of students, the search for the 'grand theory', the social dimension to the practice of science and the learning of science, the role of the teacher, the scope of the utility of constructivism, the status of constructivism with teachers, the impact on teacher development and links to progressive education. These main criticisms, and a constructivist address to them, are now discussed.

Loosely Defined Terms

One of the main criticisms of constructivism has been the use of loosely defined terms, for example, 'active' and 'construction'. However, as Duit (1994) points out, this so-called looseness or vagueness has also been a strength, for it has allowed a creative development of thinking within the broad frame of constructivism, which would not have been possible in a more closed theory, with precise definitions. We agree that more well-defined use of terms is now sought by those working within and without the field of constructivism to prevent this powerful and useful view of learning being thrown out 'with the bath water'. With respect to social constructivism, answers to the following questions would address some of the currently perceived vagueness: What is socially constructed knowledge? How is this knowledge constructed? What criteria are used to judge the worth of socially constructed beliefs and knowledge? Are these fruitful questions to ask?

The Ontological Issues of Realism and Relativism

The constructivist perspective, particularly the social constructivist perspective of knowledge and learning, is sometimes critiqued as involving a relativist view of knowledge creation. The issue of relativism is currently being debated and argued in science and science education, and it is largely unacceptable to many in science education. But a socially constructed view of scientific knowledge and students' scientific knowledge need not imply relativism — a realist position can be adopted (Osborne, 1993; Driver, Asoko, Leach, Mortimer and Scott, 1994). But both the realist and relativist positions are alternatives to empirical and positivist views.

The realist-relativist distinction may well be a false dichotomy. There are other ontological and epistemological positions being developed and as debates in the area are still to be clarified, we do not wish to take up a position ourselves at this time. Moreover, we look to our philosophically inclined colleagues to see if they can develop an ontological position to underlie the conceptual development and personal and social views of learning being researched and developed in science education, rather than throwing out the constructivist view of learning completely.

Making Sense

A constructivist approach to science education emphasizes 'making sense': both making sense of the everyday world and making sense of science. However, such an approach runs a risk that it might be inferred as promoting a view that science and learning proceed by an empirical-inductivist route. A constructivist view of learning does not advocate this. 'Making sense' is a phrase used to indicate the construction of knowledge by the students as part of their learning. The inputs into the construction of knowledge may be those sensed by touch and sight in terms of observations of the physical world but they may also be inputs from the social world sensed by sight and hearing of communication. Moreover, the empiricist label is difficult to sustain if a social constructivist position is adopted. 'Making sense' can also refer to the cognitive processes of reflection and reconstruction which can take place in the absence of any sensory input (Osborne, 1985).

The criticism is sometimes linked to curriculum debates with the misleading statement that 'anything goes' and students will not learn the content in a state or national curriculum if they are 'making sense for themselves'. However, teachers who view learning and teaching from a constructivist position are morally and (often) legally committed to helping students to construct meaningful understandings for themselves of the scientific concepts in the curriculum. A view of learning from a constructivist perspective is not the same as discovery learning — the teacher intervenes when necessary to engage with the thinking of the students (Bell, 1994a). More research on the interventions of the teacher needed to promote conceptual development is required.

Theory Adjudication

Another criticism levelled at constructivism is that it lacks a theory of theory adjudication for learners. Many of the major concepts of science, when originally invented, conflicted with common sense when applied to everyday events. It is therefore not surprising that students find it difficult to bring together, and resolve the conflict between, the 'everyday view' and the 'science view' of a phenomenon, which requires either rejecting one in favour of the other or clarifying the context in which to use each. Teaching based on a constructivist view of learning certainly needs a way of theorizing about how students test out their ideas and the ideas of others.

In addition, the notion of adjudication of newly constructed knowledge by a group as well as an individual needs to theorized.

Science Curricula

A constructivist view of learning is sometimes critiqued with respect to the content of curricula. All science curricula are predicated on providing young people with an understanding of the main concepts and procedures of science. Indeed, this is probably the only chance that many students will ever have of coming to understand this socially constructed and valued knowledge. In any curriculum writing exercise, the question of what aspects of scientific knowledge will be listed (given that all scientific knowledge cannot be included) gives rise to intense debate between the various stakeholders in the exercise. Constructivism has been criticized in this type of debate for the length of time required in a classroom based on constructivist views of learning which prevents all the currently perceived central concepts from being fully addressed.

In most curricula, there exists no clear rationale for what is deemed to be central. Moreover, constructivists have a research base that is too small to inform current debates on the content of curricula (Bell, 1990). Even if constructivists had more data, the task of justifying concept inclusion must be addressed more widely, by others involved in the curriculum development process, for example, employers and parents. If all the concepts are genuinely seen as vital, then, given the fixed timetable of curricula, a suitable response from constructivists must be to provide more research evidence to support the existing claim that teaching approaches based on a constructivist view of learning ultimately saves time because the quality of learning is improved and therefore less 'revision' is needed. However, a more appropriate response would be to decrease the number of concepts for inclusion using the aims of science education as the criteria for selection. The inclusion of concepts in a 'science for all' curriculum would be different to those in a 'science for future scientists' or in a 'science for the most able' curriculum. Most state and national curricula do not address this issue and blur the problem in an attempt to satisfy all stakeholders in the curriculum development exercise.

Progression in the Curriculum

Current constructivist views of learning are criticized for not providing any guidance on how to fulfil the requirement that national or state curricula indicate a progression of teaching or learning. As argued in Chapter 1, progression seems to have arisen as a demand on the curriculum from concerns about accountability. We argue that progression is not necessarily an inherent part of a view of learning, but that a view of learning must interface with this predominant concept in current curriculum development.

The Capabilities and Learning Styles of Students

Accounts of constructivist views of learning rarely take into account the literature on different learning styles. Whilst some students thrive on a diet of sceptical inquiry, others prefer to receive didactic exposition; some like to know the 'whole story' at the outset of a learning sequence, while others prefer to proceed in a linear fashion. In addition, the constructivist accounts to date do not address the development of reasoning skills of students, as researched by the earlier Piagetian studies, and little progress has been made in linking the research on the role of metaphors and analogies with a constructivist view of learning. The challenge is to include accounts of these findings on learning in constructivist views of learning (Resnick, 1991) or to argue that they need not be addressed as in poststructural critiques of the dualism of personal and social (Gergen, 1985) or to accept that constructivism gives only a partial account of learning.

The Search for the 'Grand Theory'

Constructivism has been critiqued as a partial account of learning and knowing; it is a cognitive approach to learning, based on a rational style of thought (McComish, 1994). It has little to say about the affective aspects of learning, non-rational thinking and skill learning, or about culture and power in the classroom (O'Loughlin, 1992a). From our perspective, this is one of the biggest challenges to constructivism from those working within its framework — that it does not address the non-rational, affective and intuitive aspects of learning. However, we would take issue with the assumption that there is something called a 'grand theory of learning' yet to be invented, and agree with Joan Solomon (1994, p. 17) that 'to equate the absence of such total coverage with theoretical error illustrates once again the overblown expectations that have accrued to constructivism'. It could well be that there will be several theories of learning, each giving a partial view. What is needed in science education, are overviews of learning that articulate better the non-rational thinking, the affective aspects and power relationships involved in learning science.

The Social Dimension to the Practice of Science and the
Learning of Science

The criticisms here are that the present practice of science education based on a constructivist view of learning does not fully recognize that the emergence of the agreed meaning of concepts in science is a social process; and that the learning of those concepts is best undertaken within a social framework. This appears to be a confusion in the minds of the critics between personal and social constructivism. The adoption of some history and philosophy of science approaches would meet the first problem, whilst the second is addressed by a social constructivist approach to teaching and learning. As indicated previously in this chapter, we agree that many accounts of learning and constructivism in science education over the last decade have focused more on the individual, at the neglect of the social. This mirrors the wider situation in psychology. Accordingly, we have outlined in this chapter a social constructivist view of learning.

The Role of the Teacher

Critics have suggested that in teaching based on a constructivist view of learning, the teacher is a neutral facilitator who does not intervene or tell the students any science. This criticism may be applied to a discovery view of learning, but not to a constructivist view. In teaching based on a constructivist view of learning, the teacher interacts with the students' thinking and facilitates the students' thinking and learning. The teacher does not stand back at all times. The teacher may tell and explain the science to students, but the teacher may also not tell the science to the students immediately, instead asking some questions or suggesting some activities to get them thinking. A constructivist view of learning does not dictate or imply a particular teaching approach (Millar, 1989). As Duit (1994) states 'constructivist teaching and learning approaches aim at helping students to make the constructions that lead to understanding of the scientific point of view' (p. xxxvi). It involves both the student's own activity and the guidance, mediation or intervention of the teacher. There are different ways this guidance, mediation or intervention might be linked with the student's learning activities. We suggest that further research on the nature and effectiveness of the teacher guidance, mediation and intervention is required.

The Scope of the Utility of Constructivism

The goal to 'find out what the students think and start teaching from there' is claimed by critics of constructivism to be impractical given the high student to staff ratios in many classes. To deal with this criticism, one could accept the current ways of organizing learning and teaching in most schools, for the sake of argument, and advocate techniques which elicit students' existing thinking with minimum use of teacher time, such as self-diagnosis, paper-based materials and computer-managed schemes. However, the criticism arises from a general misunderstanding that to be a teacher who holds a constructivist view of learning is to use a particular teaching sequence and set of activities, which are to elicit the prior knowledge of *all* students in the class. In contrast, we view teaching based on a constructivist view of learning as a particular mind-set of the teacher, who plans for and uses interactions with students' thinking, to elicit, intervene and engage with the thinking and under-standings of the students towards the currently scientifically accepted conceptions.

The advocacy of learning through eliciting, challenging and questioning others' conceptions and beliefs must be treated with a degree of circumspection. Much teaching based on a constructivist view of learning involves the students' public questioning of the teacher and other students, but in many societies this is considered grossly offensive and culturally inappropriate (Moli, 1993). It may also be counterproductive to a gender inclusive curriculum (McComish, 1994). The valuing of the ideas, experiences and opinions that girls bring to the classroom by teachers and boys is not dependant only on how well the girls clarify and communicate their ideas. A suitable response is needed to this issue, perhaps based around the idea of self-reflection, although doubt is not a universal concept. Finally, it must be said that there is a need for longitudinal research on whole cohorts, to determine the effectiveness of approaches to teaching based on a constructivist view of learning.

The Status of Constructivism with Teachers

It is sometimes said that constructivism is put forward as a fact rather than as a set of allied theories, such that teachers are asked to believe it as truth. The criticism also includes that converted teachers have a sense of 'evangelism'. Typically many teachers' response to using constructivist ideas about learning and associated teaching activities is strongly positive: it matches and enables the achievement of their professional goals. The teachers who have used teaching approaches based on a constructivist view of learning usually report improved learning (both learning conditions and outcomes) and classroom management of their students. However, it must be pointed out that if teachers wish to reject a behaviourist view of learning (which many do), a constructivist view of learning is the only credible alternative available.

Impact on Teacher Development

The criticism here is that in teacher education undue attention is paid to teaching activities based on a constructivist view of learning for the classroom and that insufficient time is devoted to teachers' own understanding of the scientific concepts that they are to teach. There does need to be a balance in pre-service and inservice education of teachers of science between learning science and learning new teaching activities. Primary teachers value learning more of the science in the curriculum, as well as learning that the teaching activities they use in other curriculum areas — for example, small group discussion activities — are appropriate for learning science. Secondary teachers appreciate learning about new teaching approaches to engage the students in thinking about the science to be learnt and to update and extend their scientific knowledge. Both kinds of teacher education need to be available for teachers.

Two other points can also be made in response to this criticism. First, this attention to classroom process (particularly for secondary teachers) would not be needed in teacher education if the school and higher education which student teachers had previously experienced had been conducted on constructivist lines, so that they were familiar with the approach from their own experience. Secondly, if teaching approaches to learning science based on a constructivist view of learning were used in primary, secondary and tertiary education, teachers would have a better understanding of the concepts of science and the nature of science.

Links to Progressive Education

Constructivism is often associated with progressive science education in general (Duit, 1994, p. xxxiii), with Dewey being described as a constructivist (Phillips, 1995). There are strong relationships between the 'science for all' movement (Fensham, 1986), including girls (Bell, 1988), and constructivism. But it would be incorrect to use the term 'constructivism' for all progressive developments in science education (Duit, 1994).

In summary, we include in our social constructivist view of learning with respect to teacher development, the following points:

- Knowledge is constructed by people. This is termed the trivial component of constructivism by von Glasersfeld but as Solomon (1994) points out it is an ill-founded description. It is the most widely referred to aspect of a constructivist view of learning in science education.
- Construction and reconstruction of knowledge is both personal and social.
- Learning involves the interaction of the personal and the social construction of meanings, and both may be changed in the interaction.
- Socially constructed knowledge is both the context for and the outcome of human social interaction. The socially constructed knowledge is an integral part of the learning activity.
- Learners as developing people have partial agency. They are partially determining and partially determined. The teacher development necessary to address the agenda of teachers outlined in Chapter 1, requires teachers (and others) to change the culture of what it means to be a teacher of science and for teachers to be positioned in the reconstructed culture.
- Social interaction — for example, in dialogues, accounting and narratives — promotes learning of socially constructed knowledge, personal construction of meaning, and the reconstruction of social knowledge.
- Learners can reconstruct their knowledge through reflection. Metacognition is an important part of learning and can involve reflection on the degree of understanding or the nature of the thoughts.
- Knowledge is not something in the world to be discovered (as in a discovery learning approach). We do not learn by 'reading the book of nature'. Rather, people construct mental representations of phenomena and these mental constructions are constrained by how the world is (Driver, Asoko, Leach, Mortimer and Scott, 1994). In particular, scientists conduct experiments in order to test the degree of fit between their constructions and how the world seems to be. Relativism is 'tempered by stability which is achieved by the individual in relation to his or her experience' (Confrey, 1993, p. 4).

Both a realist and a relativist position can accept that we can never directly know the 'real world' or an 'absolute' truth. A suitable approach to the issue of realism versus relativism might be to follow Kelly (1969), that is, to put the matter to one side; or von Glaserfeld (1991), that is, to reject the concept of reality; or to see the debate as still in progress.

- All the approaches to constructivism take a similar view on communication: a directly transmitted and received message is not possible, there exists only an active construction of meaning by the hearer. Teacher development must allow for messages to be produced in a variety of forms and for hearers to discuss their constructions of the messages.

- Teacher development as learning by teachers needs to take into account the existing knowledge, experiences, opinions and values of the teachers. This will include their prior knowledge of teaching and learning, and the nature and status of knowledge. It will also include taking into account their ways of learning. In doing this, teacher development convenors or facilitators need to expect and plan for unintended learning outcomes.

- Teacher development as learning needs to take into account the existing socially constructed knowledge of what it means to be a teacher of science.

- Learning by teachers in teacher development situations is occurring within wider social and political contexts. These need to be addressed, not ignored.

Other Perspectives on Teacher Learning

In the above summary, we have outlined our view of learning to underline teacher development, one that we call a social constructivist view of learning. One of the criticisms of constructivism in science education is that it does not include aspects of learning researched outside the literature on constructivist views of learning. In this section, we review those research findings that are commensurate with a constructivist view of learning and teacher development. We do not attempt to add these aspects to a constructivist view but to alert our readers to the research findings. Some ideas from the fields of adult learning, from studies in learning styles and strategies, and from empirical work on learning-to-learn are discussed.

The Teacher as Adult Learner

It would seem entirely proper to view the learning of teachers, to a first approximation, as one example of the learning of adults in general. However, they have engaged previously in far more deliberate learning and teaching than the average citizen has, and may therefore be more influenced by the process and content of that prior learning. Knowles (1989) saw the learning of adults as distinct from that of children. In his so-called andragogical model, he makes a number of assumptions: that adults need to know the purposes for which they are learning something before they are willing to invest a lot of effort to learn it; that adults, being accustomed to making their own decisions in everyday life, learn best when they have the greatest degree of self-direction over the nature, pace and approach of their learning; and that adults learn best when addressing tasks and problems which they perceive to be real and which arise from, or otherwise relate to, the demands of their everyday lives.

In our view, the distinction represents a false dichotomy, for these assumptions about the conditions needed for high quality learning apply equally to adults and to young people. Knowles' (1989) prescription lacks an awareness of up-to-date approaches in school-level education, particularly those based on a constructivist view of learning. Many adults do bring a much larger amount of experience to their studies than many young people, which is certainly a valuable resource on which to draw. A group of teachers will have highly diverse backgrounds, accompanied by strongly held knowledge, skills, and attitudes, especially about the nature of teaching and learning. These experiences must be acknowledged, drawn upon and evaluated, if successful learning is to take place.

One aspect of prior knowledge and experiences to be attended to in teacher-development activities, is associated with teachers' views of what constitutes teaching and learning activities for teachers as adult learners. Teachers, like other adults, are facing the same life challenges of sustaining financial independence, sustaining relationships of various kinds with other adults, bringing up children, and the like, but they may differ from other adult learners in two key respects. First, they will have had considerable experience of tertiary (and adult) education. The principles of adult learning may well not have informed the way that they were taught when in higher education. They may thus bring to their teacher development activities expectations about what constitutes 'proper' teaching and learning for adults which are very different from those set out above. Secondly, their own practice of teaching may not be informed by the above assumptions, which we believe to be applicable to learners of all ages. Therefore, the prior experiences and views about teacher development activities held by teachers engaging in professional development activities may be at odds with those being advocated as a result of the research findings in this book. For example, teachers may not value listening to other teachers talk of their teaching if they come expecting to listen to an expert on new ways to teach science to students. An aspect of teacher development is therefore to acknowledge and address the concepts and beliefs about learning already held by teachers.

As well as their views of learning and teaching, how teachers as learners view the nature of knowledge is of interest. Perry (1970), later supported by the work of Jacques (1991), found differences among undergraduates in the ways that they view the nature of knowledge and approach learning. The nine 'positions', as seen from the perspective of the individual concerned, are illustrated with two of the nine positions:

> There is a right and wrong to everything. Authorities, whose role it is to teach the answers, know what these are, and, if I work hard, and learn the right answers, adding more and more to my stock of knowledge, all will be well.

Some uncertainties and differences of opinion are real and legitimate. But this is a temporary situation for authorities who are still searching for the right answer.

The notion that different people may hold differing views on the nature and status of knowledge may also be applied to differences between the ways of knowing of women and men (Belenky, Clinchy, Goldberger and Tarule, 1986).

Learning Strategies and Styles

In addition to knowing something of the circumstances which will support the learning of teachers as adults, it is valuable to know more about how they actually go about the learning tasks that they undertake. Much of the work which is centrally relevant to this issue has been done by Marton (1988), Pask (see Daniel, 1975; Ogborn, 1993), and Entwistle (1988). Indeed, it is the model by Entwistle (1988) which enables all this work to be synthesized.

In this model, adults are said to adopt one of three strategies when confronted with a learning task. Two of them, the 'surface' and the 'deep' strategies were identified by Marton (1988), whilst the 'strategic' approach was identified by Entwistle (1988). In surface-level processing, the learner (in this case, teachers) is primarily concerned: to complete the course, programme or extended learning activity; to avoid failing the course; to cover and pay equal attention to all the content of the course; to find the 'right' answers which are imbedded within the course; and to assimilate unaltered chunks of material by learning the course content verbatim. In deep-level processing, the learner is primarily concerned: to extend an already-present interest in the subject matter of the course; to obtain as much personally relevant, perhaps vocationally relevant, knowledge from the course as possible; to build up an overall picture of the content of the course; to identify the arguments which lie beneath the central point and the logic involved in them; to clarify unclear points, and to question the conclusions. Whilst some people seem to use either a surface approach or a deep approach irrespective of the nature of the task, others use the two approaches in a flexible combination dependent on the perceived nature of the task: this is the 'strategic' approach.

Reliance on the surface approach is of little benefit in teacher development when viewed from a constructivist perspective. The memorization of fragmentary facts would seem to offer an ineffective way of addressing the issues which are central to growth and development as outlined in our model. However, the deep approach has much offer. The work of Pask (see Ogborn, 1993) has shown that such an approach can be implemented in two distinct ways: by 'operation' learning, in which the learner proceeds by understanding each element in a chain of logical argument in turn; and by 'comprehension' learning, in which the learner first seeks to form an overall view of the material to be learnt by cross-relating the ideas involved. Inevitably, some people can deploy both of these strategies: they are referred to as 'versatile' learners. They are, overall, the most effective because a deep level of understanding is acquired, which integrates principles with facts and uses evidence to develop arguments.

Overall, the most successful learning strategy seems to be Entwistle's (1988) 'strategic' approach, which makes use of both the surface and the deep strategies, and which engages in 'versatile' learning within the latter. The outcome of such learning will be a variable level of understanding, depending on what the learner feels can and should be achieved within the context of expectations set by the course organizer. The overt adoption of course designs, teaching strategies, and expectations of the nature of learning, which promote the use of the strategic approach, is both feasible and effective (Sheppard and Gilbert, 1991). It is an engagement of teachers with the ideas and activities being suggested in a programme that will promote the teacher development we see as being required for the improvement of science education.

Metacognition

The term metacognition can be used to refer to learner's awareness of their thoughts, beliefs and ways of coming to know about the processes of learning and teaching. Reflecting on one's beliefs about teaching and learning activities (for adults and school students), the status of knowledge, and learning styles can be seen as an aspect of metacognition that is important to the teacher development process. This importance can be said to apply to pre-service teacher education (Gunstone and Northfield, 1994) as well as in-service teacher education. Harri-Augstein and Thomas (1991) have also pointed out that people's capacity to learn may be inhibited by a range of personally held beliefs about learning and about themselves as learners, which may include beliefs about the nature and scope of what they are capable of learning. People may believe that certain topics can only be understood by specialists in those subjects, such that their own understanding of them will be necessarily limited to an introductory, or partial, understanding. Their beliefs may also concern the circumstances in which their own learning can take place. Individuals may believe that learning can only take place in circumstances deliberately contrived by another person, that is, by a teacher, or that these beliefs may be about the circumstances in the outside world and in the person's internal world needed for learning to take place. People may believe that learning only takes place if there is some idealized state of synergy between the structure of events in the outside world and a personal readiness to learn about those events. People may have a poor understanding of their own learning processes, believing that they have a limited capacity for learning, either generally, which they explain as a lack of 'intelligence', or specifically, which they explain as a lack of 'talent' in that subject area.

Harri-Augstein and Thomas (1991) believed that the quality and quantity of an individual's learning can be improved substantially. They saw this as achieved by acquiring a greater dependency on oneself, as opposed to others, for an evaluation of the quality and quantity of any learning achieved. They advocate that self-management of learning must be aspired to and achieved, with each person seeing learning as including changes in personal thinking, feeling, and perceiving, rather than only in terms of the external performance of tasks. This outlook would entail the development of a clearer perception of how one learns. The development of an ability to perceive learning as a process rather than only as the attainment of a pre-specified outcome is also seen to be helpful. This would involve developing a greater self-awareness of the ways in which learning takes place while it is occurring. An individual could, with great profit, come to see the acquisition of learning skills as the key to the development of an infinite capacity for learning. This realization will take place as those skills are progressively developed. Lastly, the learner might come to view learning as an activity undertaken intentionally. Again, the issue of self-awareness and self-management is to the fore. As mentioned previously, this view of learning is based on a strong sense of agency, supported by the concept of individualism.

In order to reflect on these beliefs about learning and to develop improved learning skills, Harri-Augstein and Thomas (1991) advocate the development of the ability to hold 'learning conversations' with oneself: a permanently sustained dialogue within oneself about the nature of learning itself. This view is built on a series of assertions which echo those expounded above: that learning is the construction of meaning; that meaning is a relationship between the knower and the known; that meaning itself cannot be transmitted, merely represented; and that conversation involves the negotiation of meaning, which is transformed by that process. The implication is that the mind of an individual (the knower) can construct meaning by contemplating experience (the known). Moreover, within a learning conversation, an individual represents that meaning to self, thereby both transforming it into a series of generalizations and becoming more aware of the processes involved. Conversations with others, as projections and interpretations of meaning, are an invaluable aid to learning.

It would thus seem beneficial, in terms of both developing learning-to-learn skills and knowledge as components of teacher development itself and as a skill that could be passed on to students, to develop the art of learning conversations in teachers. Conversations with others would enable both the personal clarification of meaning, as well as enhance one's ability to conduct learning conversations within oneself.

Narratives

Narration is a form of conversation. Telling a narrative involves recounting and restorying past experiences and the processes of constructing shared understandings, constructing mental models for representing and organizing experiences, recalling, summarizing and communicating (Cortazzi, 1993, pp. 1–4). Hence, the telling of narratives or anecdotes may also be useful in the teacher development situation to help teachers reflect on, evaluate and develop, their beliefs and actions on teaching, learning, and other aspects of science education. In this sense, telling narratives can be seen as a part of the learning process when viewed as a social process, and as a part of the development of self-identity as social, interpersonal and relational (Bruner, 1990, pp. 99–138). Personal and social development are intertwined in telling narratives because, as Clandinin and Connelly (1991, p. 259) state: 'deliberately storying and restorying one's life is . . . a fundamental method of personal (and social growth): it is a fundamental quality of education'.

Telling narratives, then, can be seen to facilitate both personal and social construction of knowledge (including self-identity). While the study of teachers' narratives may give researchers insights into teachers' culture (Cortazzi, 1993), the sharing of narratives amongst teachers may enable them, themselves, to construct and reconstruct their own culture of what it means to be a teacher of science and to reconstruct their sense of self. Examples of telling narratives in teacher development situations can be found in Clandinin and Connelly (1991), Mattingly (1991) and The Mathematical Association (1991).

Critical Inquiry

In the first chapter, we outlined some of the areas for professional development currently sought by teachers. Teachers also seek skills and theoretical frameworks that will enable them to engage in a life-long process of professional development in order to address adequately both present and future challenges. Forming a clear view of the expertise involved in teaching, deploying enhanced knowledge and skills within a sustained programme of curriculum development, presenting that professionalism to all those who have a legitimate interest in the issues involved, and defending opinions and actions against criticism, all require that the learning of teachers be given a high priority in order that they can be obtained.

The metaphor needed to underpin such learning is 'the teachers as critical inquirer'. According to Jane Gilbert (1994b), such a view conceptualizes teachers as:

> . . . professionals who think critically about themselves as practitioners, and about the contexts in which they work. The ways in which teacher education is practised are seen as reflecting the particular social conditions, political structures, and social interests within which it operates. The relationship between teacher development, schooling, and the rest of society is emphasised. An important part of the critical perspective on teacher development is the notion of teacher empowerment. A central focus in the change process is given to teachers as professionals and as human beings in a social and political context. (Gilbert, 1994b, p. 21)

The notion of the teacher as a critical inquirer is best approached through a consideration of the 'reflective practitioner', which is a concept that has received considerable attention over the last decade or so, in teacher education and elsewhere, as a result of the writing of Donald Schön (Schön, 1983, 1987, 1991). It has gained prominence at the expense of the then-established approach, which required a novice professional to learn sequentially theoretical knowledge, then applied knowledge, and then how to use that applied knowledge in practice. Jane Gilbert (1993) has summarized the criticisms that Schön levelled against this established view:

> Firstly, there is an assumption that professional knowledge can be produced in isolation from the situation in which it is to be applied. This assumption does not take account of the way such knowledge is embedded in a socially structured context by a community of practitioners and exercised in the institutional settings particular to that profession (Schön, 1987). Secondly, there is an assumption that practitioners work by applying scientifically derived theoretical knowledge to their practice. This is an inadequate description of the ways professionals work. It is more accurate to describe their work as based on their own, largely tacit, knowledge of what they are doing and trying to achieve. Professional knowledge is not a systematically organised body of theoretical knowledge, but is more accurately described as a shared body of inherited practical knowledge. Thirdly, there is the assumption that professional competence and technical problem solving competence are the same thing. This assumption does not take account of the way problems arise in real world practice situations — not as givens, but more accurately as 'messy', 'indeterminate' situations arising as a result of conflicting values. These problems are resolved through what Schön calls 'artful competence' — a non-technical, non-rational, process . . . (Gilbert, 1993, pp. 30–1)

Schön advocated a very different approach, based on the premise that, when actually practising a profession, an individual displays: knowledge-in-action; reflection-in-action; and reflection-on-action.

- **Knowledge-in-action**
  Schön (1983) saw this as involving:

  > . . . actions, recognitions, and judgements which we know how to carry out spontaneously; we do not have to think about them prior to or during their performance. We are often unaware of having learned to do these things, we simply find ourselves doing them . . . we are usually unable to describe the knowing which our action reveals. (Schön, 1983, p. 54)

- **Reflection-in-action**
  This involves the exercise of analysis, judgment, and action, in a framework of 'thinking on your feet'. Building on the ideas of Dewey, Grimmett (1988) suggested that reflection-in-action could be considered in terms of the following elements: being perplexed by the teaching situation; seeking to recall a somewhat similar problem, previously solved, and considering it as a metaphor; reframing the problem through the use of the metaphor;

thinking through alternative solutions, including their consequences; and taking action by use of the emergent solution.

- **Reflection-on-action**
  This is the version of reflection-in-action which can take place after the event: for example, when thinking through the events of a day. It would be much more deliberate, extend over some period of time, and perhaps lead to changes of beliefs and to resolutions to act similarly or differently in future.

A major challenge for teacher education has been to operationalize these concepts and precepts. As Grimmett (1988) remarks: 'Central to the process (of reflection) is the paradox that one cannot know (whether a solution is appropriate) without acting and one cannot act without knowing'. Notwithstanding this paradox, the approach has been widely used. Zeichner and Tabachnick (1991) have identified four traditions which have emerged, since Schön's early work, in the preparation of teachers to engage in reflection:

1. an academic version that stresses reflection upon subject matter and the representation and translation of subject matter to promote student understanding . . . 2. a social efficiency version that emphasises the thoughtful application of particular teaching strategies that have been suggested by research on teaching . . . 3. a developmentalist version that prioritises teaching that is sensitive to students' interests, thinking, and patterns of developmental growth . . . and 4. a social reconstructionist version that stresses reflection about the social and political context of schooling and the assessment of classroom actions for their ability to contribute towards greater equity, social justice, and humane conditions in schooling and society. (Zeichner and Tabachnick, 1991, p. 3)

The first three notions of the reflective teacher are based on a personal, individual view of learning, in which the individual is able and willing to do reflective thinking, and take action in particular ways. It is these meanings of 'reflection' that are often appropriated by those with technicist views of teacher development (Gilbert, 1994b) in their ongoing search for new and more powerful ways of achieving teachers' compliance with implementing new research, development or policy. Only the fourth notion can be linked with a social view of learning and with the notion of the critical inquirer.

Adopting the notion of reflective practitioner must be seen against a backdrop of the criticisms that have been made of the approach. Smythe (1992) has identified four problems. First, the wide acceptance of the approach as the basis for professional development could lead to the insistence that all teachers develop and use the skills entailed — that is, there would be a pressure to conform. Only a far wider use of the approach than occurs currently would make this a possibility. Secondly, the vagueness of how the features of reflective practice are defined could lead to its use for a variety of concealed purposes, because each of Zeichner and

Tabachnick's (1991) four traditions rests on unstated value systems. Certainly, the reasons underlying the adoption of any one of these traditions should be known to those involved. Thirdly, the process may be inadvertently self-destructive for teachers. As Smythe (1992) comments:

> Individualising the problem of 'quality' and 'excellence' in schools by leaving it to individual teachers to reflect on their practice is handing them an instrument that many will turn on themselves in the hopeless search for what's wrong with schooling. By labelling the problem in this way (i.e., the need for teachers to be more reflective about teaching), we have neatly quarantined the problem. Portraying the problems confronting schools as if they were due in some measure to a lack of competence on the part of teachers and schools and as if they were resolvable by individuals (or groups of teachers), is to effectively divert attention away from the real structural problems that are deeply embedded in social, economic, and political, inequalities. (Smythe, 1992, p. 287)

Fourthly, adopting the concept of reflective practitioner may lead to an undue emphasis on pragmatic solutions, and thus to an over-valuing of what works in practice at the expense of what is right in principle.

To these potential problems, Gilliss (1988) has added two pragmatic criticisms. The groups from which Schön (1983) drew his original examples, such as musicians, were students who were highly skilled in the basic technical competencies of their professions before they reached higher education. By contrast, even experienced teachers sometimes do not have a complete curriculum knowledge of their subjects. Moreover, the development of the reflective practitioner involves access to a highly knowledgeable and skilled tutor: such people are in short supply.

If teacher development is to include the development of the reflective practitioner, then these shortcomings need to be minimized. Smythe (1992) describes four sequential, general types of activity for teachers, each of which entails one facet of reflection: describing (what do I do?); informing (what do these actions mean?); confronting (how do I come to do things this way?); and reconstructing (how might I do things differently?). Similarly, Louden (1992) talks of four forms of teacher action within which reflection is embedded: through introspection, where the teacher thinks about problems, events, and their meaning; the use of replay and simulation, so that prior performance can be analysed; through inquiry, where some form of data collection and analysis takes place; and through spontaneous action in the classroom. With the exception of the last form of action, these activity types and purposes lend themselves more readily to the development of reflection-on-action rather than to reflection-in-action. All are capable of explicit presentation to participants.

If a reflection-on-action session of one teacher is to be shared by a number of teachers, then there is a need to have the original classroom situation available to all in the greatest detail. An excellent approach, but one for which use is limited by technical problems, involves the discussion of a videotape of classroom activity and of the recollection of what the teacher was thinking at the time (see Erickson and MacKinnon, 1991).

Many reflection-on-action sessions make use of written materials, in the form of diaries, journals, or case study accounts, which Grimmett (1988) has suggested may be used in one of three ways. First, written materials could be copied as accounts of model or ideal practice, which in practice in so far as it can be done, might elicit reflection. Secondly, a series of accounts of case studies might be used to stimulate an appreciation of the importance of specific contextual issues during their comparative evaluation. Thirdly, written materials could serve as a source of insight for the direct appreciation of personal practice. A teacher is being invited to view the materials as a metaphor for their own practice. The materials may be used to inspire questions about personal practice, or may cause the restructuring of some personal experience, or a re-examination of some taken-for-granted belief. Another approach to sharing the experiences of one teacher with a group, is through the use of narratives (Bell, 1994b).

The choice of methodology will depend on the purpose for which reflection-on-action is being undertaken. Louden (1992) talks in terms of four purposes which a teacher may be addressing during reflection: a technical purpose, where an established theory is being checked for validity; a personal purpose, where some understanding of private importance is being sought; a problematic purpose, where some problem in professional practice is being inquired into; and a critical purpose, where some underlying issue of the conditions or purposes of schooling is being addressed.

In different ways and to varying degrees, this reflection-on-action approach and the related approach of action-research have underpinned much of the most respected and influential research and teacher development work in science education over the last fifteen years: including the work by the Children's Learning in Science Project (CLISP) and the Science Processes and Concept Exploration Project (SPACE), in the United Kingdom, the Learning in Science Projects (LISP) in New Zealand, and the Project for Enhancing Effective Learning (PEEL) in Australia.

The development of the reflective and critical inquirer is congruent with the challenges being addressed in this book. The value of reflection, as a professional skill, in the evolution of the 'teacher as critical inquirer' is evident. However, the notion of critical inquirer embodies the idea of social reconstructionism. That is, the aim of critical inquiry is the empowerment of teachers as professionals to critique and act in the social and political contexts in which they work. A part of this is reflecting on the political ideologies underlying the different approaches to science education. In this sense, reflection is not about the technical concerns of whether an activity works in the classroom or not, but about considering and taking action on political questions in science education, such as gender, race, and class issues, excessive central-government control over the curriculum and accountability in the teaching profession.

Reflection is a skill which is inherently part of constructivism, particularly personal constructivism. A social constructivist view of learning and knowing is better able to be related to the notion of critical inquiry and social reconstructionism.

In summary, teachers can use reflection and critical inquiry as the basis for their own conceptual development and for contributing to curriculum change. It is a valuable tool in the examination of their role as a teacher and in reviewing their classroom activities. Most importantly, the reflective practitioner has the capability to review the assumptions and expectations of political contexts, for example, 'New Rightist' inspired prescriptions, and social debates, for example, the inclusive curriculum. The 'appropriateness of response' to proposed changes may well be related to, or arise from, the form of reflective activity that is undertaken.

The notion of the reflective practitioner supports and enables the teacher as critical inquirer. Our position is that teachers today are being challenged to critique the social and political contexts in which they work. An understanding of the hidden values and ideas underlying new policy initiative, such as, the New Zealand Qualifications Framework, is essential not only to evaluate the educational worth of the new policy or innovation, but also to understand the pressures and problems being projected (inappropriately) on teachers by the wider society.

Summary

What, then, is a suitable interpretation of learning on which to base a view of teacher development? We include in our view of learning and development the following:

- The development of self-identity as a teacher of science is a part of teacher development. What it means to be a teacher of science is socially constructed and a part of the culture of science teaching. During teacher development, this culture and socially constructed knowledge will be renegotiated and reconstructed. An individual teacher will be constructing for himself or herself a self-identity as a teacher and be positioned within this culture. Teachers need to be contributors to the reconstruction of the culture if they are to be empowered and engaged.
- Knowledge is constructed by people.
- Construction and reconstruction of knowledge is both personal and social.
- Learning involves the interaction of the personal and the social constructions of meanings, and both may be changed in the interaction.
- Socially constructed knowledge is both the context for, and the outcome of, human social interaction. The socially constructed knowledge is an integral part of the learning activity.
- Learners as developing people have partial agency. They are partially determining and partially determined. The teacher development required to address the agenda of teachers outlined in Chapter 1, requires teachers (and others) to change the culture of what it means to be a teacher of science and for teachers to be positioned in the reconstructed culture.
- Social interaction — for example, in dialogues, accounting and narratives — promotes learning of socially constructed knowledge, personal construction of meaning, and the reconstruction of social knowledge.

- Learners can reconstruct their knowledge through reflection. Metacognition is an important part of learning and can involve reflection on the degree of understanding or the nature of the thoughts.
- Teacher development as learning by teachers needs to take into account the existing knowledge, experiences, opinions and values of the teachers. This will include their prior knowledge of teaching and learning, and the nature and status of knowledge. It will also include taking into account their ways of learning. In doing this, teacher development convenors or facilitators need to expect and plan for unintended learning outcomes.
- Learning by teachers in teacher-development situations is occurring within wider social and political contexts. These need to be addressed, not ignored.
- Teacher development as learning needs to take into account the existing socially constructed knowledge of what it means to be a teacher of science.
- Teacher development can be viewed as reflective and critical inquiry, within the social and political contexts of teaching and education.

This chapter has explored a view of learning that is based on a consideration of human development and the development of self-identity, a social constructivist view of learning, and reflective and critical inquiry. This view can be related to the model of teacher development outlined in Chapter 2, indicating the interwoven and interactive nature of the three aspects of teacher development. Social development as part of teacher development involves the teachers contributing to the renegotiation and reconstruction of what it means to be a teacher (of science, for example). It also involves the development of the ways of working with others that enable the kinds of social interaction necessary for the renegotiating and reconstructing of what it means to be a teacher of science. Personal development as part of teacher development involves each individual teacher constructing, evaluating and accepting or rejecting for herself or himself the newly socially constructed knowledge about what it means to be a teacher (of science, for example), and managing the feelings associated with changing their activities and beliefs about science education, particularly when they go 'against the grain' (Cochran-Smith, 1991) of the current or proposed socially constructed and accepted knowledge. Professional development as a part of teacher development involves not only the use of different teaching activities but also the development of the beliefs and conceptions teaching, learning, science and science education, underlying the activities. It may also involve learning some science.

4 'Feeling Better about Myself as a Teacher' and 'Better Learning'

In the previous two chapters, the importance of social, personal and professional development as aspects of teacher development was discussed, as was their inter-woven nature when viewed from a social constructivist view of learning. In this chapter, two research findings on teacher development which informed the model and the view of learning are presented. The two findings are labelled 'feeling better about myself as a teacher' and 'better learning'.

'Feeling Better about Myself as a Teacher'

One of the factors that helped teacher development was that the teachers reported that they were 'more like the teachers they would like to be' and that they 'felt better about themselves as teachers' as a result of changing their teaching activities (Bell and Pearson, 1993a). For example, one teacher felt that the new teaching activities and roles for the teacher enabled her to be more like the kind of teacher she would like to be:

> ... I hated school. I did well at school but I was so frustrated ... I was bored ... at school. (I ended up doing teaching) because I felt there had to be something better than what I got and what my sisters got. That was my prime motivator really, for ever going teaching ... I get so frustrated when I see me doing what I got (at school). And so for me, this is some way of helping me become what I think a teacher should be. (16/M2/91)

> [The first part of the transcript code indicates the teacher who is quoted; the second part indicates the interview (I), survey (S), programme session (P) or meeting (M) in which the comment was made; and the last part indicates the year.]

Another stated:

> For me, knowing all of this here about the role of the teacher, this gives the impetus to do what I want to do in the classroom. I want to fulfil those roles and for me, the interactive approach gives me a vehicle to do the best way of fulfilling those roles. (15/M1/90)

Other teachers felt that they were better teachers because of the new activities they were trying out; for example:

I definitely think I am a much, much better teacher than I ever used to be. (7/I5/91)

I still go back and do it again on the Monday. It is a good way to teach and I like doing it like that for the reason that for the majority of the kids there is something in it for them. And while the demands are different and while sometimes it can be quite stressful, you get the positive vibes. (5/I4/91)

I am a lot happier with the job that I am doing. It certainly changed that. I mean I am surviving to the end of the second term without having a nervous breakdown, so I must be doing all right. I think it has made me a lot happier with the job itself and that therefore has taken off a certain amount of stress. (11/I3/91)

I think that is my motivation, wanting to do what I do better and that is what drives me on, I guess. I am really looking forward to it. (14/I4/91)

'Feeling better about myself as a teacher' was seen as a pay-off to keep on changing even though changing their teaching was considered to be intensive and energy draining; for example:

And you have to have strong positive relationships with your children and you often have to be one ahead, looking all the time thinking 'how can I challenge that child, how can I develop that further, what could I do?' So I think this is sometimes where you want to be a constructivist teacher but you get tuckered out, you get absolutely exhausted and so it (more traditional teaching) is a bit easier sometimes, of course, we all do it. (3/I11/91)

Sometimes it can be quite teacher intensive in that you are giving, giving, giving. I mean kids are wanting things from you, sometimes it is physical things like they need felts or they need rubbers and scissors and glue and sellotape and they need to be able to go to the library and permission to do this and they are always at you. And if you are doing it really well and then you are spending a lot of time interacting with them when they are doing their work and sharing things with them. Sometimes at the end of the day after you have had a Dean's meeting all lunch time, you are just drained and sometimes it is good to be able to pull out a work sheet or a task that they can do independent, that they can do quietly without you having to relate to them in a very big way. I think that is a concern in the school. It wouldn't only be me, it must be lots of other teachers that feel that sort of pressure of being, not necessarily up-front, but just it is hard work dealing with children on a one-to-one relationship . . . and hav(ing) to interact in that very close way is hard. (5/13/91)

But despite this, the teachers continued to develop their teaching because the pay-off of 'feeling better about myself as a teacher' was stronger. 'Feeling better about myself as a teacher' enabled social, personal and professional, development.

The goal of the teacher development programmes, run as part of the research project, was for the teachers to develop their teaching to take into account students' thinking. To do so, they used the activities suggested in and modelled on, the teacher development programmes (Bell, 1993b). The aspects of teaching commented on by the teachers in terms of developing or changing their role as a science teacher were viewed as:

- teaching as researching: finding out what the students are thinking;
- teaching as responding: interacting with the students' thinking;
- teaching as assessing students' thinking;
- teaching as managing learning; and
- teacher as learner.

The following quotations from interviews and surveys illustrate some of the teaching activities and the roles of the teacher discussed by the teachers and which contributed to their 'feeling better about themselves as a teacher'. The teachers tended to emphasize the new activities and did not talk much about former teaching activities that they continued to do, for example, experiments, practicals and field trips. A full documentation of the new activities and roles can be found in Bell (1993a).

Teaching as Researching: Finding out What the Students Are Thinking

The teachers stated in interview that they had changed their ideas about teaching and their classroom activities to include finding out what the students were thinking; for example:

As a teacher I have more flexibility, taking far more notice of what the kids know, which is something I never did before, bothering about what they come into my classroom with and what they knew. And now it is always asking at the beginning of things — 'what do you know, what does this one word conjure up to you', even if it is just those spider diagrams and having a look and going from there, just looking at that at the end of a unit and having a look to see what changes they have made, what additions and what sort of developments in understanding they have got, misconceptions they might have come in with. So that is really new for me, because I hadn't ever done that before. I think that is the most helpful too. And I think that kids really respond to that because they think, well, they are not so dumb, what they know the teacher is actually using, starting with that. And I think if I was a student in the class I would feel more inclined to want to do something more than to just sit there being told 'do this, do that, okay pack up now, now write this'. (12/I5/91)

The value of finding out what the students are thinking was voiced; for example:

The children are getting a lot out of it and I feel I know them better and that is a pay-off. And it is a big one if you are a teacher because of having all these children and you know whether or not they learned what you have in the textbook or can do the experiments that you have asked them to do today, you sit this experiment, you know whether or not they can do that. You find out if they have got other things in their heads. Because when you do an interactive thing, they are surprising, children will come up with surprising ideas and that is the real pay-off, that you know more about your students as you are going through it. And that is the pay-off for me because I always want to know what is going on in kids' heads. That is probably the main one. (8/I3/91)

It is neat to see the kids actually respond. You sometimes don't acknowledge that they — well I guess lots of teachers don't acknowledge that they actually have some knowledge already and they have experiences and they are involved with people who have had experiences, especially in this health and disease. It was interesting the depth of knowledge that collectively the class had. (5/I3/91)

The different ways of finding out about students' thinking were mentioned by the teachers as they talked about their teaching in the interviews. These included seeking further information or explanation and listening in classroom dialogue with an individual student, students writing in thinking books or journals, spider webs and concept maps, and brainstorming; for example:

We did centrifugal force ... with the work experience kids ... and when I asked them 'how many examples can you think of this sort of movement being used in everyday life' they came up with eight. I have never had that many for using centrifugal force ever. . . . I think of the dryer, the washing machine and a few things but these kids came up with eight. Helicopters were the same thing. And they could group them into things that were just for moving or things that were separating ... I went around the science teachers and asked them and they could come up with one or two. One came up with three, one came up with none ... I said 'well my work experience unit kids, they got eight' and I don't think it made the teachers feel very comfortable, it made them feel inadequate ... I was absolutely staggered. (12/I3/91)

Teaching as Responding: Interacting with the Students' Thinking

The teachers (and the curriculum) were intending that the students learn the scientific ideas and not be left just to clarify their own ideas. The complex teaching skill that the teachers were asked to develop during the programme was that of responding to, and interacting with, students' ideas.

In responding to, and interacting with, students' ideas, the teachers were encouraged to acknowledge that they had heard or read the students' ideas (That's an interesting idea), seek further clarification (Cars are living. What tells you that?), question the students' ideas in a supportive way (Cars give out waste fumes or gases. Is this the same as people breathing out?), propose a counterview (Cars are not living as they are not made of cells), help the students test out an idea (How could you test out that idea?), ask the students to broaden the range of applications of an idea (Are all moving things living?) or ask the students to differentiate an idea (Is a car living in the same way that a cat is?). They were also telling and explaining the science to the students. Often in interview, the teachers described their interacting with, and responding to, the students' thinking in terms of 'getting the students thinking'; for example:

> This is part of what I see as what we have been on about with the constructivist . . . Developing the student's ideas and doing that through questioning and actually trying to get them to look more deeply and expand their questions so that they can develop their ideas. I see that as basically what we have been trying to do, isn't it? (1/I12/91)

The teachers indicated that they were questioning and challenging the students' ideas more. As well as teacher–student questioning, student–student questioning occurred; for example:

> I always did a lot of motivation and I always did a lot of leading the children into things but I guess what has happened now is that they have caught up to me and so it is more of a shared thing without me, perhaps, being the dominant. But I always encourage the children to speak and have a go and question and I always lead that. But I think probably what has happened is that I don't have to have so much input into it now. And that was obvious today, even in the session today, because they were almost taking over, talking about it to one another. And so there has been a shift there, probably in my role. (3/I12/91)

It was a skill with which most teachers felt a need for more practice; for example:

> I still don't think I am good at that. That is still something that I need to work on. I am not good at probing deep into where the kids are thinking. I feel it is just a superficial 'well what do you think about it' and 'where

do you get that idea from' but I just don't feel as if I have — maybe that is enough, maybe what I do is enough but that is just something that I don't feel I am getting right down to. And I still tend to at the end of the day, sometimes I want to tell them what I think. I struggle with that one. (5/I4/91)

The teachers explicitly mentioned they were trying to get the students 'to think for themselves'; for example:

Well now, if kids ask me what the answer is, what is the answer to that question, why is this so? I would have told them the answer in the past. And now sometimes I do tell them the answer but it is not straight away, there is a path before I actually get there. (5/I3/91)

I guess I am (now) allowing the children to — I am providing them with a situation where they can, themselves, build on their knowledge, whereas before I was building on the knowledge . . . (5/I2/90)

Teaching and learning activities used to 'get students thinking' that were mentioned in interviews were starter or experience activities, spider diagrams or concept maps, brainstorming, language activities, linking school science ideas to students' everyday experiences, students doing practical activities, students not copying notes off the whiteboard or overhead projector, creative writing, encouraging students' questions, role plays, involving students in the planning of their learning activities, asking the students to reflect on their own learning and on the teaching activities, and student science log books; for example:

They had logs, the logs were wonderful. The information that you handed us out . . . about keeping a log — I gave them that information, exactly the stuff that you had given us and I said 'now I want you to keep a log of current scientific events'. Some of them would check the newspapers every day, some would do it once a week, some would do it once a month and that really fascinated . . . they would come along and say 'hey, did you see what was in the paper about this' and 'what do you think about that' and they really got involved in the science scene and that was an excellent way of doing things. (11/I3/91)

Another activity used to 'get students thinking' was the students testing out their own ideas; for example:

We had at one stage, thirty candles going . . . We got to a point where I got the whole class together with a discussion looking at the observations they had made and it came down to the fact that in their view the wax was nothing more than to support the wick, hold it up, and it slowed — because the flame melted the wax, the melting of the wax slowed the burning down. So we made a candle out of sand and that burned down quickly until it reached the sand and went out. I said 'what is the difference between that and a wax one, it just supports the thing?' 'Oh no, but that didn't melt', so that was important. . . . in the next period they came up and they said 'oh yes, we could make one out of ice'. So that left them a bit of agape because they had said that it should work and yet it didn't. Which was neat really because it came to the point where they could follow something through and then they got conflicting pieces of information. We went through and we wrote down all the observations that they had made in their books and put them up on the board. We tried to have a look at all of that again and some observations that they had made, which they had just discounted last time, now became very important in what they were doing . . . (14/I2/91)

In summary, a role of the teacher discernible in the teachers' comments was that of getting the students thinking. This role was one that they felt helped them 'feel better about themselves as teachers'.

The teachers acknowledged that a part of getting students to think was teachers and students valuing the students' ideas and skills. This valuing of students' ideas and skills was communicated to the students by the teachers and students listening and responding to a student's ideas in a constructive way, and by the teacher showing an interest in the students' ideas; for example:

Oh, because I value what kids know already . . . Ever since I started teaching I always get very, very upset with anyone, kids or adults, who tell me they don't know anything or they don't value the learning they have already had. The fact that they get up each day and get dressed and come to school, they all know heaps. And this way I can actually get kids — the confidence thing — that is my reward. (8/I5/91)

This valuing was also communicated by encouraging the students to value their own and others ideas, by accepting students' ideas as a useful contribution to classroom discussion even if their ideas are not scientifically acceptable (note that accepting 'wrong' ideas as contributions to the classroom debates is not the same as leaving students with 'wrong' ideas at the end of the teaching unit), and through the expectation that all students will have an opportunity to contribute their ideas and thinking to the class discussions.

The teachers still felt they had a role in giving the students information as a part of getting them thinking. In other words, students could get their information from the teacher as well as other sources, such as books, scientists, and parents; for example:

Some kid talked about today, that the colours are different wave lengths and immediately one kid said 'What is a wave length?' In that particular case no one could really — they were able to explain it a bit — and I said,

'I think I know something about it, do you want me to say something' and so I got up and actually talked to them about the fact that scientists think light travels like this, like a wave. And I said they call a wave length from crest to crest and some waves — and I told them about the electro magnetic spectrum and how at one end of the spectrum they have got long wave lengths and at the other end they have got short wave lengths and the different colours — it is just all to do with their wave length. They were quite happy on that. But I felt that was okay, I was coming in as an information giver. I said to them 'Do you want me to tell you about it?' 'Oh yes'. And I thought, well their interest was caught, they were going to listen to me, and they did. (7/I2/91)

Teaching as Managing Learning

Another teaching activity that the teachers felt good about was that of managing. All of the teachers mentioned in the interviews that they, as teachers, continued to see themselves as a manager in the lessons; for example:

I feel that the management and what is going on in the classroom is my responsibility. I feel that really strongly, and I would say that my employers would say that was my responsibility too. And I think, too, my personality — I don't like things totally out of control. But on the other hand I am prepared to let — I enjoyed the light unit and as far as I was concerned that was letting go of a lot of control. But the kids still had certain ground rules so I was maintaining control of my ground rules. But it certainly wasn't me up front directing all the time. (7/I4/91)

Although the lesson was less teacher-directed, the teachers were still in control; for example:

I will be in control of the whole situation but you don't make it that obvious to kids. But to me they have got to be on task with what they are doing or else why are they here for? They can play cards at home or they can stay at home. (10/I6/91)

The management had changed to become more that of managing for learning and not just management for good behaviour. The managing for learning had several different aspects to it — planning, structuring, being sensitive to student groupings, facilitating discussion and helping individual students.

The teachers mentioned that planning was a part of being a teacher, who has a constructivist view of learning, although the planning required was different to that done previously. The planning done was not so much the sequencing of ideas to be taught but the planning to take into account the students' thinking. The teachers planned to elicit the students' thinking; to help the students to clarify, reflect on and evaluate their own ideas; to enable the students to find out what other people, including scientists think; to help the students to modify their ideas if need be; and to accept and use new ideas with confidence. For example:

> I don't know whether I shared it a few months ago, at the end of the course — about this whole difference in planning for me, just working through the whole differences of planning units and things — it actually is in a totally different way. I need to look at situations that will bring these ideas up, where these ideas are gives a starting point for kids to start thinking about these ideas or what are the activities or what are the stimulus material that I need for that. That is really the planning stage. And the particular direction or the particular way we go through the topic — what comes first, what comes second is not my choice, that is where the class as a whole or individuals in the class — how their brain comes at that question or at that phenomenon. Which is probably quite often different from the way I would approach it because of what I know and my experiences. (14/I5/91)

The planning was seen to involve deciding (sometimes with the students) on the broad learning goals as indicated in the syllabus or school scheme; selecting learning activities that promote conceptual development and which provide opportunities for the teacher to interact with students' thinking; and selecting assessment activities. The teachers also thought of further investigations to get the students thinking. For example, they wrote activities on cards, which would be given to a student with the comment, 'This may help you find the answer to your question.' The teachers also gave thought to ways to help the students think about their alternative conceptions. The specific activities were not always preplanned but thought of when the teacher had obtained information as to the students' thinking.

The teachers commented that they felt uncomfortable with the change in what was meant by planning. They may have felt that they were not planning; for example:

> The planning stage (is) totally quite different and for a while I was really worried that I wasn't doing any planning. 'This is terrible, what am I doing, I am not sitting down filling in my plan book', but when you come to grips with 'hang on', actually you still are planning and you are still a professional, what you are doing, you are not slacking off. In fact you are putting as much work into planning what is going to happen and planning the sort of ways in which they are going to be looking so that you have got the resources available. That is your job, your job is a supply job, a resource person job and a guider with some of these things. But you are not necessarily the driving force — 'today we shall do this, tomorrow we shall do this and if you didn't pick it up I am sorry but . . . here is a homework sheet, try and work it out.' The planning has to be there in the

beginning, I have got to know where we are going. Really it is more resource gathering, the planning you have got to think through. The whole planning process is different. (14/I5/91)

The teachers may have felt that they did not know exactly what they were going to be doing in the lesson and that they did not know the direction the lesson might take; for example:

But you can see in the more traditional lessons — there is quite a detailed sequence of what I am doing, whereas with the fourth forms all I do is list them (the learning goals). Because you really don't know where the lesson is going. Although I am finding that doing the concept map at the back has given me a sense of structure. I think it is giving the kids a sense of structure too, they sort of know the areas that they have looked at and where there are gaps. (7/I2/91)

In summary, planning was viewed as an activity which the teachers did. But their view of planning had been reconceptualized. Previously, their view of planning was based on planning a sequence for the teaching of the ideas; for example, teaching about producers, then consumers, then decomposers. They, therefore, knew beforehand what activities would be in each lesson and the direction of the lesson. Now their planning was done both before and during a lesson as they needed to obtain information from the students as part of their planning. They planned activities to find out what the students were thinking and they planned to respond to, and interact with, the students' thinking. As they found out about the students' thinking, they were able to think of activities to aid the students' conceptual development. They planned to manage the learning as well as the behaviour. They also planned to provide structure, attend to groupings, facilitate discussion, and to help individual students. Furthermore, they planned for the students to cover the curriculum.

The teachers mentioned the need to continue to give some structure to the lessons to attend to such concerns as sequencing, pacing and time management. Although this aspect of teaching is not specific to teaching approaches based on a constructivist view of learning, teachers felt they still needed to do this to support students' learning, particularly when the changes in their teaching required changes in the students' learning activities. When to end a topic and move on to another area in the syllabus, was a concern for some teachers, as was setting time limits and maintaining a variety of learning activities.

Being sensitive to student groupings was seen as another aspect of the role of teacher as manager. The teachers mentioned in interview (in response to an interview question) that they considered student groups in the classroom; for example:

What ways has my teaching in the classroom changed. I now have my class set out like this, I have it in groups. Whereas before when I first got into teaching it was always in big lots like horseshoe shapes and them sitting along benches, so that has changed. I still do that at the beginning of the year just as a settling down thing right at the beginning but when we get into real teaching and learning then I find this a better way to organize the structure of my room. (14/I5/91)

Groupings were made to take into account increasing student involvement, the learning activities themselves, size, prior experiences, group skills, and gender concerns. Other aspects of the role of the teacher of managing mentioned by the teachers were the facilitation of classroom discussion, and helping individual students.

Teacher as Learner

Another new role mentioned by the teachers that helped them feel 'better' was that of teacher as learner. Many of the teachers said that they were learning alongside the students in the classroom at times; for example:

They bring things to you. That is the thing that, I think, is a real plus and I still think it is worth saying again. They begin to see you as a person who is interested in learning as well as a teacher and so they will bring you things that they have seen and heard and tell you things they have seen and heard. Where, if you are just a teacher, they tend to assume that you know that already and you miss a lot. It is actually supporting if someone says 'I read this in the *Listener*, Miss, did you?' or 'did you see that programme and it was about' and *Beyond 2000* is actually very good for the source of these things. And they actually feel that you are interested in learning that or you probably have seen it but just in case you might like to know. They feel they can safely provide you with some information. They don't feel that you will say 'oh yes, I already knew that', that sort of thing. Or somehow they don't assume any more that you do know everything. I had a long discussion with someone who has got different ethnic origins, from overseas, who says he feels he must be able to answer every question before he could teach a subject. I thought — I would assume that you would need a good knowledge of the subject, I don't dispute that you have to be qualified, but I would strongly dispute that you have to be able to answer all the questions. And life is a lot more interesting if you don't. If you do you cut yourself off from learning and that is a plus for all this — as a teacher you become a learner too and that is a huge plus for me. (8/I6/91)

To be learning from and with the students was important in that it indicated a new kind of relationship between the teachers and students. This new kind of relationship contributed to the teachers feeling better about themselves as teachers; for example:

. . . the role of the teacher was no longer standing up the front with all little minions down on the desks . . . it (the new teaching approach) breaks down the barriers, it puts everybody on the same footing. (11/M2/91)

I am finding that my teaching is very exciting and I think that in those classes where I am actually using constructivist teaching I think there is a much, much better relationship between myself and the kids. (7/I2/91)

Well it is far less teacher-directed, me at the front. There is a lot more of students getting on with tasks at their own pace and me going around as a roving trouble shooter. That has had lots of spin-off in the sense that on the whole I don't have the behaviour problems and it has been interesting that in the last unit I did on reproduction, in part of that where I was up front and we were all going through the same task sheets, the same activities, that is when I struck trouble with behaviour problems. (7/I5/91)

Well they expect things to work that way now and so if, for some reason, that your life is getting really, really busy and you want to just kick back into textbooks and say 'okay read this today and answer questions seven, eight, nine and four', it doesn't go down very well. They realize that 'hang on, we are just marking time today'. But in some ways the relationship that you built up, you actually build up a much better relationship with your class, with the people who are in your class. It is no longer just a class, you know the individuals a heck of a lot better, and so even when that does happen they sort of understand that a bit better. (14/I5/91)

. . . you are relating to them on a different level. I think that science unit on matter — when I was up the front of the science lab and I gave them directions and, I mean, I felt a bit strange and I didn't really know what I was doing. But I just followed what was written down on paper. Whereas this . . . into a completely different role — side by side with them. Often the level of knowledge can be quite equal. You can be learning along with the children, so obviously your relationship or teaching roles are going to change a lot. (3/I9/91)

In discussing the relationships with their students, the teachers were indicating that they were still 'in control' but the lessons tended to be less teacher-dominated.

In summary, a factor that helped teacher development for the teachers was not just getting information about the new teaching activities, but also trying them out to experience 'feeling better about myself as a teacher', 'being more like the teacher I would like to be like' and 'being a better teacher'. The reasons why the teachers tended to feel 'better about themselves' included that the teachers:

- found value in listening to the students rather than just talking at them;
- knew their students better, were pleasantly surprised how much the

students knew about different topics and that they now had a way to communicate to the students that they valued what the students brought to
the lesson. In many cases their respect for their students' knowledge had
increased;

- enjoyed being able to gain insights into what was happening for the students as they were learning;
- felt good about being able to develop a greater sense of trust that the
students would learn something;
- appreciated spending more time interacting with the students' ideas rather
than interacting with them for organizational or management reasons. The
teachers reported less need for behaviour management;
- enjoyed having fewer demands being made directly on them by the students
as the students were thinking more for themselves and were less dependent
on the teacher;
- appreciated that the responsibility and energy for keeping the lesson moving did not rest solely with the teacher, as the students were taking more
initiatives in the lessons. The teachers felt they had to spend less time and
energy motivating the students to learn;
- felt that the new teaching activities did not mean that they had to stop
doing some activities which they felt to be central to their view of what it
means to be a teacher. They still felt that there was a role for their teaching
activities of giving some structure to the unit of work, explaining some
science, planning, covering the syllabus, attending to student grouping in
the lessons, facilitating class discussion, and assessment. They still felt that
they had control over what was happening in the lessons and that they were
doing those things required of them by the students, school, parents and the
Government;
- learnt alongside the students. They enjoyed being learners themselves and
they appreciated the lessening of the expectation that they had to know all
the answers; and
- enjoyed the different relationships with the students. The teachers felt that
they related and talked with the students in a different way. They felt the
new teaching activities had enabled them to work more alongside of the
students rather than from the front. They felt good because the students
were enjoying being in their lessons.

'Feeling better about myself as a teacher' arose because the teachers had
changed what they did in the classroom, especially the way they interacted with the
students, and they had changed their ideas and feelings about what it meant to be
teaching and to be a teacher. If the teachers had not made these changes, they
would not have experienced what it felt like to be a 'better' teacher. If the new
teaching activities had not helped the teachers to 'feel better about themselves as
teachers', then the teacher development would not have continued. In changing
their teaching, and accepting the changes, the teachers were reconceptualizing and
reconstructing what it means to be a teacher of science. For example, for many

teachers, it now included finding out what the students are thinking, responding to students' ideas, valuing students' own ideas, planning differently, and assessing for conceptual change.

'Feeling better about myself as a teacher' can be related to professional, personal and social development. The teachers' professional development can be seen in their learning about and using the new teaching activities that led to the teachers feeling better about themselves as teachers and in their changed conceptions and beliefs about teaching and the roles of the teacher. Social development can be evidenced in the reconstruction of what it means to be a teacher. For example, being in control in the classroom is a central facet of being a teacher. The new teaching activities did not diminish this role, although it was manifested in different ways and the notion of 'being in control' was reconceptualized. Finding out what the students were thinking became an accepted part of 'being a teacher of science' — the notion of 'being a teacher of science' was reconceptualized by the individual teachers and reconstructed collectively by the group. The existing culture of teaching and what it means to be a teacher was well-known to the teachers, and against this background they had to evaluate the new teaching activities that they were trying out. Both their own conceptions and the socially constructed knowledge changed. In addition, each of the teachers had to match their views of themselves as people with their views of what it means to be a teacher and the kind of teacher they would like to be (Begg, 1994). This can be considered an aspect of personal development.

'Better Learning'

Another factor that helped the teacher development (professional, personal and social development) was that the teachers felt there was 'better learning' occurring in the lessons (Bell and Pearson, 1992, 1993b). When talking about the classroom feedback they had received on the new teaching activities from students, the teachers often talked about the 'better learning' that was occurring. That 'better learning' was occurring, was perceived by the teachers as a reason to continue to implement the findings of the previous Learning in Science Projects, despite the difficulties with a new teaching approach and with changing. The 'better learning' was perceived as a pay-off; for example:

> Because it makes us enjoy our job much more. We see kids learning and enjoying their learning, then I can justify getting up in the morning. No matter what goes on in the staffroom, I can justify my being at school and enjoying my vocation if I see kids learning and enjoying learning. (14/M2/91)

The comments made by the teachers indicated that what they called 'better learning' included the establishment of better conditions for learning and the achievement of better learning outcomes.

'Better Learning' Conditions

The better learning conditions included increased enjoyment; social cooperation; ownership; student confidence; student motivation.

Increased Enjoyment

Initially, the teachers commented that there was more enjoyment of science and implied that better learning was occurring, for example:

> I equate a lot of learning with, if someone is enjoying it you seem to . . . delve into it more to get more enjoyment out of it. (4/I6/90),

> Well I asked them, I said, 'who enjoyed the torch unit?' — or the light unit it was called, 'who learned something?' (10/I2/90)

Enjoyment was seen to result from students researching their own interests; for example:

> Well when I had the animal research topic going and they were doing endangered species, every parent at the parent interviews mentioned that, every one of them without a doubt. I was really surprised and I think it was that the kids were really excited about it and they obviously talked about it at home. And so I think they can see their kids being enthusiastic about it and I think that is what they were keen on. (4/I5/90)

> Well there was better learning, there was more enjoyment. You didn't have to battle with them to try and do things because they were responsible for what they decided to do . . . so it was more beneficial for me to teach. You got much more feedback from the kids because they were allowed to discuss things and they were more actively encouraged to discuss things. (17/I1/90)

Another teacher also described the enjoyment experienced by students who had been engaged in the learning activity:

> The satisfaction that you see from the kids when they have found out something, or discovered something or made some connections that they hadn't previously thought about rather than you telling them and them discovering that for themselves. The kids coming up and just saying 'I enjoyed that lesson' or 'that activity was a neat thing', those sorts of things. (5/I2/90)

Later on in the programme, a teacher acknowledged that enjoyment does not necessarily equate with better learning:

In the junior school especially, if kids can enjoy their science, if they can walk out of a classroom at the end of a period and have enjoyed themselves and when they line up for the next period, if they are keen to get in the classroom, then I think I am 80 per cent of the way there. I am winning. I am winning with those kids and if I can add some learning in there as we go along, which I guess that also is really important. It is no good just having a room where we have a lot of fun and muck around and nothing goes on in the brain . . . (14/I4/91)

Social Cooperation

Increased cooperation was perceived between students with the introduction of the new teaching activities, which teachers related to improved learning. In one situation, where experimental equipment had to be shared, the teacher noted:

The groups really worked together although they were doing different things to make sure the other group wasn't impeded by their space . . . I didn't expect that would happen. If you were to ask me I would say that it would have happened the other way. People in such a hurry to get their experiment done, they became aggressive to someone in their space. (4/I5/90)

Other teachers saw the advantages of interaction within the groupings:

They were all helping each other. They were working in groups and there was a lot of talk. (18/I1/90)

The kids all being involved, the kids working together in little groups sharing little bits of information. (5/I2/90)

Another teacher clearly stated the advantage of the new teaching activities:

It is a great socializer, it really is a great socializer for making them realise that everyone has got something to contribute. It also makes them respect other people more and realize that the seats of learning don't belong just in certain heads in the room. (8/I2/90)

Ownership

The teachers saw that when students were engaged in the learning activities, ownership of work was enhanced. A relationship between ownership and improved learning was suggested in the comments of teachers; for example:

I know that children learn better and are more interested if it is something that they are interested in. Kids write better when it is their choice, most kids write better when it is their choice. (3/I4/90)

One teacher found during a teaching unit:

> That they were keen and another indicator would be the fact that people
> who didn't normally carry out experiments or if they do they just muck
> around and fool about . . . were actually doing something useful. So some
> of the kids who don't normally do anything at science, or get very little
> out of it were actually becoming involved because they were able to choose
> their own thing and they saw it as their problem . . . And in fact one of the
> girls said that she enjoyed this type of approach because she is able to find
> out things for herself, the things she wanted to do. (9/12/90)

Other teachers commented on the students' increased ownership of the work
and the increased responsibility for their own learning; for example:

> . . . it is a classroom change. They don't come in with a 'how can we get
> out of doing any work?' which they used to see videos as. That is common
> in children when you say 'today we are going to have a video'. 'Oh cool,
> we are not going to do any work' . . . They are not really interested. They
> see TV at home. If it was a good video, an interesting video about what
> they had been doing. If I said 'now that we have done this much of stuff
> on wheelchairs and disabled we will have a look at a video and see some
> people in wheelchairs', then they are very focused. That is fine. But if you
> just say 'I am going to show you a video now because it is the end of term,
> something to relax and watch', they are not particularly interested. They
> would rather be doing what they are supposed to be doing, but not what
> I think they are supposed to be doing, what they think they have got
> involved in. They would rather just keep doing it. And I am relaxed, it is
> amazing. (8/16/91)

> I noticed when I was doing — the sixth formers wanted to do some chalk
> and talk work after they had done two units of this interactively and I think
> they really wanted basically a rest. I noticed the deterioration or the non-
> involvement and the non-participation of kids in the class when we drifted
> back into that way because they didn't own it. (5/14/91)

Student Confidence

The teachers stated that using the new teaching activities resulted in the students
gaining increased confidence in themselves and implied a link with increased learning; for example:

> And I have seen quiet kids respond to this whole change in emphasis, to
> the taking responsibility for their own learning and I can think of one
> really good example where (being asked to defend their theories on what
> makes the light bulb glow) — one girl who at that point had hardly said
> boo all year, stood up, not physically, she was on her own against the rest
> of the class. I can only explain it . . . she was taking charge of her own

thing, 'this is what I think and this is why' ... It gave her the courage to be able to stand up and say 'I disagree with 90 per cent of the class'. (13/I1/90)

There is one lad that I am thinking of in particular that has never given any real interest to science ... and he got really fired up about this ... His past term exam mark was about 30 something ... he has just got so much more interested in science and got 55 in the last exam and he is one of the real successes that I am sure is purely because we had that bit of time when he suddenly saw the relevance of what he was doing and was able to think for himself. (17/I1/90)

Explanations for these changes were given as personal growth:

It is self-esteem, I think, with the kids. It builds their self-esteem immensely. Some of the kids that just had no confidence have just got so much confidence in themselves now ... The ones I noticed were my fifth-formers. The ones that have done nothing all year and have been a pain, actually work and actually went away quite confident that they were going to sit the exam this time instead of wagging it like they did last time. They actually knew they knew something. (12/I1/90)

Motivation

Teaching based on a constructivist view of learning was also seen as improving student motivation generally and, therefore, learning; for example:

Well they see more purpose in it. When they own that question that they want an answer for they are as keen as mustard to do it. (10/I2/90)

The teachers also commented; for example:

I think the big difference is perhaps the motivation where because they are actually finding out and finding answers for themselves, there is maybe an increase in motivation and that would therefore aid learning. (1/I5/90)

I think we are breaking through some unseen barrier for learning. I can't really explain what it is but I think we refer to it as the blinds going up, or their eyes sparkling instead of glazing over, but there is some blockage there to learning that this somehow gets past. (11/M2/91)

Learning Outcomes

Increased enjoyment, social cooperation, ownership, confidence and motivation were aspects of the students' learning considered initially by the teachers as feedback that the new teaching approach was of value. They are conditions for learning consistent with the model of learning developed by the Learning in Science Projects (Osborne and Wittrock, 1985). In terms of learning outcomes, many teachers indicated that the strength of the new teaching activities was in the development of students' learning skills; conceptual development; and in improved results on tests and examinations.

Learning Skills

The teachers commented that the students were learning skills such as asking questions, discussion skills, writing skills and metacognition. Asking questions was seen by some teachers as a better learning outcome of the new teaching activities; for example:

> I think they are asking better things. They will go straight, direct. What things they want to know about has been a surprise. You kind of have a closed vision of what you want to know and what you think children want to know and you get quite a surprise at what they want to know about something that you felt was quite obvious to them. (15/I1/90)

The teachers noticed that the students were generally discussing the topic more and exchanging ideas; for example:

> Well the first thing was — the animated discussion that was taking place during the whole assembly and reassembling process (of irons) which was on task. They weren't talking about the movies or anything like that, they were actually on task with it because it was a very good focusing thing. When they got to a new bit, they would be talking and thinking, now what was this for, and so on. (22/I1/90)

Writing skills were another example of learning skill outcomes enhanced by the new teaching activities, as was metacognition about learning; for example:

> The sixth-formers have got an exam in a couple of weeks time and (A), one of the things she was saying to me was 'how do you actually learn for exams?' and we talked about some study techniques and she said 'you know, it is really interesting, the work that we did on our own, that interactive material' she said 'I am having no trouble at all with that'. She said 'it is there, I understand it, it makes sense to me, I can retain it' but she said 'when I look at some of the work that we did prior to that or some of the other things that we have done and' she said 'it is really hard to learn that'. So there is those sorts of comments. (5/I4/91)

Development of the Students' Concepts and Ideas

The teachers commented on what they thought the learning gains had been in terms of conceptual development; for example:

During the course I saw evidence of their changing views. We went to the library and they had to research different answers and it was interesting to see that when they had first had their preconceived idea that they wrote down and they went to the library and actually found it wasn't the actual answer, they did change their perception. (20/I1/90)

The teachers also reported that the students were better able to transfer and use the new ideas being learnt; for example:

When students take something that you are talking about, come back and tell you about something in their own environment which ties into that, there has got to be learning going on. That is one way of telling, when they actually are approaching you on an informal basis and tying in what you are talking about in the classroom with what is in their life, then they have made a link between what you are talking about here and really you are separating out the intricacies of what you are talking about in the classroom, you get down to the nuts and bolts of things, normally. And so if they are getting some of the nuts and bolts and they are actually tying in their environment things that are going on, that is good. 'Sir I get an electric shock when I touch the electric fence' and so we can talk about electricity is and things like that and 'well why do you get a shock and why do you get a bigger shock when you have got wet feet or wet gumboots or if you are wearing dry gumboots why don't you get a shock' and they ask you those things. Learning is going on there. (14/I4/91)

Also reported was the increased retention of new ideas; for example:

They keep things in their minds longer in terms of — you could be finished a unit and maybe three of four weeks later they find something that is relevant and so they mention it again . . . So that is not necessarily more learning, it is not necessarily they know more about electricity but it is more that the things stay in the front of their mind. It seems to be more useful. Does that make sense? (8/I3/91)

Attainment in School or National Examinations

Some of the teachers mentioned the students' increased achievement in school and national examinations as evidence of learning outcomes, for example:

When I gave them their tests back and I said 'how did you feel about that' there was a comment from at least half a dozen that said they had never scored so well in science and they were really pleased. (7/I2/91)

I must admit I was really happy with my fifth form. When I just had last year's lot that I kept dabbling with and thinking 'well, I will try this and see if I can squeeze this around the exam paper'. And then we get that curly exam paper at the end of the year and my kids did pretty well. With C2 material, we were getting B1s and B2s at the end of the year and I was really happy with what they had achieved. I was actually quite stunned with some of them. They coped better with the strangeness of the paper. (12/M2/91)

In summary, when talking about the classroom feedback they had received on the new teaching activities from students, the teachers spoke of 'better learning'. That 'better learning' was occurring was perceived by the teachers as a reason to keep on using the new activities in the classroom. The teachers were comparing their perception of the learning occurring as a result of the new teaching with that obtained by the former teaching. The 'better learning' was seen as a pay-off to keep on developing their teaching. Initially, the comments about 'better learning' included those related to better learning conditions (enjoyment, social cooperation, ownership, student confidence, motivation), while later on the comments were more about those related to better learning outcomes (learning skills, conceptual development and results in tests and examinations) and indicators of learning.

It would appear that teachers tended to focus more on feedback about learning conditions than learning outcomes in the classroom. This is not surprising given the demands of managing the behaviour and learning of over thirty students, and teachers expressed concerns about assessment when using the teaching approaches based on a constructivist view of learning. The teachers had expressed a need for assistance in assessing conceptual change, particularly in the secondary school, where formative assessment is interfaced with summative assessment for national awards (Bell, Pearson and Kirkwood, 1991).

There is, however, a danger that in attending primarily to learning conditions, teachers equate the better learning conditions with better learning outcomes. Hewson and Hewson (1988) argued that many teachers believe that a causal link exists between teaching and learning activities and learning outcomes. That is, if the students have carried out a learning activity, for example, a 'stick and paste' activity or 'filling in the blank' activity, then learning will have occurred. They claim that this belief arises from confusion between learning-as-task (learning activities and actions) and learning-as-achievement (a result, an outcome, identified by the learner achieving some end state). Marks (1989) suggested that, as the principles of learning play an important part in pre-service teacher education, teachers may tacitly apply these principles and, because they are encouraging motivation, participation and satisfaction, assume that learning outcomes will follow. While this may be so, there is no indication that conceptual change will occur unless teaching and learning activities plan this as an outcome. Cole (1988) in her review of teacher thinking, noted the implicit theories, attitudes and beliefs that teachers hold. She regarded teacher practice as an expression of various forms of teacher 'knowing' and describes this as 'complex, dynamic and personally construed activity' (p. 26). Her research focuses on the way teachers read 'situational cues'; coming from the students — their behaviour, responses, progress and attitudes — or from other aspects of the environment — interruptions, classroom noise level, the time of day, and the weather, or from the teachers' own estimations or feelings about the situation. This professional knowledge about learning activities may not be linked with learning outcomes.

In a quantitative study on interactive decision-making by science teachers, Butefish (1990) observed that very few decisions that were made in the classroom were related to learning outcomes. The vast majority of decisions related to keeping the students engaged in learning activities, keeping up the pace of the lesson and creating a supportive atmosphere by rewarding effort and giving personal encouragement. Recent research by Nuthall and Alton-Lee (1990) indicated that the behaviours that are observed in the classrooms by teachers are only indirectly related to learning in students. What teachers observe and comment on are just 'signs and symptoms' of learning processes in action. As they note 'some [of the signs and symptoms] are subtle and fleeting, like smiles and chewing a pencil top; others are more obvious and substantial, like writing, reading and arguing with a peer' (p. 566). Wheatley (1991) suggested that in many classrooms learning is not the goal, time on task is. Marshall (1988) asserted that many teachers' actions in the classroom are based on the metaphor of classrooms as 'workplaces' not 'learning-places'. Consequently, effective learning is seen as occurring when students are working enthusiastically and purposefully, when they are engaged in the task. When the metaphor of the 'classroom as a workplace' is used as a basis for teachers' actions, then the constructivist view of learning as conceptual change is inappropriate and overlooked.

In summary, the above data and discussion on 'feeling better about myself as a teacher' and 'better learning' illustrate the notion that teacher development can be viewed as professional, personal and social development and that these aspects are interwoven. The main reason why teachers engage in teacher development is to be able to do a better job — to be a better teacher and to get better learning by their students. The feedback that the teachers received from the students that the learning was 'better', and that they felt better about themselves as teachers, kept them changing despite the uncomfortableness of changing. They were using new teaching and learning activities in the classroom; reconceptualizing their own ideas about teaching, being a teacher, learning and others aspects of science education; and reflecting on, and evaluating, the results of using the new teaching activities both in terms of their own views of themselves as teachers and the socially constructed knowledge about what it means to be a teacher of science.

5   Feedback, Support and Reflection

Three factors that the teachers reported as helping their teacher development were feedback, support and reflection (Bell and Pearson, 1993c). In this chapter, the ways in which feedback, support and reflection contributed to teachers' learning and the three aspects of teacher development — social, personal and professional — are discussed.

Feedback

The teachers in the research project commented that feedback was an important part of the teacher development process. As they tried out new teaching activities, they sought and valued feedback as to their development or, as one teacher said, 'How do I know if I am a LISP teacher?' The responses they received as a result of changing their teaching, were largely positive and encouraged them to keep on changing. For example:

> . . . having done it and discovered that I felt comfortable with it, that it got results that I hadn't been able to get in the old way is a powerful trigger to keep trying, to keep on slotting in those sort of techniques. And every time it is successful then it reinforces for you that it is a good way to go. (5/I5/91)

> [The first part of the transcript code indicates the teacher who is quoted; the second part indicates the interview (I), survey (S), programme session (P) or meeting(M) in which the comment was made; and the last part indicates the year.]

Feedback is used here to mean the responses obtained by the teachers to their existing and new ideas, feelings and actions from others. The feedback given and received on the teacher development programme helped in the professional, personal and social development aspects of teacher development.

Feedback helped the teachers' professional development in two ways. First, the feedback on their existing ideas and actions tended to help the teachers to clarify the problematic nature of science education in their classrooms. Secondly, the feedback on the changes appeared to give teachers information about the extent and nature of the changes and enabled them to compare the actual changes with the intended ones. For example:

> Well sometimes you don't know you have changed. I takes someone else to come in and observe you to realize that you have changed quite a bit and there are lots of things that are happening. (3/I12/91)

The responses of others were perceived as giving professional feedback on whether existing or new teaching activities were 'working' in the classroom. 'Working' meant working with respect to classroom management, students' learning and the match with their own values about people and education. The responses gave suggestions to the teachers for modifications and further changes.

The feedback was also viewed as helping personal development. Responses to their disclosure of feelings helped the teachers gain support and to know that they were not alone in undertaking the change. This feedback helped the teachers develop in a personal way to manage the change process and to increase their self-esteem, confidence, and sense of competence. For some, the feedback gave confirmation and permission to use ideas and actions that they felt to be alternatives to mainstream ones. Others felt that the feedback communicated that others respected and valued their ideas, feelings and actions. That the responses from others resulted in the teachers feeling better about themselves as teachers, was feedback to keep on trying new activities in the classroom. For example, one teacher felt the feedback gave her confidence in her own ideas:

> (The feedback gave me) confidence definitely. I look back on what I was like and, believe it or not, I had no conversation at all when I came back teaching. I used to dodge social events because I had no conversation. It is hard to think of at the moment, isn't it. I can usually find something to say. But it does encourage you to have more confidence in what you say, your opinion is just as good as everybody else's and this is what this approach does bring out for the kids as well as the teacher, that people can be wrong, people don't have to be right all the time and what they say needs to be thought about, needs to be considered. So that is important in this way of thinking. (11/I4/91)

The feedback also contributed to the social development as part of teacher development as it communicated to the teachers something of the socially constructed knowledge of teaching. The responses of others were seen as feedback on the acceptability of changes they had made in the classroom, on the way they conceptualized teaching and learning, and on their competence as teachers. The teachers found it helpful to know how others perceived their teaching (both theoretical ideas and actions) and themselves as teachers. The teachers were also renegotiating and reconstructing amongst themselves what it means to be a teacher of science and the feedback gave them an indication of the acceptability of anything new. Hence, giving and receiving feedback was an aspect of the social development of the teachers.

Receiving feedback was dependent on others responding to what the teachers did or thought. When others were encouraged or given the opportunity to respond, as they were by working in collaborative and interactive ways on the programme, the teachers received feedback that helped them develop. The teachers felt they got feedback on their changes from the other teachers on the programme, which they valued as feedback from others who were going through similar experiences; for example:

> What else did I need to change? Feedback of people who are doing the same things, who are going through the same experience, talking to them, mutual feedback, we understood each other, we knew the stresses involved and it was over a long period of time where you could work through things and needed time to set out some new scheme of work, set out something I wanted to trial for myself, have time to do that at my own pace and then have time to reflect and talk to others about it. And get that feedback, yes, that positive feedback that comes when other people are doing the same sort of thing. I didn't get a particular lot of feedback in my own school here. I think that would have helped, but in some ways maybe it was okay because I didn't particularly mind going cold turkey on it without feedback here. In some ways it was probably good because I was doing it on my own in isolation, more or less, and so people didn't really bother me too much and they didn't ask those questions — how is it going today, absolutely awful. (14/I5/91)

They also got feedback indirectly from the group's collated responses to interviews, surveys or post-box activities run as workshop activities. The feedback here was the extent to which their thinking matched or did not match that of others in the group. The shared understandings about teaching science were used as templates by the teachers to evaluate themselves and the changes they made.

However, other teachers on the programme were not the only people who gave feedback. The teachers commented that they received feedback from the students. The teachers indicated that feedback on whether the changes in their teaching activities were 'working or not' came mainly from the students. In fact, student feedback was the main source of feedback and for some teachers the only source of feedback outside of the group; for example:

> . . . I get heaps of feedback from the kids, heaps of feedback that this is the way that they like to do it, this is the way that they like to learn, that they feel comfortable, that they feel that they are achieving something. (8/I6/91)

Other teachers in the school gave feedback to the teachers; for example:

> Other staff making comments from something kids have said. That is really nice when you have someone else say 'so and so came and told me

about what they were doing, and they were trying to tell me because I know nothing about it'. That is really nice especially when the teacher knows nothing about science and they were getting quite interested about what they were being told. (12/I5/91)

Feedback also received from student teachers; for example:

(And the) student from teachers college, has commented on my questioning, the open-ended sort of questioning. The way the children become more involved. He said 'you do a lot of talking and a lot of discussion where the kids are'. Like you get, as if it is part and parcel of your teaching and you don't really consciously think about what you are doing and it takes somebody to make you think 'oh yes, I am going in the right direction, what I am doing' but sometimes I don't know whether I really have changed that much. I don't consciously think about it. (3/I12/91)

Parents were another group of people who gave feedback; for example:

The general comments — there was a third and two fourth forms — talking about the fourth forms — the comments I got were things like 'oh my daughter really likes science now. What class are you going to be teaching in the fifth form (as) she wants to make sure she gets into your class?' which really blows you away as a teacher a bit. You think that they would have 'had enough please, and we want to change', but that sort of comment — and 'yes my son isn't really enjoying school at the moment except for science, he is really enjoying what he is doing in science', or 'enjoys you as a teacher', or 'he just enjoys science, being turned on to science'. And without a lie, there were at least four different parents, that is parents of different kids, who gave comments of that type. 'My child is really enjoying science' and at least two, if not three of them, were girls who for the first time were switching on to really enjoying science. (14/I4/91)

Feedback was given by others to the teachers and was important in influencing the development of the teachers. In summary, giving and receiving feedback fostered all aspects of teacher development — professional, personal and social.

Support

Support was also perceived as important for professional, personal and social development. Support is variously defined in the Oxford dictionary as 'keep from sinking or failing; enable to last out, keep from failing, give strength to, encourage; lend assistance; assist by one's presence . . .'. Weissglass (1994) described it in this way:

Support means different things to different people: respect, encouragement, good instructional materials, time to reflect and plan, opportunity
to learn, changes in policy, time to share information, opportunity to be
listened to about one's problems, goals and dreams. . . . One form of
support — the opportunity to be listened to and to release emotions —
is often neglected . . . People are able to change unproductive practices
when they are listened to as they talk about their actions and how their
previous experiences are influencing their current practices . . . The change
process is accelerated when it is safe to release emotions . . . The only
way that there will be enough attention to fuel the change process is if
people develop the ability and the commitment to regularly take the time
to pay attention to each other. (Weissglass, 1994, p. 226)

McCarty (1993) suggested that the support that is needed for professional
growth includes helping teachers feel:

- Safe. Nobody who feels personally, socially, or professionally threatened,
  that is — fearful of the consequences of acts — will make changes in what
  they believe or do. The provision of support must, then, be conducted so
  that each teacher feels free of fear.
- Recognized as a valued individual. People are willing to change when they
  feel valued. Thus the provision of support must recognize and value the
  contribution of each individual to any corporate activity.
- Connected to others. Inclusion and affiliation give an individual a
  sense of safety and being valued. Thus teacher development activities are
  most effective when a sense of mutual support and corporate activity
  is nourished.
- A sense of power over their own ideas and actions. The converse, powerlessness, stultifies initiative and reduces the likelihood of sustained change.
  Teacher development activities must, therefore, explicitly seek to empower
  individuals in respect of ideas and actions.
- That their professional lives and judgments are meaningful. A sense of
  futility is a massive inhibition to change. Teacher development activities
  must enable teachers to generate a sense of meaning and significance in
  respect of their professional values, judgments, and actions.
- A willingness to take risks. Change implies the possibility of both success
  and failure. Teacher-development activities must therefore offer individuals
  scope to experiment, such that success is possible and can be identified,
  and they are aware of what protection is provided against the consequences
  of failure.
- That models and mentors are available. Change seems more achievable if
  an individual has access to both a model, a person who has made the
  change aspired to and who exemplifies what change entails, and mentors,
  peers who will provide collegial support in seeking personal change.
- That counselling support is available. A counsellor, an individual who can

help another identify and address problems, would be helpful to a teacher seeking to make some substantive change, particularly one that addressed a core construct.
- A sense of fun. Change does seem more easy to make if it can be viewed through, and analysed with a sense of humour and with fun.

Support and feedback are related but not all feedback is supportive and not all support comes from feedback. Moreover, support for change and growth needs to be distinguished from support for no growth. Some teachers might seek support for their stance of not engaging with change from like-minded colleagues and the talk may be about 'the latest bandwagon', or that they had 'tried this in the 1960s and it didn't work'. Innovative teachers and teachers wanting to change their classroom practice need the support of others who value what they are doing. Without support, teacher development is less likely to occur. In this sense, support involves others — it is a social phenomenon.

The teachers indicated that they valued support for personal, professional and social development. Comments they made suggested that they appreciated the personal support received during the programme to deal with the negative feelings associated with change and with doing something different to what others did (or wanted them to do). This personal support was important to maintain self-confidence and a sense of self-worth, as the new activities in the classroom may not always work the first time. It included support for accepting criticism, disclosing feelings, acceptance of beliefs and feelings, confirmation that they were not alone or unique in their personal experience, validation of procedures followed and outcomes achieved, and encouragement and confidence to innovate.

Personal support was perceived by the teachers as helpful in dealing with criticism. One teacher felt that attending the programme had helped her feel more confident after her confidence had been eroded by the criticism of a parent:

> I was not confident, when I went to that course last year. I was not terribly confident because in my third year back, in my second year of teaching seventh-form chemistry, I had a particularly belligerent parent . . . and that completely destroyed my confidence. Every time I would say something I would get half way through a sentence and think 'oh my God, is that right?' because you had that sort of hostile presence there. You only need one experience like that and boy you are very careful what you say. You don't try anything new in case you fall in. So I think you have to have confidence in yourself and your own teaching before you try something new, a new technique. (11/I3/91)

Many of the teachers felt supported when they could disclose and share their feelings about changing; for example:

> What I thought about last night — I think I expressed one of my thoughts during the session when we had the sharing time about feeling

more comfortable in a non-threatening situation and relating it to students. I thought it was quite a relevant point when [A] was talking about how he is very up-front in his teaching and he is right up there. I shared with the group about how I felt quite threatened about the whole course and being with those sorts of people but the way it has been handled and the situation, it is a lot more comfortable way to learn and I wonder whether we should do more of this in teaching. (3/I5/90)

It was important that the teachers' feelings were accepted and not pooh-poohed or dismissed; for example:

I have spoken to [B] but then she just doesn't have any perception of what I am trying to get at, at all . . . I am a bit loathe to expose things that I think are important to people who don't . . . I am a bit more sensitive that it is falling on really unfriendly ears at times. (16/I5/91)

Having someone accept that this was the way the teachers felt or believed was validating to them as people. Acceptance here did not necessarily mean agreement but acknowledgment that this is the way the teacher thought or felt. Acceptance was often conveyed when teachers were asked for their opinion or advice; for example:

(What sort of things did they do to support you?) I suppose just by asking my opinion about things. (7/I5/91)

Another form of support was in others giving confirmation that the teacher was not alone or unique in her or his personal experiences. For example:

It is the sort of self-esteem thing that you were able to talk with people about what you had done, talk about the things that had worked and the things that hadn't worked and to know that you weren't the only one who had difficulties. There were other people who didn't always find that everything that they did worked. (5/I5/91)

Validation of action taken and outcomes achieved was seen as giving support; for example:

But that was supporting because they (the other subject teachers of a class) asked me why I was having fewer problems (with the class). And any time that someone actually acknowledged that you are doing it right, or doing something that is working is support. They don't necessarily have to say 'oh what science are you teaching' or 'are you an interactive teacher' or any words or jargon. It is just acknowledgment that something is going on for you. (8/I6/91)

Similarly, support gave encouragement and confidence to innovate; for example:

> Those discussion times were really important to me because it helps keep
> you interested in what you are doing. You think 'oh well, maybe it wasn't
> a bad idea, okay well I will keep going at this', if I might have felt a bit
> lost thinking 'I would just like to throw this bit away'. So that was really
> important, it gave you the inspiration and the impetus to keep going. If
> you were a person who is quite happy about trying change and not feeling
> threatened by it, that keeps you going and I think with people who don't
> feel comfortable like that, they feel quite threatened and I think they
> would get a lot of benefit out of that sort of support. (12/I5/91)

From the comments made by the teachers, the researchers felt that teachers
tended not to receive this personal support to any large extent in the school setting.
Some of the teachers commented to us informally that they would not seek support
through disclosure of feelings from the head of department or one of the management team as the disclosure could be taken as a sign of weakness, rather than as
a natural consequence of undergoing change. If the teachers did receive this kind
of support, it was from a family member, a colleague who was also a close friend,
or from others on the programme going through the same experience. School-based
teacher development needs to consider ways to provide support by middle management and in ways distinct from staff appraisal.

Support for professional development was sought by the teachers. While the
support of friends and partners was also valued, the support from other professionals
in the same field was seen as important; for example:

> Well, I needed the ideas. The reason why I joined the course at the begin-
> ning was because I was dissatisfied with how I was teaching and there
> must be some new ideas that would get me out of the rut basically. But
> the thing you need is the group support because the first time you try it
> the kids don't know what you are talking about and you are unsure yourself
> and it goes down like a lead balloon, I tell you. And you think 'oh', so you
> have got to have that support to keep you going, to make you try again.
> The fact that we were coming back every week, I had to have something
> to talk about every week and therefore I thought 'well I will try again'.
> And so it was the incentive to keep going. Once you kept going and once
> you had a success then the success encouraged you to keep trying again,
> because you knew you could do it. But if it is something that you try and
> it doesn't work and you haven't got that support, then you are not likely
> to go back and try again. You are going to say 'well I haven't got time
> to stuff about, I am going to do it the old way and get it finished and that
> unit is over and what is the next unit'. We just haven't got time. So the
> course going on week after week was essential because it kept you think-
> ing about that sort of approach. You go to a one week course or a one-
> day course. Yes, you might get fired with enthusiasm and you might go

back to school and try it once and if it doesn't work you put that on the back burner and you go off and do something else. (11/I4/91)

The support for change and innovation in teaching science did not come from all colleagues and these teachers sought support from like-minded teachers, 'teachers like me'.

Professional support was perceived by the teachers as sharing professional knowledge — sharing teaching activities, solutions to problems and theoretical ideas. Sharing teaching activities was seen as supportive, for example:

I have actually enjoyed the interaction and swapping of ideas. It gives you ideas as well. Everybody has got a different way that they do things and different ideas and come up with things which perhaps you wouldn't have done or thought of. (1/I7/90)

Support was also seen in sharing solutions to problems; for example:

When things go well you get a lot of support and hip-hip-hurray type stuff from the group. You have got something to say and people are interested in what you are talking about. But if something goes wrong you have got lots of people to get ideas of how to fix it up from. I found that a real plus. (11/M1/90)

Sharing primary and secondary teaching expertise was perceived as supportive; for example:

Really I guess for me the high point would be — what I got most from, was actually talking to other teachers and I think partly it may be because I am a first-year teacher and partly because it was also good to talk to the primary and intermediate school teachers who were teaching in a different style from what I have to. But I got most of my ideas, and what I learned, came from talking to them, hearing what they were trying out. (13/I1/90)

Support was also gained through sharing theoretical ideas and experiences. Some teachers commented on how the programme had helped them to have a professional conversation with a colleague (usually someone else on the programme) as they had a common interest or experience; for example:

Yes when we left, [A] and I went back together, and we had a good talk about it actually, about just what technology is. (4/I2/90)

As the previous quotations suggest, the teachers found being able to talk with other teachers about what they were doing and with other people, such as advisers, supportive of their changing:

I really enjoy hearing what other people are doing and I like the interaction that has been going on and hearing about the problems or the joys that (others are) having. And I am not alone in these things, the ups and downs that I am having. It is good. (15/I2/91)

I found the discussion quite essential really because it is — you need a bit of raw courage to go out of the security of a textbook and go into something that is totally unknown and the first time I tried I really didn't have a good experience at all. But because of the encouragement of the group and you get various ideas from various people around the group, then you think well I will have another go. And I think coming back each week it made you think at least once a week about this new approach and about what was going on in the course. You had to have something to say, for a start. But it really gave you the support that you needed. I didn't have another teacher in my school that was on the course which was perhaps a disadvantage, looking back on it, and so I tended to use other people at our weekly sessions in that respect to give me confidence because I found it was really quite scary to leave your textbooks behind, to leave your dictatorship from the front behind, to risk having chaos in your classroom, to try something new. So I found the weekly sessions really quite good and the discussions. (11/M1/90)

One of the things — reflection we tend to do at the start of each session — is to reflect on what we have been thinking the week before and sharing ideas, although it is a little bit more on what we have been doing. I think that is quite a valuable little session that we usually have ten or twenty minutes beforehand. (1/I8/90)

Well I think one of the things I find good is when you have got other people to work with and you can prepare things as a team, as a group. Because quite different ideas come from different people. You sort of look at things and, I suppose, you get a little bit tunnel vision in some ways. You see things in a particular way and then somebody else will turn around and look at something completely different and yet it is totally related. I think that is quite good. Also if you can work together as a team preparing materials, because with a lot of these starter activities and things like that, there is probably going to be a lot of getting gear together and that sort of thing and if you can work together on it and perhaps prepare resource kits that go from one year to the next, that should end up saving a lot of work in the long run. That sort of thing, I think, is really important. (1/I6/90)

Support for social development as a part of teacher development was also valued. Support for social development can be seen as support for the social construction of what it means to be a teacher of science and support for interacting with others in collaborative and interactive ways to enable that support to be given. For some teachers, working in this way was initiated and established during the programme. Others were able to get support from existing relationships or colleagueships. Receiving support did not happen in all situations. The programme modelled for the teachers new activities and ways of giving and receiving support. (These are further discussed in Chapter 7.)

The teachers commented that they received support from other teachers on the programmes; for example:

> I think the camaraderie of that big group was a strong factor in all (our) development. The sharing of ideas, the realization that others had the same sorts of problems and also the chance to look at a problem from a different angle, to hear someone else's point of view on a particular problem, someone else's solution to a particular problem. (7/I1/90)

> That has had its spin-off in the sense of we have formed good friendships. [A] and I have swapped a few resources, but again the nature of — we are both HODs, it is just trying to get together. We are just so busy, and there are a multitude of other bits and pieces that kept them away I am afraid. But we have good social professional contacts now and that has certainly strengthened that. And certainly we know, in terms of scheme development and so on, that we are thinking along similar lines, I know that I could always say to (her), 'have you got anything on a particular topic, what do you do in this area', for example (we) are collaborating with quiz projects. (7/I5/91)

However, support was given to some teachers by a close colleague or buddy in the school. Having two people from the one school on a regionally based programme, or the whole staff in the school-based programme, was felt to be beneficial; for example:

> Having someone in the same school who knows what you are on about, can understand your ideas and what you are aiming at. Or if you are not sure where you are going being able to talk about the idea and they say 'well how about this, have you looked at it this way' . . . Nothing really formal. Like I always sit down at lunch time or after school or we get on the phone at night and sit for half an hour or an hour discussing this, that and the other. We are both running out of time at the moment with all the end-of-term things, with parents evening and careers evenings, organizing and that sort of thing. (12/I4/91)

Interest in what they were doing from others in the science department, was seen as supportive; for example:

> (A new teacher) is really interested in what I am doing and, again, she has come in and she is struggling to familiarize herself but she has actually

stated that she has come to this school because she knew that I was associated with the learning in science stuff. She was interested to get in with all that. (7/I5/91)

Support from other staff in the school was mentioned; for example:

(The principal) stood up and she said she had this certificate (of involvement in the research project) to present and I thought 'oh yes' and I was sitting back there half comatose at morning tea time and she started talking on and I thought 'oh my God'. But it was quite good really because people wanted to know what it was all about and were interested that you did something out of school. A lot of them simply wouldn't dream of taking up anything out of school hours. (11/I3/91)

Another source of support mentioned was family; for example:

I tell (my partner) he gets to hear it all ... And he is quite good actually because he suggests other things as well that I don't see in terms of things — not experiments to try but ways to deal with things .... putting a different perspective on something, that is really important. (16/I5/91)

My Mum is a primary teacher and a girlfriend is a primary teacher. Sometimes I talk about things with them, say 'what would you do in primary schools with this idea or that idea?' And they are more flexible thinkers than secondary teachers. And I have got lots of good ideas off them. (12/I5/91)

Students could also provide support; for example:

Apart from others in the group, and (buddy), the kids. And that is really neat when the kids support what you are doing and feel it is constructive. That made doing things easier because if the kids were going to turn around and say 'well we are not doing this, we just want our notes' then that would make life pretty hard if you are not that sort of person. (12/I5/91)

Support from the school management was felt to be valuable; for example:

With (the deputy principal) there has been a few discussions. Not a lot of discussions but she has been aware of what we have been doing and it fits in to what the school is about and encouraging the children to be responsible for their learning ... it was useful because we were doing earthquakes with the fourth formers when she came in and so she picked up on that and was quite intrigued with what the kids were doing. And then she came in and taught in the unit in the fifth-form science with the kids. She was amazed at the very open way that the kids responded to questions and were free and giving of all sorts of information to her which she was quite chuffed with. (5/I5/91)

Our assistant principal sent a student teacher to see me about how to teach interactively. Quite good for the self-confidence at the end of a long term. (14/S3/91)

One teacher found support from within, based on her confidence and belief in what she was doing:

Last year I probably had a little bit of support from my colleagues at the Intermediate. But I haven't really had any support this year. The only thing that supported me was my belief in what I am doing, that is a personal thing and the course, being able to talk about it at the course with the course members. I suppose a little bit at home, talking about the things that I have been doing at home. I just think basically I didn't have that much support . . . It was basically myself and what I have learned that made me change and also perhaps being able to sound off at the course. (3/I12/91)

Opportunities for the teachers on the teacher development programme to share and discuss what they were doing in the classroom, the new teaching activities they were using, the 'better learning' being obtained and the difficulties they were experiencing with the new activities enabled the teachers to give and receive support. Giving and receiving support facilitated professional, personal and social development.

Reflection

Another factor that was seen as helping teacher development was reflection. The teachers used the word 'reflection' in a broad sense to refer to thinking about teaching practice and ideas (reflection-on-action), reflection-in-action, and reflection as critical inquiry (Adler, 1990). The teachers commented that reflection had promoted their learning; for example:

I think this sort of developmental thing has been really, really valuable and it has been really good to have your . . . input and actually having to do this focusing in on and then asked to think about and having to identify in your mind what it is that has been going on. It is a very powerful thing to do. (5/I5/91)

I have looked at the way that I behave with management and control type things, but no I have never really looked at how I ask a question or whether I am introducing somebody else's ideas and trying to focus on that. No, I have never done that and I have found that really useful. (16/I4/91)

They commented that reflection had helped their professional, personal and social development. Reflection had helped their professional development, for in implementing the findings of the Learning in Science Projects, teachers were being asked to change their ideas and beliefs about teaching, being a teacher, the role of the teacher, learning, the learner, the nature of knowledge, the nature of science and the science curriculum, and to change their activities and roles in the classroom. Beliefs and actions are inter-related, as one teacher acknowledged:

(The programme) gave me the confidence really, and it also gave me the time to think about . . . Like before, you asked me what my views are on something — it is not until you actually start thinking about it that you have to crystallize those views into words. I guess that the way that you perceive something comes through in your actions. You might not have actually crystallized that into words but you still think it even though you haven't got the words to think it. And it comes through in the actions or the behaviour that you do, in the way that you might approach things but now, at least I have thought about — well I haven't thought about all the things because it hasn't come up yet, but I have thought about some of the things and I guess I have crystallized them in my mind and it makes it a lot easier to justify what I am doing. And in fact some of the things that I have wanted to do, I now feel justified in doing because I have had the time — we were pretty busy in that course — but you would be surprised at what goes on in the old ticker when you are sitting there and you probably don't even realize it. (14/I1/90)

Changing ideas and beliefs may involve the clarification of existing ideas and beliefs, evaluation of and dissatisfaction with existing ideas and beliefs, construction and consideration of new ideas, acceptance of new ideas and modification of existing ideas and beliefs. Reflection also involves this form of thinking and in connection with classroom practice. Therefore, the process of reflection was promoted in the programme sessions as a way of helping teachers think about their classroom activities and the beliefs associated with those actions. Most of the teachers indicated that the programme had helped them develop their ideas and beliefs about teaching. For example:

Before I was probably pretty cynical about, say, teachers college and education generally speaking and new modern ideas about how you should teach and things like that, I was probably pretty wary or cynical of those. Which wasn't helped by the other teachers around the place, they would say 'oh yes, all this modern education rubbish'. So I have really changed my tune as far as those go and I can see that there is — well I am certainly able to see, in this particular, probably partly with assessment procedures and in-service courses on assessment and also with the LISP (Learning in Science Project) course especially that there is quite a bit that you can do and also the TET (Teacher Effectiveness Training) business. I found that quite interesting as well. So I began to realize that I would have to make up my own mind about them rather than listen to other people's opinions of them. I went to this with a pretty open mind, quite keen, and so I think that was a good way to go into it and I have gained a lot out of it. (9/I2/90)

Not only did this teacher reflect on new ideas presented to him, he accepted and owned some of those new ideas as well. During the programme, the teachers had reflected on and, to varying degrees, modified their views on different aspects of science education. A full account of the topics the teachers reflected on can be found in Bell and Pearson (1993c). Topics included teaching, learning, the curriculum, the aims of science education, the nature of science, assessment and gender issues. For example:

I guess I see it as an unclouding, I guess . . . in my mind. I had a perspective on learning which was innate, but not very well expressed. In fact, when I went to teachers' college I had a whole lot of ideas of how education should happen given to me. And in some ways, over time and over practice and over this course at looking at things, some of those have fallen away and what is me as a teacher has become more clarified. (14/I4/91)

The teachers also commented in a way to indicate that the programme had helped them reflect more on their teaching activities and that this reflection had been helpful in their professional development. However, many of the teachers indicated that they usually thought about what they did in the classroom. This thinking about practice was with respect to whether 'things were working or not':

Because I already did reflect . . . Just in the ongoing way — in the class I do my sort of two ticks or three ticks system or big X through, 'don't repeat this' on my plan book. I sit, I just have my last year's plan book sitting under this year's one because I don't have unit plans and I look at something and I go by the evaluation of that and what I remember from it to decide how I will do the unit this year. That is a reflection because the things have still stuck from last year when I did it, they will determine whether I do it or whether I modify it. (2/I13/91)

The reflection done by the teachers as part of the programme helped them to see what was happening in the classroom as problematic — that is, as requiring improvement:

I guess it (the programme) has made me re-evaluate some of the things. It has caused a few problems and it is unsettling in some ways. But it is

good in that it perhaps makes you re-evaluate some of the things you are
doing and perhaps look for new ways of trying to tackle things and do
things. But some of the time you think 'are you doing it right' — it has
put a lot of doubts about a number of things which you have done in the
past . . . well this is what you are going to learn and go through and you
do a . . . and at times you think 'well is this what I should be doing or
should I be going back to some of the old methods and going through and
getting some of this material'. There is still those doubts and ambivalence
about things at times. (1/I12/91)

The programme also helped the teachers to think about their teaching activities
in relation to their views of teaching and learning, and other aspects of science
education:

Well I think the whole course has been influential. I mean obviously I
wouldn't go back every week, (if it wasn't). I think I would have dropped
out. I used to feel tired but once I got there, there were things that happened that I really enjoyed and especially on the way home that helped me
do it. So this year especially, just that bit on learning, what is learning and
how do I know that my students were learning? That made me think and
reflecting. Reflecting on what I have done and where my kids are at. I
probably haven't done a lot of that, I am always so busy and wondering
about what is going to happen next and your planning. I don't think we
sit back and think about it at all. (3/I11/91)

The reflection also helped the teachers to put new ideas into action:

I had the framework and now I am just seeing how they become classroom
realities. (2/I4/90)

And to be honest, my ideas have changed. My ideas haven't changed, the
idea that my ideas can be applied has changed. That is the big change. I
always knew that they don't learn as well — if you do something for
someone they do not remember it as well as if you let them do it themselves. But I would still have said 'well we haven't got time, the fifth-form
science syllabus is so full I have to go through it this way and have to get
the content across to them' so that is an excuse for not trying to do it by
any other approach. I think probably I am now a lot more aware. (8/I2/90)

Reflection also promoted personal and social development. When the teachers
were reflecting on what ideas they owned and having to give an account of those
beliefs to other colleagues, the reflection was contributing to personal development.
Reflection on, and evaluation of, new social constructions of what it means to be
a teacher of science can also be seen to be a part of personal and social development. The criteria used to determine whether a new teaching activity 'works' or

'does not work' in the classroom can be seen as socially constructed and negotiated. For example, a new activity that results in an increased noise level in the classroom may be considered to be 'working' by some teachers but not by others. The former may interpret the noise as associated with talking for learning, whilst the latter may see it as indicating poor behaviour management. The culture of teaching is a powerful influence on determining the evaluations as a part of reflection.

This evaluative thinking about classroom activities, undertaken with a view to improving the teaching and learning activities for next time, continued after the programme:

> Every time I do something and I sit back or as we go through I will think 'oh well this didn't work' and maybe I should write them down but I am not a person for writing anything down. I am not very good at writing things down, but as I go through things I tend to look at it and think 'next time I will try that instead of this'. (16/I5/91)

The programme to some extent had changed the criteria used by the teachers to decide if something was working or not. For example, as discussed in the previous chapter, by the end of the programme the teachers tended to use better learning outcomes more than better learning conditions as indicators of learning. Hence, reflection was important in the personal and social development aspect of teacher development — in the construction of new social knowledge about being a teacher of science and in the individual teacher accepting or rejecting the new knowledge.

Comments were made by the teachers about factors that helped them reflect, including time and the opportunity to sit down and think; the timing of the programme in their professional life history; communicating their ideas orally and through writing; and reading the articles given out on the programme. The teachers valued the opportunity to reflect provided by clarifying their ideas when talking with others. For example:

> I think you do it (reflection) internally, you do it with yourself, but to actually verbalize the things, to actually talk them out with another person is a much more powerful reflective mechanism . . . Articulating your thought, because when you are thinking, sometimes you don't actually set aside time to do it, it is done while you are running around doing other things and a thought runs through your mind. I don't sit myself down in a quiet place and take ten minutes, which we should do of course, sit down and work it through in my mind. It is on the trot. So actually sitting down and talking with somebody is good clarifying stuff. And they have input too so there is somebody to bounce their ideas off, an opportunity to modify and change. (5/I5/91)

The social and normative dimension of reflection was evident in the comments made about the sharing sessions in the programme:

It is basically listening to what the other ones are doing . . . and you reflect that back to what you have done in the past or what you are going to do. You think 'oh yes, my thinking is like theirs' and if it is not you have still (have the opportunity) to ask them. And it has been very valuable that. (10/I4/91)

Summary

In summary, the feedback, support and reflection helped the teachers to develop socially, personally and professionally. Feedback, support and reflection helped the teachers to change their ideas and classroom practice — their ideas and actions. They aided the teachers in renegotiating and reconstructing collective knowledge about what it means to be a teacher of science. They also helped teachers reconceptualize for themselves what being a teacher of science means. The feedback and support were able to be given to, and received by, the teachers through the interaction with others, especially the other teachers on the programmes. Interactive and collaborative ways of working enabled the feedback and support to be given and received. The teachers also commented that this way of working with other teachers aided reflection. While, for some teachers this collaborative and interactive way of working was not new, for others it was, and the programme enabled them to develop new ways of working with other teachers.

6   Managing the Change Process

Personal development is a part of teacher development and one aspect of it is managing the feelings associated with changing classroom activities and beliefs about science education, particularly when they go 'against the grain' (Cochran-Smith, 1991). Dealing with the emotional issues, conflicts, uncertainties, pressures, stresses, anxieties and worries which arise from changing is a part of personal development. An inability to manage these feelings may result in teachers becoming disengaged (Claxton, 1989, p. 3). The teachers' personal development was centred around their enhanced well-being. In this chapter, we look at the data from the research project relating to this aspect of personal development and explore the feelings associated with the change process, the teachers' views of changing, the requirements for change, managing the students' responses to change, knowing about the change process, and being in charge.

Feelings Associated with Changing

Changing their teaching required the teachers to manage the positive and negative feelings associated with changing. The teachers' talk in the programme sessions and in the interviews gave indications of the feelings involved in the change process for them — both positive and negative (Bell and Pearson, 1993d). In the ninth session of the 1991 programme, the teachers did a workshop activity on the change process, in which one of the questions in the post-box activity was about the feelings associated with the change process. The teachers' written and anonymous responses included:

Very positive, I like the challenge.

Challenged, anxious, determined, excited.

a) positive, excited, somewhat bewildered (at times) . . .

Good — just a little cheesed off if I'm too busy to keep it going *or* too exhausted. It is exciting and provides a real incentive to keep trying to change.

'Worth a crack, Nigel', occasional elation or 'oh, __, that crashed' because risks put you more on the edge.

Uncertain when first trying ideas. Lost at times, not sure what happens next. Pleased when things go well.

... Quite happy but slightly apprehensive about not always following through an old 'proven' (to you) method of teaching ...

Sometimes inadequate.... (all/P9/91)

[The first part of the transcript code indicates the teacher who is quoted; the second part indicates the interview (I), survey (S), programme session (P) or meeting (M) in which the comment was made; and the last part indicates the year.]

While they had positive feelings and experiences, the teachers also said that they felt uncomfortable about making changes, because they felt out of control and inexperienced. For example:

There were times when I felt quite threatened or quite uncomfortable with the things that I was going to have to do ... How am I going to do all this ... I won't feel comfortable, I won't know what to say, I won't know what sort of questions to ask the kids. It will all get out of control because they will be doing a hundred and one things ... It was like being a new teacher again ... It will be all right, it will be all right, it is just that I feel like a new teacher out of control. (5/I2/90)

They also mentioned being annoyed and frustrated; for example:

Totally frustrating at times because the kids are not moving (forward in their learning). The most frustrating part is the questions they set, if they can't find quick responses to them. (10/I4/90)

Comment was made on feeling low when things did not go smoothly; for example:

(So what were the low points then, what were the lows?) It is when I get the days where they have asked for things they want to know, or they have got ideas that they want to carry out and I need more equipment than is available, more resources or the library is booked and it would be the ideal time to go on with what they want, is to go to the library but it is not available. The system here is the English classes are booked in permanently and we fit around them and so your flow gets interrupted. Those are the low points. Or the technician is sick and you thought you were going to do this hands-on thing and it is period one and you don't have time to do it yourself, which you would have if you had known, just those sort of glitches. It is not really in the theory or in the teaching process, it is in the practicalities of it. (8/I3/91)

Feeling scared when they were working with unknowns was another factor mentioned; for example:

It was fairly scary at the beginning because I have seen my Mum teach that way for years and my girlfriend. I don't know if I could handle that because we are not taught how to do that and what to do, how to recognize things and how to build on kids' confidences and get them motivated. (12/I2/91)

(Going through that experience in the programme with the irons) . . . just being asked for some equipment from home sort of freaks you out because you didn't know what you were going to do and that just lets me feel what we do with the kids in the classroom and it can be quite freaky that. You are put on the spot, see and no adult likes to be put on the spot like that. (10/I6/91)

Teachers commented on feeling insecure when they did not feel confident and things were not working out; for example:

Whether you managed to try — or succeed in what you were trying to do. It is difficult when you are still learning a process that you are not terribly confident with yet and until you get to that confidence level — well if it doesn't work, what the heck — it is a bit unsettling there. But, no, I am a lot happier now than I used to be. (11/I4/91)

I feel a lot more confident this year, but I don't know whether that is because everything was new last year, like the whole of the syllabus and everything was completely new. So I don't feel quite so scared when things don't work. It is a scary feeling because, like if you are not actually sure what is supposed to be happening anyway and when it doesn't work then — I got a bit concerned whereas at this stage if it doesn't work then I just say to the kids 'that one was a bit of a bomb, we will have to try that again this way'. (16/I2/91)

Another uncomfortable feeling mentioned was being insecure when they did not know the answer; for example:

I think people are very scared of beginning to admit that they didn't know anything or they were failing. (10/I6/91)

Being able to live with these feelings was important if the teachers were going to persist with changing; for example:

(The) first time I tried that particular approach the kids just didn't know what I was talking about, it just went down like a wet balloon. So I had another go with a different class in a slightly different way and they were a bit better so I thought 'oh well, perhaps it will work'. But then it was really the third time that I tried it, with the second class again, and it was the same topic but it was a different starter, that things started to roll. Once things started to roll I was right. Once you actually got into it. But I think it is quite insecure to start off saying 'there are going to be questions I can't answer', that you are going to establish the fact that you don't know everything, that there are going to be lots of kids coming at you with different questions all at the same time. I think until you cope with that once, you are going to be hesitant at even trying. (11/I2/91)

Confidence in yourself, a willingness to change or a willingness to try something new and give it a real go, not being easily put off when it feels a real failure, that is important. Having support from the group, like having (A) to talk to and others saying 'oh well, a bad day' or this, that or the other and others contributing. But it would have been really easy to give up — I mean the students aren't going to respond the way we were expecting them to straight away so it would be easy to give up and say 'oh well, these kids won't work this way'. Patience, being able to persevere with it and try to make a difference. (12/I5/91)

Acknowledging that having positive and negative feelings is an integral part of the change process, is a part of teacher development. In particular, the negative feelings need to be seen as a part of the change process to be managed, rather than as an aspect to be avoided or ignored.

Views of Changing

Some of the teachers who changed, implied in their comments and actions that they viewed the changes as challenges rather than problems or threats; for example:

It is the challenge of trying out new things and it is the opportunity to share the things with other people, to bounce your ideas off other groups of people. In the second session with the teachers from the other schools, that was the natural move for me with them, for me in that small secure school-based thing, to then meet with other people who were along the way and to have their feedback and their input — that I found extremely stimulating and valuable. So for me there were two things to it, the challenge of actually doing something to change what I was doing in the classroom and having people to run those things by from day to day. (5/I5/91)

The teachers in the research, as volunteers, were honest and aware of the situation in their classrooms and had accepted that change was necessary:

> ... the kids were obviously not responding to what I was doing very much. They were sitting there being very lethargic and it was coming from me and not from them. And they were sort of sponges, I suppose, and really didn't see where they were going or any relevance. (1/I3/90)

In addition, they had a desire and commitment to change:

> (I came on the programme to) avoid stagnating! ... To be revitalized? i.e., to be made to examine what I am doing and how effective it is compared to other methods available. (8/S1/90)

The teachers also felt responsible to do something, rather than attribute responsibility for change solely to others, for example, school management and students:

> (Obviously there are big changes in the way you teach, what did you feel that you needed before you made those changes?) I needed some encouragement, or support. I needed to feel comfortable in my own mind that it was a good move and I guess I knew that what was happening in my classroom at that particular point in time was tired and jaded and I needed to take responsibility for that. And what I have found is that what you people offered was something that I could work with. (5/I5/91)

Requirements for Change

The research findings indicated that there were several requirements to be met if teachers were to be able to change their classroom activities and ideas about science education. As already discussed, managing the feelings associated with the change process and viewing the change as a challenge rather than as a problem were two aspects of this. Another requirement for change was planning and visualizing what alternatives might be like in the classroom. In doing so, risk was minimized. Planning involved being as organized as possible and being mentally prepared — thinking it through and knowing what to expect; for example:

> It wasn't easy because I was threatened a bit because I didn't know the direction the lesson was going to take. We become very secure if we know the direction our lesson is going to take. And if you don't know that, even though you may know a lot of background theory, know enough to answer kids' questions, there is that little niggle of uncertainty in the back of your mind. I felt that to some extent, although I enjoyed hearing the kids respond and when they were positive at it I felt good. (21/I1/91)

The teachers commented on the time and energy required for changing; for example:

> It is an incredibly tiring process re-evaluating what you are doing and becoming disgruntled with it to the point where you want to change, yes. It can be very difficult. (14/I4/91)

> It is hard sometimes. The days just go choo, choo, choo, choo, choo and I feel that by Thursday when I go into your meeting I am often just spaced out. (5/I3/91)

Some appreciated the need to look after themselves through a change, with time for relaxation, support and friendship (Claxton, 1989).

The teachers felt that they had to be prepared to take calculated risks; for example:

> I think you take risks when you find that the method you are using at the moment isn't getting through, and you are quite prepared to have a go at something new to try and break through the barrier that seems to have built up. (11/P9/91)

Having courage was also seen as important; for example:

> Once you have been through it once, and I think you have got the courage to do it again. I think it is quite courageous to try and get out of your rut. It is cosy in a nice little rut where you just go in there, spout forth, walk out — 50 per cent of them pass. (11/I2/91)

They also believed that they had to have ownership of their professional development; for example:

> I guess it is that whole ownership thing. I am here 100 percent because I want to be (here) now. And I have done some things and now I want to work out some of these other finer points now. I feel really positive about going through the course again this year, about putting things into practice in my classroom. (14/I4/91)

The teachers commented that before they did something different in the classroom, they needed to feel confident — confident that they could maintain classroom control, that the students could do the new activities and that their reputation, mana and status as a teacher remained intact. For example:

> What way has my classroom teaching changed? I will have to collect my thoughts here. I think it has changed in terms of my confidence, being prepared to try things that aren't down the straight and narrow learning

objectives, not only because I know more about it, I am more familiar with it — and I don't think that is entirely it — it is the fact that I have been with other people who are changing things. My backup that my philosophy of what it is all about — even if it isn't what is written in the school scheme as acceptable. And I certainly was concerned about that last year in a way that it hasn't concerned me this year. A heck of a lot more confident to ask questions from the kids without worrying that I don't know the answers myself. I don't think I know a lot more answers than I did before but I don't feel quite so concerned that I don't know the answers in the way that I did, I tended to last year. I think that is because of the confidence. (16/I5/91)

Knowing of someone else's success was a part of feeling confident; for example:

(My views on teaching have been) strengthened because there are other people doing it and I know that it works. (16/I4/91)

I think there needs to be more evidence of the sort of teaching going on and the results of it being shown in forms that teachers recognize, like kids' work, science projects or just an ordinary classroom teacher talking to the rest of the group saying 'I tried this and these are the sorts of things that happened, here are some of the things I tried. This worked, that didn't work.' (7/I5/91)

Linked to managing and living with the feelings associated with changing, was the teachers' clarifying of their values about teaching and science education. One teacher stated that he now had to act on his basic philosophy and this was underlying his desire for professional growth:

It has become more important to actually do what I want to do. Do you understand what I am saying? It has become more important that my practice reflects what I believe I should be doing . . . I am sure that given enough time — you see I only taught for a year and then I came into the course. If I had got to the point now, yes, I actually think I probably would have been pretty dissatisfied. I actually would have been looking for my own answers, looking for my own answers as to how to do that. (14/I5/91)

The teachers also welcomed a gradual pace of change and being able to control the pace:

That was a big plus, the fact that it went on week after week after week after week with the same people, you got to know them really well, they supported you, you supported them and you had the encouragement to keep trying. Whereas in a one-off course — like I went to this chemistry conference in the holidays and there were lots of ideas there but there were too many ideas at once. I have got a heap of stuff over there that I have got to go through and sort out all the notes and what I can use and what I can't. Whereas if you just had one thing and did it thoroughly week after week, you would establish that form of activity really well. Instead of having lots of ideas and then being left in a limbo to try them on your own. (11/I2/91)

They welcomed being able to decide when they would take the plunge and use a new activity. They appreciated being able to manage the risk and the changes.

The challenge to teacher development is to enable and operationalize these requirements.

Students and Change

Helping the students to deal with the change was seen as an important factor in promoting change. Not only did the teachers have to change their teaching activities but that the students had to be accepting of the changes in terms of what they consider to be 'good' teaching practice and 'good' learning activities; for example:

I see this whole approach as sort of a two-stage thing. First of all building up the teacher's confidence in it and then secondly getting the kids to accept it. (17/M1/90)

The teachers commented that the need for a gradual change arose not only because of the teachers changing but because the students were having to change as well; for example:

I have found that you can't have something new like that for more than about three or four weeks, people will tolerate it for three or four weeks and then they really want to get back to something a little bit more traditional or recognizable. So you have got to intersperse it, I don't think you could do it all the time or you would think you were a pain. (11/I2/91)

The students appeared to require support to change the way they viewed teaching and learning. Change was facilitated if the teachers were sensitive to the students' response to change and the need for students to understand and accept the reason for the changes; for example:

I think also doing it at the beginning of the year and telling the kids 'well I am going to try different things during the year, things that you might not be used to' and giving them a little bit of warning. (12/I5/91)

Change was facilitated if the students were aware that the new teaching and learning activities helped their learning:

Yes, yes with the class (I have) talked about what is learning. Some of the ideas we talked about on the course — what is learning? . . . I may have told you the story in passing before about coming back from being away for a week. (I had) to set relief work and so it was not interactive, it is just 'here is a textbook, just keep quiet for an hour please with the relief teacher and don't bug me too much'. (I came) back and (found) them saying 'oh you are back, great' . . . instead of going 'oh groan, you are back again' 'Why is that?' 'Oh well we are going to do some learning' . . . 'well hang on, tell me, what sort of things did you do while I was away?' 'Oh I wrote things out and copied things down'. (I asked them questions such as) 'Do you think you learned much?' 'Nope'. 'Why not?' . . . 'How do you learn, what is it that happens in the classroom that you think, that you perceive as what allows you to learn the best?' (14/I5/91)

. . . They said 'oh this is too hard, this is too hard'. But at the end of it they acknowledged that it was the better way to go because they had actually had to work through in their own mind, much more so if they had just copied a pile of notes down off the board. (5/I5/91)

The teachers also commented that the change was facilitated if the students knew what was expected of them; for example:

The students have to know what is going on. For you to be able to change what you do, they have got to be predisposed to the fact that things are going to change otherwise the ground rules have been changed and they don't know where they are. (14/I5/91)

Trusting the teacher, even when he or she did things differently to other teachers, also helped; for example:

I think it is the maturity, I think it is the greater maturity of the kid that you are able to say to those children 'I am going to try something different. It may not seem that you are learning very much initially but as we move along the way you will see that it is a better way of learning'. I guess, because they are sixth-formers and they know who I am and they know where I fit into the school — for them they know that there is a whole lot of things that go on and learning that goes on outside of the classroom. They know who I am, they know that I won't be telling them a load of rubbish so they feel comfortable with that and are prepared to move with you. You can't tell that to third-formers. (5/I5/91)

Acknowledging and facilitating the student change in the process of teacher development are major contributing factors to the long period of time required for teacher development. Teachers' change is always mediated by how they think students (and parents, management and others) will respond to their changing and how they actually do respond. Teachers will seek feedback on classroom behaviour management, learning outcomes, student enjoyment, and the extent to which they are respected and liked by students. Feedback from students about the changes is a key factor in determining the pace of change and an important reason why the pace of curriculum change in education cannot be compared to changing the production line in a factory.

Knowing about the Change Process

Knowing about other aspects of the change process was seen as important for personal development by the teachers and researchers in the research. Knowing that others were experiencing the negative feelings as well as the positive ones helped. It also helped to know that changing required taking calculated risks, planning and knowing what else to do, having courage, confidence, control of the pace of change and ownership.

Knowing that there are increasing degrees of competence as one moves from being a novice to an expert, contributed to starting and sustaining professional development. As changes do not happen overnight, a 'not so polished' outcome is acceptable if viewed as a step towards becoming an expert. Not meeting with instant success is also acceptable; for example:

> Well, I am certainly much happier with what I do in the classroom, much more so and I feel a lot more confident and a lot more skilful now than I used to, now two years have passed, about the processes. I am still not always — the questioning techniques on that one-to-one when you are dealing with those one or two children and you are talking through things with them. I still need to work more on that. I guess it is a fine line between frustration for the kids and that sort of probing questions and the sorts of deep questions that get that gut response out of the kids, I am not always good at and that is something I still need to work on. (5/I5/91)

Another aspect of promoting the change process was for the teachers to reflect on, clarify and discuss the change process with others in the sharing sessions. It was particularly important to know that personal beliefs about oneself and others can militate against change (Claxton, 1989, p. 112; Claxton and Carr, 1991, p. 4). Some of these beliefs include:

1 'Thou shalt not make mistakes' (forget people's names, misread classroom situations, make slips of the tongue, get the answer 'wrong'). Your worth depends on your *success*.

2   'Thou shalt not act out of character' (surprise or disappoint yourself
    or other people, change your mind, shift your ground). Your worth
    depends on your *consistency* and *predictability*.

3   'Thou shalt not be confused' (not have an answer, be half-baked, feel
    at sea). Your worth depends on your *clarity*.

4   'Thou shalt not be afraid' (uncertain, anxious, apprehensive, insecure,
    timid). Strong feelings are immature and should be covered up. Your
    worth depends on your *cool*. (Claxton and Carr, 1991, p. 4).

If teachers are to change their teaching, then these injunctions must be disobeyed
and the task is to provide a context in which these personal beliefs can be over-
ridden and change engaged with.

Knowing about the change process also involved knowing that learning to be
a teacher was an ongoing process over their career and not confined to pre-service
teacher education. Hence, a way to enhance teacher development was learning-to-
learn as adult learners. The teachers were learning about the change process and
how they as teachers were changing and developing. This meta-knowledge is a part
of the teacher development process and, moreover, is seen as empowering teachers
in their ongoing development. This goal of empowerment shaped the aims, activities
and facilitation of the programmes in the research. The programmes enabled teachers
to feel included as part of the group; contribute to the programme and to feel that
their contributions were valuable to the programme, for example, feeling that their
opinions, ideas, teaching activities, suggestions in decision making, and initiatives
were worthwhile; experience competency in teaching; develop a sense of ownership towards their own development; address their concerns and needs; volunteer
for the programme or an aspect of the programme; negotiate the content and form
of the programme; determine the pace and nature of the changes; reconceptualize
their view of teacher development; view themselves as learners; innovate and be
creative, rather than only implement given strategies; and feel that the changes are
possible and beneficial in the current school and political situation.

The teachers appreciated being given space to decide for themselves, the pace
and nature of the changes they would make to their teaching in the classroom,
within the broad framework of the programme. For example, the teachers felt their
development was hindered if they were told by the facilitator to try a specific
activity in the classroom before the next session. They felt their development was
supported if the facilitator gave them a range of activities to try out over the time
of several sessions. They were then able to select which activity they would try,
given the contexts in which they were teaching. Teachers appreciated the opportunity to manage the risk involved in changing what they did in the classroom.

The teachers were able to contribute to the programmes by talking about what
they are doing in the classroom, providing their ideas and opinions for discussion,
giving support and feedback, and negotiating the content and ways of doing the
activities. The teachers gained much from each other as they did from the facilitator.
The act of contributing was seen as empowering by the teachers. Merely responding to the facilitator's questions or directions was seen as a contribution of lesser

value. Once the teachers contributed, they were able to be given support and feedback, which were important to their development. In this way, they were contributing to the socially constructed knowledge about what it means to be a teacher of science.

The desired teacher development was not achieved by trying to force the teachers to change. Although the facilitator was explicit about her expectation that the teachers would try out new activities in the classroom, and although the programme had a structure and goals, the precise direction of any change was not predetermined by the facilitator. The teachers needed to be convinced about the need for change, and to determine the direction of the change, before they would engage in any development activity in such a way that they would learn.

Summary

In summary, the personal and affective are aspects of knowing and learning in the context of teacher development. But to address the personal in teacher development programmes, we must also address the social. Learning and knowing (for example, in a professional teaching situation) are not solely rational, logical activities, with affective dimensions. They involve the social renegotiation and reconstruction of what it means to be a teacher of science, including the construction of the teacher as a learner and someone who is changing his or her practice and beliefs throughout his or her career. Moreover, as stated in Chapter 3, we adopt the position that the individual has some degree of responsibility and agency in the change process, while we also accept that an individual teacher has limited power to change the culture and socially constructed knowledge.

7   Using Anecdotes

In the previous three chapters, the role of 'better' teaching and learning; feedback, support and reflection; and managing the change process in professional, personal and social development; have been discussed. In this chapter, we will consider a teacher development activity that has enabled these factors to be operative.

Many activities were used in the programmes to introduce the teachers to new teaching activities and new theoretical ideas, and to help them reflect on, and change, their classroom practice. The teacher development activities included workshop activities (Bell, 1993b), keeping journals, modelling the new teaching activities, developing curriculum materials, readings on different aspects of science education and the change process, and school visits (Bell, 1993a, pp. 258–78). Other aspects of the programmes were also commented on favourably by the teachers and included being part of the group, the atmosphere of trust and support, the facilitation, the expectations with respect to the goals of the programme, time and timing, and the degree of structure to the programme sessions.

However, the activity that the teachers in the research project most valued was talking and listening to other teachers. Most teachers saw it as an important way to learn and develop (Bell, 1993a, p. 277). One way the teachers talked with other teachers was by using anecdotes (a narrative of a significant event) to communicate what they were doing in the classroom (Bell, 1994b). Telling anecdotes is an everyday way to make sense of our experiences to ourselves or to add sense to what has happened to us. In telling an anecdote, a teacher can talk of experiences and actions and become aware of the beliefs, assumptions and feelings underlying them (Mattingly, 1991).

While anecdoting has been used as a research tool in teacher education (Clandinin and Connelly, 1991), telling anecdotes can also be used as a learning tool in the teacher development process itself (The Mathematical Association, 1991; Mattingly, 1991). 'Deliberately storying and restorying one's life is . . . a fundamental method of personal (and social growth): It is a fundamental quality of education' (Clandinin and Connelly, 1991). The anecdoting fostered cognition as a social process. The anecdoting and accounting provided the interaction necessary for cognitive development and enabled the tacit knowledge, values, norms and morals of teachers to be discussed, renegotiated and reconstructed.

In the early programme sessions in 1990, both facilitators noted that the teachers tended to use anecdotes about their teaching, students or events in the classroom and school, to communicate with each other in the workshop activities, in informal conversation over afternoon tea and on the telephone. This tendency was utilized deliberately in the later 1990 sessions, and in 1991 and 1992, to help the teachers share with the rest of the group what new things they were doing in their classrooms, as a part of assisting the teachers to develop their classroom actions as well as their ideas.

With regard to the aspects of the teacher development programme that helped them, the teachers most often commented on the sharing sessions. These began each of the two-hour weekly sessions and lasted from 15–120 minutes. They gave the teachers the opportunity to share with the others what they had been doing in their classrooms and talk about events, successes, problems and concerns with a new teaching activity; issues in science education (for example, gender, examinations, the curriculum or classroom management) and their feelings about changing. The teachers made the decisions about what was going to be talked about. The talking in these sharing sessions tended to be centred around telling anecdotes.

The interviews with the teachers indicated that they benefited from talking and sharing ideas and experiences, and that this was achieved predominantly in the sharing sessions. The sharing sessions and the telling of anecdotes were valued for the opportunity the talking (and listening) gave for giving and receiving support and feedback, sharing new teaching activities, sharing feelings and reflection. For example:

> The sharing of ideas, people given the opportunity to come and express their feelings and describe their successes or failures they have got is absolutely essential because I think that involves people. And it makes them feel good if they can share it with others. I think that is important that people need to feel good about what they are doing. (Why is it happening on a course?) On a course like this — I think it is because it is a group of people who are all involved in a similar task. We have all got the battlefront to go back to. It is the fact that we are all in a circle, in a large group. The whole atmosphere of everybody has got something of worth to say, that accepting atmosphere is very important. And I think that these are people who obviously want to know more about how to teach more effectively otherwise they would not have gone on the course . . . Well I think the camaraderie of that big group was a strong factor in all their development. The sharing of ideas, the realization that others had the same sorts of problems and also the chance to look at a problem from a different angle, to hear someone else's point of view on a particular problem, someone else's solution to a particular problem. (7/I1/90)

> Really I guess for me the high point would be — what I got most from — was actually talking to other teachers and I think partly it may be because I am a first-year teacher and partly because it was also good to talk to the primary and intermediate school teachers who were teaching in a different style from what I have to. But I got most of my ideas, and what I learned came from talking to them, hearing what they were trying out. (13/I1/90)

[Each quotation is identified by a code. The first number in the code identifies the person quoted. The teachers are identified by a number. (F) is the facilitator. The second part of the code indicates the number of the session in the teacher-development programme or the number of the interview with that person. The last part indicates the year in which the data was collected. For example, the code (7/P3/91) indicates a quotation from teacher number 7, in programme session 3, of the 1991 programme. The code (7/I1/90) indicates a quotation from interview one with teacher 7 in 1990. The dots (. . .) indicate that the transcript has been edited for ease of reading].

The sharing sessions were included in the programme deliberately and based initially on a constructivist view of learning. Talking with other teachers was a means by which the components of teacher development of support, feedback and reflection happened. Fuller documentation is given in Bell (1993a, pp. 279–319).

In the following sections, the structure of the anecdotes is described together with the different ways anecdotes were used in communication and in the learning process. The way the teachers were facilitated to go beyond the anecdotes, to give support and feedback, and to reflect is also discussed.

The Structure of the Anecdotes

There tended to be four aspects to using the anecdotes as a means of talking in the sharing sessions:

- describing the context in which the episode occurred;
- giving the details of the episode;
- stating a response cue, which indicated to the other teachers the reason the anecdote had been told and which invited an appropriate response; and
- the responses made to the cue by the other teachers and the facilitator.

For example, this is an anecdote told by an experienced and competent teacher, who shared with the group her experiences and problems with using the new teaching approach. Firstly, she set the *context* for the anecdote:

Could I start the ball rolling because I have really got an immediate need. Last period today I decided that the new topic with my fourth form was going to be light. I thought 'right, I am going to try this one interactive'. The last one I taught reasonably conventionally, although I tried the circus (activity) and I was really pleased with that. But this time I thought well I had tried the earthquake interactive approach, I will try something I have never gone into before, so I thought I would try light. Light can be a bit of a bedlam with the fourth form. (7/P5/91)

Then, she gave the *details* of what had happened:

> I knew there was a survey, one of the LISP (Learning in Science Project) working papers is on light, and there is a survey at the back of it. So I used that. Basically the survey consisted of about ten questions and they are all about — you see these little stick figures and there is a candle — and the kids are given four choices. You are sitting watching the candle in the middle of the day. The light from the candle stays with the candle, the light from the candle comes half way up, the light from the candle comes right up to you and stops or the light from the candle keeps going until it hits something. So they had a whole lot of questions . . . So I divided the class up into groups and they each had their own copy and as a group they all had to come to a consensus about the answers. Or I said if you didn't agree amongst yourselves that was fine. So I let them go for about fifteen minutes and most of them answered it in about five minutes. I brought them all back into a big group and we started through. I asked one group to give their answers for the first three. Well there was this (huge) argument started up, they were to-ing and fro-ing and it was really hard to control because it was a mixed-ability class and there were really bright girls who were really strong in their ideas and they were calling across each other and even some of the hard nuts were doing the same . . . They were not listening, they were all over the show.

> Anyway, we eventually got through it all and most at the beginning thought the light stayed on the candle, that it didn't move out. Then it was pretty obvious, they started to draw in all these other experiences and when we got to the cinema screen, for example, one girl said that the light must go out to them because if you are sitting by the screen and you look back you can see all the people's faces, they are lit up by the screen so the light must have gone out to their faces. By the end of it all, most started to think, well maybe the light goes right out until it hits something. So that was okay. You could see that a lot of them had obviously constructed new ideas.

> Then I stopped it all and I started to ask them, did they have any questions? And some of them got quite belligerent 'you know the answers to these' they said, 'you know the answers'. I said there were lots of things about life that I don't know . . . I managed to convince some of them that I didn't know everything about it, but there was this belligerent lot who knows that I know something about light. And then some of them said 'she is going to make us answer all these questions for homework'. So what has eventually happened is that the class was really rowdy and unsettled by the end of the whole thing. There was . . . a lot of constructing going on but it has ended such that a large number of them are a bit belligerent about it all . . . (7/P5/91)

The teacher then gave a *response cue* to communicate the purpose for telling the anecdote and the kind of response she was seeking from the other teachers:

> I am wondering what I am going to do with all these questions. So I will have to go back tomorrow and somehow convince them to go to the next step, which is 'let's find out the answers to these questions'. (7/P5/91)

The teacher was thus seeking specific suggestions about what to do next.

The last aspect of an anecdote is *the response to the telling of the anecdote*. This was often a discussion between the original teacher, the other teachers and the facilitator. The interaction went from the anecdote teller to another person, back to the teller, to another and so on. The discussion did not tend to go around the circle but back and forth between the anecdote teller and the others. In this example, another teacher responded first by sharing her own experiences and feelings as a learner herself, thereby affirming the teacher's concerns:

> You dare not leave them with all the questions because that is never . . . when I came to that course . . . a few years ago, all you got was questions, you never rounded off to an answer and I found that, myself, totally frustrating. I was just about ready to throw things. I was absolutely frustrated because there were all these questions and you were all eager to find an answer and nobody ever got to the answer. So you have got to, somehow, get them to the next step. (11/P5/91)

The original teacher then went on to speak about her own possible solutions and thereby cueing in the other teachers again to her request for specific suggestions:

> Well my thoughts are — I have got a collection of books on light and we have got a couple of school texts that have got a lot of experiments on light so I am thinking that I will get the kids to decide which questions they would like to investigate and then I might go around and interact with the groups and say 'well, I know there are some experiments, I have seen some experiments here.' (7/P5/91)

Other teachers, affirmed these suggestions based on their own experiences and provided alternatives:

> Yes, I did exactly that and I set things up on cards and I sat them up in the corner and I said 'these may give you some answers to some of your questions' and that was good because it started them off and then they went further than that. But that is what I did because they really had no idea where to go or what to do or how to find out . . . (3/P5/91)

> You could use the circus type ideas and . . . unless you are confident enough to let them go off and do their own investigations. I think you are better

to do — I did with my fourth-form last year and I found that really quite difficult in that the belligerent ones didn't do anything and the other kids did their own thing . . . So that if you did something like what (she) was talking about, saying 'some of these will help you answer your questions.' And you have a circus type thing again. (16/P5/91)

Get them to write their question down on a piece of paper, one per piece of paper and then stick them on the wall. And even the ones who are getting (cross) about it, and then say 'right, when you have found the answer to that question, take it off the wall and write the answer on the same piece of paper' and that seems to control it a little bit more. It gets away from the sort of cross purposes, when they can actually stick down — and say 'right I am going to answer that question if I can' and they take that question and they work through that and then they put it back on the wall. 'That is my answer' and they put it back there and then they will go on to a different one. It just controls the questions. (11/P5/91)

The original teacher was able to redefine the problem during this discussion:

That is not my problem because I am all geared up for light, I have got all the light sets, I have got all the books and I have got all the experiments and the rest of it. What is really worrying me is that there are some cynical girls, I think, who have seen through my strategy . . . My worry is that they will see this as another ploy to 'oh I have to do some work'. (7/ P5/91)

The facilitator asked the group to stand back and reflect on the purpose of students investigating the answers to their own questions and on the change process:

I am just wondering whether we need to go back and stand back and think what is the whole purpose of doing this. We may need to have a debate with the students about why we are actually doing this — you know you talked about the double change where students had to change their view of teaching and learning too. Most of you found that (the) students' view of teaching was 'you tell me, so if you know then why aren't you teaching?' So I am wondering whether there is a case for, when this arises, saying 'look I do know the answers to some of those questions but the point is I am not learning here, you are' and get them to think about what learning is and the way they might go about learning. I am not quite sure how you would do it, but I was just wondering what you are meeting might be them changing their view of teaching and learning and feeling a little uncomfortable about the whole thing . . . are they aware that the agenda has changed? (F/P5/91)

Other teachers offered support and suggestions of how to respond to the 'cynical' students:

You could start tomorrow by what you think learning is and how do you think you learn and when do you learn best and maybe even have group discussions and have a report and bring it all back and then relate it to what you are trying to do. (3/P5/91)

With my girls I just told them right up front the first time we arrived 'I enjoy learning' and I talked about the fact that I get excited about things that I haven't found out before and that the whole idea of science is for them to learn something and every time they come across a question that means they want to find something out and if they ask interesting questions they will find out interesting things. If they ask boring questions, they won't find out anything interesting. That is why I ended up with that dilemma of them wanting to ask their questions when I didn't want them to ask any questions. Just being up-front and saying that 'I don't have to come here to learn, it is you who is coming here to learn, and this is a way, hopefully, by which you are going to be able to relate what you are learning to something that you want to know'. (16/P5/91)

I think they have to learn how to learn. I have found that with my sixth-form technology group. I had to teach them, if you like, how to learn on their own, how to actually do experiments and question and look for answers. Instead of just rubbishing and putting things down or ignoring they actually had to learn to do things on their own. For so long they have sat there like large sponges and just said 'slurp up'. Now I have actually turned around and said — pretty cold turkey the way I did it actually — 'you have got to investigate something, you have got to lead your own learning, if you like. I can give you all the information, all the things to look up, I can direct you where to look, but you have to take responsibility for your own learning' and that was something that they had to take on board before I could even start them. (11/P5/91)

The original teacher continued, describing some of her students' views on light that she had elicited in the lesson:

Initially their ideas were that light during the day didn't travel out from the candle but during the night it does travel. 'So light does travel but only in certain circumstances.' And 'do you know why it doesn't travel during the day?' Because 'all the light out there pushes it in and keeps it in the candle'. All the light out here in the day. And then one kid suddenly said 'but the light must travel to you because if you are in a lighted room and it is dark outside you can't see the things outside but if you are outside in the dark, you can see things inside the lighted house. Therefore the things in the lighted house, the light must have come to you because you can't see out in the dark because nothing has come to you.' So then they worked, virtually (all) the . . . opinions, by the time we got to the last question, had gone from the fact the light was stable in the candle unless it was able to escape, to the whole idea that it must always be travelling out. (7/P5/91)

Two pieces of positive feedback were given:

In terms of being a constructivist teacher you found out quite a lot of the kids' views on it. (F/P5/91)

Really . . . , maybe you have a really successful lesson, some great thinking going on too. (10/P5/91)

The teacher restated her concern:

Successful in that sense, but I have come out feeling 'where am I going to go tomorrow', but I will . . . (7/P5/91)

Another specific suggestion was given:

Why don't you just put them into small groups and they can discuss what possible answers could be. Instead of writing all the time, just make a discussion thing. (10/P5/91)

The discussion then moved on to another teacher's attempt to teach light based on a constructivist view of learning. During the rest of the sharing session, the original teacher was able to seek out further support from the group for her teaching with the class on light; for example:

Did you let on that you knew the answers, did you let on that you are helping them learn? (7/P5/91)

No, I said we would learn together. Some of the answers I know, some I don't and I said — some of the things I didn't know I said 'come on let's see if we can find some answers together.' Sometimes I didn't know the outcomes of some of the experiments that I put on the cards. I said 'let's have a go together' so it is very much a learning alongside . . . I just be open with them, I just say 'look . . .' (16/P5/91)

In the seventh session of the 1991 programme, the original teacher gave the group some feedback on her class learning about light:

The light kids are going really well and two new things that I am trying, I suppose, remember I said that in the ground rules the kids — I was going to pick on a kid or a group of kids to report back their findings . . . I am using them as teachers and it is working quite well. It usually lasts about ten or fifteen minutes, that first session, depending on how confident the kids are talking, how it interests the rest of them. But I am finding now that kids will get up and they will explain what they have been doing and almost immediately questions start coming from the other kids 'What do you mean by a wave length?' And the kids at the front are forced into a situation where they have got to explain what they mean and other kids who have possibly been exploring the same area are coming in with their bits of information. And now and again, today for instance with one of the fourth forms, they all got tied up with wave length so I then said 'well I know a little bit about it, do you want me to tell you a bit?' so I did a very quick lesson on electro-magnetic radiation and how the different waves have different wave lengths. And I told them what a wave length was and I showed them that blue light might have a wave length like that and a red light might have a shorter one or the other way around. And so they were all interested in listening . . .

And secondly this whole business is about because the kids are all off in different directions, exploring different things. I know at the end of three weeks I am going to introduce the learning objectives to them for the unit and they are going to sit a test, a conventional test. So I thought one way of keeping track of where everybody was going was to do a big concept map at the back of the room on a big piece of paper. So I have got two big concept maps, one for (each class). And I am just, as the ideas are coming, say, I have got light in the middle and it might be — most of them started off with rainbows, of course, so I have prism, rainbow, beams light and the colours and wave lengths and so on and it is quite good because each group that is getting up seems to be covering something different. There is one area they don't — none of them seem particularly interested in mirrors for some reason or other. They are playing with the lenses, they are playing with bits of glass, they have all played with the filtered colours. Quite a few have gone to lasers, very interested in lasers for some reason or other. And there was just one last thing, in terms of the learning, with a group of bright girls a tremendous amount of learning went on with refraction. They made sense of some quite important concepts. They came up with refracted ray, angle of refraction, angle of incidence, normals etc, and the animation on their faces was really neat to see. I think they actually make noises, they are quite surprised at what they have done themselves. (7/P7/91)

These excerpts indicate that the teacher had been able to further develop her teaching along constructivist lines. In an interview, she acknowledged and expressed her appreciation of group members' support and suggestions of specific activities given in the earlier sharing session:

What it (the programme) did for me, it brought me into contact with other practising teachers who were going through the same process. It was largely through listening to them, their experiences, that I have learned different techniques . . . the sharing sessions have been great. And the ability to ask them question, 'how did you do that?' And that time when I went with my problem about the light, that was marvellous, because I got two or three really good concrete suggestions. And I went straight back to the class-room, I used it and it worked. (7/I2/91)

All four aspects of using an anecdote were required if support, feedback and reflection were to be promoted by the telling of anecdotes. However, not all four aspects were included in all anecdote-telling episodes. For example, one teacher told an anecdote at the end of a two-hour session:

I would just like to share a really interesting thing that happened in the class today. My fourth-formers are doing practical with experimental things and last time they had it they all discussed what they were going to do and all their questions were written down and one lot of boys have already done, just about finished theirs and the girls have got to experimental things using food and they were going to carry these out today and work in the classroom and they were all told to come prepared to do their practical work. Well the girls were organized and they had brought food and one lot went off to the home economics room to test their things to do with pikelets and one set of girls I hid away in one of the other labs to eat chocolate for the period. And the boys were so angry because the girls were making food and they were going to eat it and they were stuck in the classroom with boring book work to do. They were really cross, but it was quite an interesting little lesson. (5/P3/91)

A context was given as were the details. However, the response cue ('but it was quite an interesting little lesson') closed the anecdote rather than signalling to the other teachers an appropriate way to respond, if in fact a response was sought. No discussion by the rest of the group followed.

Further examples of anecdotes told during the teacher-development programmes run as part of the research are given in Bell (1993a, pp. 279–319).

Types of Anecdotes Told

The teachers tended to tell anecdotes when they wished to:

- tell the others of a significant event or episode for them. Often this significant event had already been told to someone close and it was retold to the group;
- share an achievement with others. This might be, for example, when they had used a new teaching activity, such as listening more to what the students are saying for the first time;
- initiate or add to a debate on theoretical notions. This was done by giving instances to back up an idea or opinion in a discussion. It was also done

by telling an anecdote to lead into a discussion on some ideas that they were mulling over in their minds; and

• tell the others of a problem they were having in using a new teaching activity in order to receive suggestions for possible solutions as well as support and feedback.

Communicating a Significant Event

A type of anecdote told by the teachers was that which communicated a significant event to the others. For example, one teacher had shown his mother a video of him teaching and her comments had helped him to reflect on what he did as a teacher.

Well the most important thing that has happened to me this week was talking to my mother. (The researcher) has been out videoing what is going on in my classroom. I thought this is a neat idea, a neat way of just showing my Mum what I do for a living. Because they were really worried when I said 'Mother I want to be a teacher.' 'We have failed, we have failed, are you sure about this, quick get him to the doctor.' So I said 'this is me in the classroom' and she only had about ten minutes viewing and she said 'do you tell your kids at the beginning of the year that this is what you expect of them?' And I said 'no, not really'. And she said 'well that is really different, really different to what normally goes on.' And, of course, I know this but it is never clicked and we have actually talked in theory about the expectations that you have . . . It is not that you really didn't click, until like I can see in my classroom, from a different angle, I am not actually part of doing things and she said 'yes, that is really quite different, that is like me walking into somebody else's classroom and looking at it and it is quite different to what I see in other classrooms.' Now when I was up the front teaching, when I am, I don't notice that because I am too busy doing things. I thought, you are right. And she said — she seems quite happy now, by the way, and she said 'in our days it was all rows and rows and you sat there and if you went boo you got whacked over the knuckles.' So the biggest thing that has hit me this week is the fact that I have quite a different expectation. One period a day those kids see me and my expectation is way different. And in fact, the way of achieving in my classroom, getting the warm fuzzies, is not to sit still, is not to sit there and shut up and copy down things, but to beetle over to me and say 'hey, I reckon this works like this', and to talk with other people, to keep on track. Not to hit things or annoy others in their group. That is how they get my attention and the warm fuzzies come from doing those things which is way different. (14/P6/91)

The discussion that followed consisted of eight contributions, started by the facilitator with a clarification question:

What was it about what your mum saw that she thought she liked what you were doing, what particularly struck her? (F/P6/91)

I think it was in the discussion, it was finding out what kids were thinking, how they thought about things. (14/P6/91)

I think a lot of the older people were totally frustrated at school because they were never allowed to say what they thought. (11/P6/91)

We had this little discussion that ensued. She said 'you are getting those kids to think about things and be able to make their own decisions in life. They are not going to be taken in by the media that says "this is what is happening", they are actually going to be thinking about the information that is coming to them in their lives and they have to make their own decisions based on, if all goes well, based on information, that they won't just believe everything that is told to them.' I am happy with that, I feel happy with doing that for a living. (14/P6/91)

So what else did your mother pick up on, and you when you watched it, in terms of what tells me the kids are learning. Did you get any clues from some from outside your classroom? She could see that they were learning different skills, but was there anything else in terms of indicators of learning? (F/P6/91)

I haven't thought hard on that one. (14/P6/91)

Communicating an Achievement

The purpose of another type of anecdote was to communicate an achievement. The teller tended to use the anecdote to communicate the changes occurring for him or her. In one example, a teacher told an anecdote to communicate a way in which his teaching had changed:

Can I make a very small comment? At the moment with sixth-form classes — I have got two classes, the rest are doing exams all this week. What I have done is have a think about my teaching at that level, and I think my pupil sensitivity has increased. Whereas I think you tend to think you have got to get through a lesson, present that material. That is what I have done in the past. I think now that I am watching facial expressions more and if I can pick up if a kid has switched off — if a kid is interested in what I am saying and I get a facial expression that shows some sort of puzzlement I am going back and trying to dig out what it is that I am doing. Probably taking more time explaining in the multiple number of ways, giving it more illustrations and perhaps doing a lot more mini experiments.

Today, for example, dealing with equilibrium in form six I latched on a number of little mini things and in the end got quite side-tracked and ended up doing something quite different . . . The sensitivity thing, I think, is pretty important. The kids are responding positively so that they feel happier to seek help. We got onto breathalysers, which is nothing to do with equilibrium. (21/P2/91)

The discussion that followed consisted of thirteen contributions from the original teacher, the facilitator and six other teachers:

I like that, that is me when I am teaching sometimes — you call it side-tracked, I just call it a learn track. The kids cotton on to something and then they start asking questions and so the direction that you are going in goes . . . (14/P2/91)

What did you call it? (F/P2/91)

Learn track. I like that, I use that. (14/P2/91)

My daughter came to school with me on Queen's Birthday Monday because we had to have school unfortunately. She sat in the back of my classes doing her science work experiments. It was quite interesting, her comments on my teaching. I was doing that all the time according to her. She reckons the kids were sitting there deliberately side-tracking me. She said then you would come back and do a bit more teaching and then off they would go again. (11/P2/91)

It is horrible when they say to you afterwards 'why don't we ever do any work?' because I had that. We have talked about things all afternoon. (16/P2/91)

Well work is writing, isn't it? (11/P2/91)

Is learn-tracking an aspect of constructivist teaching? (F/P2/91)

Yes, it has to be. (2/P2/91)

They are building up an idea and then a question is occurring, they are trying to clarify for themselves or if something has occurred to them that doesn't quite make sense so they ask the question. I assume that is what you mean. (7/P2/91)

Yes, that is what happened to me. We were doing precipitate reactions and we ended up talking about heart attacks . . . a build up of cholesterol in blood stream and then we got on to how do you treat that. (14/P2/91)

Initiating or Adding to a Debate

Another type of anecdote was used to initiate or add to a debate on some theoretical idea. This was done by giving instances to back up an idea or opinion in a discussion, or to lead into a discussion on some ideas teachers were mulling over in their minds. In this example, a teacher made a general statement about students relating the science they are learning to their everyday world, and then told an anecdote to exemplify the general statement:

> It is nice when the kids come up with everyday examples and can equate it to something happening at home. (With) the third form we just took solids and talked about heat and what happens to the particles when you heat them. You know the standard little thing — we have got one with iron and aluminium and rust and copper . . . and someone said 'no, they can't really all be the same, well not exactly the same because that is what happens in kitchens with your pots.' Then I said 'well what kind of pots are they' and they come out with 'well there is aluminium and there is the shiny stainless, and you get ones that have got copper on the bottom too'. So we had the three. I said 'you rank those in order of which ones would burn your food the quickest' and they had to put them in order. And then they were quite happy having bets on their other three measures. (12/P3/91)

In another example of linking what was happening in the classroom to the theoretical ideas being introduced and discussed, a teacher told how some of the girls in her class were reluctant to join in. The comment was made after the group of teachers had watched excerpts from a video of a local teacher teaching interactively:

> I am just thinking of one of my fifth-form science classes where I am merely trying to get through the work . . . and I think of all those girls in there who just sit like dummies and I am not getting a response from them because I am not using this technique on that class. It takes longer, it takes longer . . . and it just makes me ask 'do you think girls learn science better in a single sex school?' I find that unless you have an accelerant class where the girls feel really on a par with the boys, they are happy to contribute . . . especially the top girls. But . . . the average girls, they sit back and . . . I consciously ask all the girls first to get a response from them. But I can see that they don't want to be asked in case their answers are wrong . . . (35/P6/92)

This account of what it was like in her classroom prompted a debate on gender issues in science education and in an adult group such as their own, with particular focus on sharing talk time and listening skills. The debate went on for five to ten minutes with eighty contributions being made by the teachers and the facilitator.

Getting Help with a Problem

One further purpose for telling anecdotes was to get help with a problem. For example, in session seven of the 1991 programme, the first anecdote was given in response to the facilitator asking if there was anything new the teachers had tried and what kind of feedback had they received. A teacher replied, seeking help with an aspect of interactive teaching:

> The other thing I tried to do was . . . with my learning assistance group I think I have identified my problems . . . And it is probably because (they) have had a lot of (experience of) their ideas not being particularly relevant and either behaving nicely . . . or being in a behaviour problem so that if you can get them to shut up and do something, you think you are winning. And so their ideas never actually have to surface. And so I was trying to find out where their ideas were at, to start from there . . . So I have tried to cut down on their book work because they switch off and trying to make more group work where one person records and the others give their writing instead of having them writing things down.
>
> And what I have found . . . is that they actually got quite cross — because at least when they did their book work they could switch off and they were just writing and I was perpetuating their behaviour anyway. And they got a bit bewildered and a little bit cross with me because I was asking them to think about things. And I discovered I really don't know where their ideas are coming from and I am not quite sure how — that is where I need a bit of help . . . like we are looking at mixtures at the moment and I don't know the questions . . . when I had the scheme and I knew what it was that we were looking at I could find out the kids' ideas about that and most of them had ideas that were around there and we could go on. If it is before that, how do you know where to start to find out what they know? Does that make sense? (16/P7/91)

In this last part of the anecdote, the teacher had given a clear response cue ('how do you know where to start to find out what they know?'), which was responded to with fifty-three contributions from six teachers, the facilitator and the original teacher, including suggestions for finding out the thinking of the students given by the other teachers:

> Could you use analogies with, say, actually have marbles and have a beaker or a cup or something or a little box with marbles all the same colour and then some marbles that are different sizes but the same colour and then marbles that are different colours and than another one where they are different colours and different sizes and simply ask them if they could separate the different ones into groups. It may be that they will pick out that the marbles that are all the same they can't separate into any sort of groups. The next lot they can separate into groups, and you could

perhaps leave them a little bit in terms of how are you sorting them? Something is different about them and perhaps lead them a little bit that way. The problem is though, have your kids got this idea, do you think, that matter is made of one continuous thing, they have not got this idea that matter is made of lots of tiny little bits? (7/P7/91)

Well maybe you need a couple of survey questions, don't you, right at the very beginning. You could say to them 'if you had a really . . .' do they know what a microscope is, have they used a microscope? You could say something to them 'if you had a really, really powerful microscope, the most powerful that you could have in the whole wide world and you looked at a piece of paper or something, what would you see?' If you could get a super, super powerful (microscope). I find with my third-formers they will say 'oh you will see lots of tiny bits'. I don't know where they get it from. They probably got it from somewhere at Intermediate School. They do seem to have some idea that if you used a very powerful microscope you would see little bits of chalk or little bits of paper. (7/P7/91)

What I would do, I would focus on the word 'mixture' and I would go to the simple bit of it, go to the mixed bit and ask them what sort of things you can mix and what happens when you do and work from there. (8/P7/91)

The one I do, have done in the past, problem-solving one — I make up the problem coming from those units, put it on the board there and immediately after that with no discussion at all they have to write down how they think they are going to solve the problem or just write down what they think about it. A simple one like 'what is a mixture' and then they write their answer. Then you go and discuss it all and experiment and whatever else, and then I ask the same question again and they record it. So I see their before and after view of it that way. It has worked reasonably well. (10/P7/91)

If you asked in your survey, first of all, what they thought using a powerful microscope what they thought a piece of chalk looked like at the microscopic level, and then you said 'take a glass of water, what would it look like on a microscopic level' and then you could say 'if you heated up that water and it became steam, what would the steam look like on a microscopic level?' That might make them — I don't know whether that might make them think. (7/P7/91)

The discussion continued on for several more minutes. The responses made by the other teachers to the original response cue of finding out what the students are thinking and what to do next, covered a number of suggestions of possible teacher activities.

In summary, the teachers often used anecdotes to get help with a specific teaching problem. Women tended to tell this kind of anecdote more than the men did. The suggestions sought were in terms of what 'I as the teacher could do'.

The Purposes for Telling Anecdotes

Telling of anecdotes appeared to serve several purposes. First, there were cognitive outcomes as telling anecdotes helped the teachers to:

- clarify their own ideas and beliefs about science, teaching and learning science, science education, and professional development;
- share their ideas with others, to listen and compare their own ideas and beliefs with others;
- construct new ideas about teaching and learning;
- link new ideas with existing ideas and modify their existing knowledge if desired;
- accept new ideas as part of their belief system;
- link new theoretical ideas with their classroom practice; and
- talk about (and value) what they were doing in their classrooms.

The sharing sessions and the use of anecdotes also enabled the teacher development to be based on the experiences and knowledge of the teachers. The teachers came to the programmes with their own existing ideas, beliefs, feelings, experiences, concerns and problems. By enabling the teachers to talk about them, the facilitator was ensuring that their experiences and knowledge were taken into account and valued in the learning or professional development process. The facilitator or guest speaker was not the only source of worthwhile ideas and activities; the teachers themselves were able to contribute to, and determine, the topics for discussion in the sharing sessions. The teachers felt the opportunities for contributing to be empowering as they became more confident that their own ideas were of value even if everyone did not agree with them.

As well as this cognitive rationale, the sharing sessions and the use of anecdotes also had personal and affective outcomes as it helped the teachers and the facilitator to:

- value what was being done in the classroom;
- value the teachers' own ideas, beliefs and values;
- attend to the feelings associated with teaching experiences and beliefs about teaching;
- share and manage the feelings associated with the change process;
- address some of the personal beliefs about themselves and about themselves as teachers;
- give and receive personal support and feedback for self-esteem, confidence and encouragement;
- confirm that they were not alone in their experiences of teacher development;

- validate the ideas of the teachers;
- empower the teachers when their contributions were accepted and valued; and
- encourage the teachers to innovate and have the confidence to keep on taking new initiatives.

There was also a social rationale for the sharing sessions and the use of anecdotes. The talking and sharing were planned to foster a sense of belonging to a group and of participating in social interactions or conversations. These were also planned to break down the isolation of teachers in classrooms, to give all the teachers attention and not ignore some, to provide a place for teachers' voices to be heard and taken seriously, to blur the distinction between novice and expert and to communicate the expectation that all participants would be contributors to the discussion and thinking in the programme. Anecdoting was the main way that the group renegotiated and reconstructed what it means to be a teacher of science.

The Role of the Facilitator

The facilitator played an important role in the teachers' use of anecdotes to talk in the professional-development situation. The facilitator focused and monitored the direction of the discussion, so that the teachers were able to give their full attention to the content of an anecdote. Facilitation was helpful to:

- encourage all teachers to tell anecdotes;
- ensure that a response cue and a resulting discussion were part of the anecdote telling episode. Often the facilitator had to give the response cue, such as 'what tells you the students are learning?';
- ensure that the resulting discussion did not move away from addressing the teller's response cue and to ensure that the discussion enabled support, feedback and reflection to occur;
- encourage, by asking probe questions in the discussion following an anecdote, a consideration of the theoretical ideas and issues introduced in the workshop sessions or that were important to the teacher development being sought;
- give summaries and overviews; and
- ensure that all who wanted to, contributed to each sharing session. This often meant rounding off one anecdote to allow for others to be told.

Facilitating the use of anecdotes in teacher development required a different perspective to that involved in facilitating the workshop activities. In facilitating the use of anecdotes, the facilitator enabled the teachers to determine the topic for discussion within the broadly agreed to framework, — that is, teaching that takes into account students' thinking — and to talk about the matters that were important to them. The points of detail and the overviews that the facilitator wished the teachers to think about, had to be fed into the teachers' discussions. In contrast, the workshop activities provided more opportunities for the facilitator to determine the topic for discussion, as well as to talk about the details and overviews that she thought were important.

Summary

The teachers in the research project commented that talking with other teachers was an important factor that helped their professional development. The mode of talking most valued by the teachers in the professional development situation was telling anecdotes (narratives of significant incidents), which were planned for, and occurred most often, in the sharing sessions. The use of anecdotes was a means by which teachers could ask for, and receive, personal and professional support and feedback. The anecdotes also enabled the teachers to reflect on their classroom teaching experiences and to consider new teaching activities. The use of anecdotes helped the teachers to engage in support, feedback and reflection which are the key aspects of promoting teacher development.

In addition, the use of anecdotes enabled the teachers to focus the discussion on teaching and what they were doing in the classroom. Classroom activities were central to telling anecdotes, enabling the teachers to share new teaching ideas, problems, and solutions that worked; to think about using new activities in their classroom; and to communicate with each other about what to expect when a new activity is used.

There was also a social rationale for the sharing sessions and the telling of anecdotes. Talking and sharing experiences, beliefs and feelings were planned to foster a sense of belonging to a group and of participating in a social inter-action, a conversation. As a deliberately planned for part of the programme, the social interaction broke down the isolation of teachers in classrooms, gave all the teachers attention rather than ignoring some, provided a place for teachers' voices to be heard and taken seriously, empowered rather than controlled teachers in their professional-development process, blurred the distinction between novice and expert and between teacher and learner, and communicated the expectation that all participants would be contributors to the discussion and thinking in the programme. Most importantly, the social interaction fostered the personal and social reconstruction of the teachers' views of teaching and learning science, and their values and norms of being a teacher of science. Cognition can be viewed as a social process, and the anecdoting enabled the collective thinking of what it means to be a teacher of science to be renegotiated and reconstructed.

8   Contemporary Contexts for Teacher Development

Introduction

In the preceding chapters, we have presented a model of teacher development based on social, personal and professional development. However, given that teacher development does not occur in a vacuum, we outline briefly in this chapter some of the wider social, economic, political and historical contexts for teacher development in New Zealand and the United Kingdom. These two countries have been chosen because we as authors are most familiar with them and because in both, recent social, economic and political changes have made marked changes in education and the work of teachers. We invite readers to compare these contexts with that in their own country. In describing the contexts in which teacher development is occurring in our countries, we essentially outline some major contemporary ways of viewing social and personal life and consider their implications for the nature and conduct of teaching and teacher development.

Teachers in the United Kingdom and New Zealand, like their colleagues in other countries, are living and working in a rapidly changing world — a world which is making increasing demands on them to change. Until recently, the voices of educationalists have been most influential in determining the direction and scope of educational change. Educationalists are those with a direct employment-related interest in educational policy and its implementation: a very loose aggregation of schoolteachers, teacher educators, educational researchers, curriculum developers, and local government school inspectors and advisers. They have arguably had more influence historically on policy formation than the ideologies of politicians, the ambitions of particular parents, or the interests of potential employers. But this is changing: the voices of politicians, claiming also to speak on behalf of parents and of employers, are being more clearly heard, at the expense of those of educationalists.

The changes teachers are being asked to make need to be seen in the context of the changes in our societies. One influence for change can be linked to the post-industrial society and post-modernism. Another is the emergence of the 'New Right' in politics generally and in educational matters particularly. As is discussed in the following two sections, these social forces vie for influence over education. Individual teachers may be personally attuned to one of these forces for change, or indeed try to reconcile them. Their professional work and development are certainly increasingly influenced by them.

Post-industrial Societies, Post-modernism and Education

One aspect of the changes influencing teachers, teaching and education, is the post-industrialist society, the key features of which include the change from a goods-producing to a service economy; the increased use and sophistication of information and communications technologies; the increase in professional and technical jobs compared to manual labour; occupational flexibility and diversity; working as a part of a team; a valuing of innovation, creativity, and enterprise; and international travel and migration.

Another aspect of change influencing teachers and education is that suggested by the term 'post-modernism'. Post-modernism is a term that defines or suggests the 'overall character or direction of experimental tendencies in Western arts, literature, architecture and intellectual activity since the 1940s' (Bullock, Stallybrass, and Trombley, 1988, p. 671). Post-modernism is often associated with a pluricultural range of styles, multiple voices, moral and scientific uncertainty, challenges to authorities, eclecticism, deconstruction, and a critique of modernism.

These two changes have given rise to new patterns of social, economic, political, and cultural relations. Hargreaves (1994, pp. 38–46) sees these collectively as constituting 'post-modernity', which he defines as a social condition comprising of social, economic, political and cultural relations, including post-modernism as an aesthetic, cultural and intellectual phenomenon. Like Hargreaves, we are primarily analysing and explaining post-modernity as a social context in which teacher development is occurring, without adopting a post-modern theoretical position. As Hargreaves notes (1994, p. 43), 'post-modernity . . . offers a new social arena in which moral and political values and commitments in education can be played out'. While some may view post-modernity as promoting equity and multiple voices, others may see it as a capitalist ploy.

Hargreaves (1994) distinguishes post-modernity from modernity, and sees it as in tension with, a critique of, and a response to modernity. Modernity can be described in this way:

> At root, modernity rests upon Enlightenment beliefs that nature can be transformed and social progress achieved by the systematic development of scientific and technological understanding, and by its rational application to social and industrial life. (Hargreaves, 1994, p. 25)

Hargreaves (1994) asserts that modernity is manifest in three arenas of action, each of which is echoed in the educational system. In the arena of economics, family and work are separated; workers carry out repetitive tasks in a precise way; the scope of these tasks has become narrower, the precision of their definition more exact, and the scope for personal input by workers reduced; and expansion is essential for economic survival.

In the *arena of politics*, the State is strong, centralized, regulatory and interventionist, with respect to social welfare, health and education. In the *arena of the personal*, there is a sense of security, sense of place, identity with a group, and well-articulated values and morals.

In recent years, a crisis of modernity has arisen, which has its counterpart in the education system (Hargreaves, 1994). The economics of modernity has produced a surplus of goods, for which no markets can be found at a price which will continue to support the factory system. The politics of modernity has been felt to be dysfunctional, with the centralized State stifling initiative and neglecting key social issues and conjunctions of issues. The organization of modernity has been seen as stifling innovation, responsiveness and entrepreneurship. In the arena of self-identity, the expression of people's innerselves was felt to be suppressed for the public face. The self was seen as being sacrificed and work becoming increasingly meaningless.

Post-modernity is, then, the social conditions resulting from the emergence of the post-industrial societies and post-modernism and in which teachers and students are living and working. In the workplace, it is characterized by occupational flexibility, such that any worker may have to discharge a wide-ranging and evolving set of tasks; work is not defined by roles but by tasks, projects and networks; a growing amount of work is part-time, temporary and contracted out; and wage arrangements are flexible, with more use of bonuses and merit pay. The organization of the workplace itself is also fluid, involving the rapid changing of the location, structure, and purpose of industrial units. For example, in some organizations, all the workers are not located on one site.

Post-modernity is also characterized by technological complexity, within a rapidly changing technological environment. For example, personal computers and telecommunication equipment are increasingly more complex and sophisticated. Technological sophistication and complexity have also in effect compressed time and space. The instantaneous communication now possible by telecommunications can engender personal anxiety through the pressure for rapid completion of tasks and decision making, the rapid pace of change, the guilt created by not keeping up, and the erosion of time for reflection on core values and relaxation.

Another characteristic of post-modernity is the globalization of markets; for example, through the creation of free trade communities (such as the European Community) and a common currency (the Eurodollar). Globalization has undermined the justification for nation states, in which the common culture and economic organization of each state has been emphasized. One reaction to this has been the intensified search for local culture and a national identity.

In our day-to-day living, post-modernity may be seen as characterized by a plurality of belief systems; the replacement of the culture of certainty with a culture of uncertainty; the discrediting of meta-theories; multiple and often contradictory positionings by people — the self is no longer defined in terms of a single position; and the blurring of the boundaries between self and the world beyond.

The nature of educational systems which would be derived from, and support, a post-modern age, is only just beginning to be teased out in theory and practice. One characteristic of such an education system would be an emphasis on young people learning-to-learn; that is, on gaining metacognition of their own learning processes. Students would relate to a wide variety of sources of support for their learning, including teachers, other adults in the community, their peers, and a range of experiences available both directly, for example in industrial settings, and surrogately through multi-media. They would have much more control over what they learnt, when, and how. They would be learning for continual learning and change throughout adult life. Another characteristic would be learning problem-solving and problem identification; selling, marketing, persuasion and communication skills; and information-technology skills. Other learning outcomes promoted would be adaptation, flexibility, creativity, innovation, initiative; self-management and autonomy, and collaboration; skills for coping with the insecurity of rapid change and shifting bases; and learning for living in a global village, such as learning a foreign language. Education in a post-modern context would also include learning for a bicultural and multi-cultural world; for inclusiveness with respect to ethnicity, gender, and disabilities; and learning the skills of critical thinking on the power relationships and ideologies embedded in policies and actions.

Post-modernity would present particular challenges to teacher development. The focus of teacher development would be on taking into account students' thinking, learning processes, gender, disabilities, cultural experiences, ethnicity and languages. Teacher development would be helping teachers to take into account contexts for learning, and to see an important part of learning as the linking of new learning with everyday knowledge and experiences. It would be helping teachers to learn a range of teaching strategies and to critically evaluate them.

Curriculum development, linked with teacher development, would be focusing on the inclusive curriculum with respect to gender, disabilities and ethnicity. The curriculum would also be promoting learning-to-learn strategies for students; teaching and learning activities that are engaging students in thinking, information skills, problem-solving, innovation and creativity; the use of information technologies; interdisciplinary studies; non-racist, multi-cultural science education; and the learning of science in indigenous languages. In addition, it would view one aspect of curriculum development as being school-based (and, in many countries, within a national framework).

Another challenge that the post-modern world gives to teacher development is to the content and ways of working in teacher-development programmes themselves. Teacher-development programmes would take into account teachers' (as learners) thinking, learning processes, gender, disabilities, cultural experiences, ethnicity and first language. Contexts for learning for teachers (as learners), would also be taken into account, and an important part of learning would be seen as linking new learning with everyday classroom knowledge and experiences. Topics for learning by teachers would include those decided by teachers' concerns and responses, and would include the learning and change processes for teachers as learners; that is, metacognition. Information skills and using information technologies would also be included, such as using Internet and e-mail to communicate locally, nationally, and internationally. The programmes would be inclusive; enable teachers to have ownership of, and engagement in, their own learning; and empower teachers as stakeholders and contributors to the renegotiation and reconstruction of the culture of teaching. The programmes would involve collaboration and negotiation. They would involve teachers learning critical reflection to clarify the core political and social ideas and values underlying proposed changes, and to clarify their own moral and ethical frameworks. It would also involve helping teachers to manage the resulting unpredictability, risk, uncomfortableness, feelings of loss of control, and spontaneity.

However, teacher development in some countries (notably the United Kingdom) seems to be moving in exactly the opposite direction, with strenuous efforts being made to reinforce and exaggerate the structures and provision of education that would be expected within modernism at the peak of its development. In other countries, for example, New Zealand, those aspects of post-modernity which are seen to contribute to economic recovery and competitiveness, are being encouraged, while others are not.

The New Right Policies and Education

In many countries, for example, New Zealand and the United Kingdom, a major change has occurred in society and in education with the implementation of the policies of neo-conservative governments. In this section, we outline these policies and in particular their impact on education.

Dale (1989) saw the State in a capitalist country as having to face three permanent problems: how to provide support for the process of capital accumulation by individuals and trading organizations; how to guarantee the context for the continued expansion of capitalism, whether in terms of existing markets or the acquisition or development of new markets; and how to legitimize the capitalist way of organizing production, including the State's own part of that broad enterprise. The public-education system, being provided by the State, and therefore a *de facto* arm of state policy, must face these several problems simultaneously. The solutions which are eventually reached may well be in tension both within themselves and between each other. Support for the process of capital accumulation suggests an emphasis on the education of an élite through a curriculum designed to identify that élite. The provision of a context to support and expand capitalism suggests an emphasis on either equality of access to educational opportunity or on equality of educational outcomes. Legitimizing capitalism can be supported by the use of the profits of capitalism to provide an educational system to facilitate the personal development of individuals as well as to produce appropriately prepared workers.

The tensions between these prescriptions for education are self-evident. In times of stability for capitalism within a state, the distribution of power between the legislature, the educational bureaucracy of the State, individual schools, and the teachers within them, achieve an equilibrium. However, in times of crisis for capitalism, which is manifest in the diverting of money by the State from the provision of an educational system, this equilibrium is profoundly disturbed. Dale (1989) cited Habermas (1976) to suggest that the State will, in these circumstances, seek both to withdraw from its extensive commitment to education and to change the emphasis from the support of individual personal development to education which will support national economic survival. In a capitalist crisis, as experienced in the 1980s and 1990s (and beyond?), the legislature of the State will seek to bring about rapid change in the educational system through laws that increase state power. That power will be used to legislate for the reduction and changed emphasis of educational provision; to have the state bureaucracy set out administrative requirements which are both more detailed and more uniformly applied; and to require schools and teachers to adhere closely to them.

In these circumstances of change, interest groups contend with each other to influence the philosophy and detail of legislation about education and its implementation. There are, according to Ball (1990), currently three broad, loosely defined, and overlapping groups contending for influence in educational policy making. Although using the example of the United Kingdom, which can be viewed as a typical capitalist State in crisis, Ball's (1990) analysis seems to apply equally well to New Zealand (Lauder, 1990) and to Australia (Seddon, 1991). The 'cultural restorationists' advocate policies which would 'return' education to its traditional role: the transmission of an idealized unitary culture, which is seen to have been a valuable preparation for a prosperous national economic life in the past and which is projected as being equally important in the future. This culture is built around external sources of discipline (organized religion, the head of State), basic skills (reading, writing, arithmetic), a knowledge of established 'facts' (of national history and economic geography), and 'high' culture (traditional literary texts). Another group are the 'industrial trainers', who seek to use education directly as preparation for an adult life of work within the established framework of industrial production. Their emphasis is on good time-keeping, a willingness to accept Fordist discipline, and the accurate performance of repetitive tasks in combination with other workers. The third group, the 'new progressives', see education as a way to prepare the young for a life of continual adaptation to changing employment and cultural norms; for example, adapting to the changes that occur as post-modernity becomes a major social context. In the current struggle for the power to set down, and to restate, policy for the educational systems in the United Kingdom, the cultural restorationists are currently in the ascendancy and the industrial trainers have some influence, while the new progressives have been marginalized to a certain degree. [Apple (1993, p. 15) has analysed, with reference to the United States, the reasons for this power shift.] The balance of influence among the three is, and seems likely to remain, fluid for many years.

Educationalists have, over the last decade or so, been able to make only a diminished contribution to policy formation in many countries. Their influence remains strong in the classroom, although that too is being eroded by accountability measures manifested in staff appraisal and national-qualifications policies. The extent of their decline in influence in policy formation varies widely, being arguably at its greatest in the United Kingdom and occurring to a lesser extent in New Zealand, but is evident in these and other countries with the restructuring of the education system in the late 1980s and early 1990s. The change was often rapid (in New Zealand it was formulated and implemented over fourteen months during 1988–9) and reflected what Boston (1991, p. 2) described as 'an analytic framework grounded in public choice theory, managerialism, and the new economics of organizations, most notably agency theory and transaction cost analysis.' This change in the education system has been part of the restructuring of the economy and the Government public state sector, following the worldwide trends in monetarism, and in response to previous social democratic governments. There was:

> a general view that state intervention to promote egalitarian social goals has caused the growing economic problems of western democracies. State intervention stifles individual initiative and invades individual rights. (Mitchell, McGee, Moltzen and Oliver (1993, p. 22)

With regard to education, claims were made that it was not fostering equity, in terms of participation and achievements, and was marked by middle-class capture; that education was characterized by falling standards, and 'inputs' were not producing 'outputs'; that it was overly bureaucratic, inefficient, and not responsive to 'users' and 'consumers' of education, locally and nationally; that it was not giving choice to parents on schooling; and that parents were excluded from decision making in education. Education was also seen as failing to provide students with skills for future employment and failing to provide the changing economy with a highly skilled workforce to compete and survive economically.

It was resolved that the way forward was restructuring education so that it addressed notions of the free market, in which education is seen as an economic commodity (Bates, 1990; Grace 1990), human nature as humans principally self-interested, and success as depending upon individual effort (Lauder, 1990). Proponents of the free-market approach to the organization of economic life argue that it has a number of advantages over the Keynesian model (Ball, 1990, p. 39). First, they believe that, by encouraging entrepreneurship, it is more effective in initiating and/or coping with rapid technological change. Encouraging individual initiative means that inequalities between individuals are both anticipated and thought desirable. The approach contains no commitments to social justice, which is seen as an advantage because such commitments would imply social change brought about by overtly political means, and are claimed to distort the operation of the economic market. The status quo with respect to wealth distribution and power is being protected. In an allied argument, the free-market approach is advocated because it is seen as containing no overt sexist or racist assumptions. The approach will also, it is claimed, produce maximum freedom of individual choice and action as external constraints are reduced to a minimum. It is said to offer greater efficiency and choice for the individual consumer as a result of competition within a market which encompasses all services, including those traditionally provided by the State. The influence of the State in all aspects of economic activity is reduced to a regulatory minimum. All in all, the free market is thought likely to produce the best possible circumstances for rapid and sustained economic growth, and is seen as intelligent, responsible and having outcomes that provide the best for people.

In general, advocates of free-market policies are said to be from the 'New Right', who feel the policies cover all aspects of any capitalist economy. Education, having a large financial turnover, is a major sector in any economy. From the New Right perspective, education is seen as a commodity. Under the dominant influence of the cultural restorationist and industrial-training groups, free-market principles now provide the major political context within which education is viewed by governments worldwide. In education (as in other sectors of the State), the implementation of New Right policies, based on free-market notions, has resulted in advisory, regulatory and delivery functions being separated and undertaken by different agencies to prevent bureaucratic capture; state educational monopolies being reduced to a minimum, with decreased budgets; services provided by the State being privatized or contracted out to private-sector providers; management skills, rather than professional and technical skills, being emphasized (and valued); management being devolved; and the quest for greater efficiency, with outputs and outcomes specified and audited (Mitchell, McGee, Moltzen and Oliver, 1993).

Another characteristic of New Right policies is what Ball (1990) so elegantly calls 'the discourse of derision'. Discourse is a manifestation of the relationship between power and knowledge (Ball, 1990). What has emerged in recent times in the discourse surrounding educational policy-making has been what might be called a 'discourse of belief': the strong, even vehement, and well-marshalled arguments in favour of a set of variously expressed educational ideals based on free-market notions, put forward as if no others could honestly exist. There are three central ideals which their proponents assert should govern policy formation. First, education should be structured in a way that will allow maximum parental influence over the quality, if not the nature, of the education schools provide. Secondly, education should be provided within a diverse range of institutions, to which admission by selection, albeit on a variety of grounds including, to some extent, parental preference. Thirdly, the provision of education should be accountable to parents, through the appraisal of teachers and through the regular testing and publication of students' achievement.

Although this set of views has been influential in many countries since the emergence of formal educational systems for all citizens, it has grown to particular prominence over the last decade. The New Right groups, including those actually within government, have come to believe that the slowing growth, and even regression, of many economies is due to the poor preparation of the young for work, to which, it is said, schools have failed to pay insufficient explicit attention. In an associated argument, the apparent fragmentation of social values in many nation states is asserted to be giving rise to increased juvenile crime rates. Again, the cause of this fragmentation is said to be schools' lack of sufficient attention to social values. Lastly, and most significantly, it is asserted that educationalists, in aggregate, are responsible for these problems and are unresponsive to the concerns of government, parents, and industry. Ball (1990) has marshalled examples of these claims in connection with the United Kingdom, whilst Sikula (1990), Dawkins (1988), and Middleton, Codd and Jones (1990) have conducted comparable exercises for the United States, Australia, and New Zealand respectively.

A 'discourse of disbelief' is directed by the dominant group against those who are assumed, often on little, if any, evidence, to hold any part of an hypothesized 'opposite' view. This 'opposite' view would have formal education structured in a way that would allow for the maximum influence of professional educators (for example, teachers, teacher trainers, advisers, and educational researchers) over the education schools provided. This provision would be made within institutions which are substantially of one type; that is, the comprehensive school to which all the children in an area are admitted. This education system would largely be accountable to professional educators through the continuous assessment of student progress conducted solely or substantially by the professional educators themselves.

The public 'discourse of derision', conducted by the two dominant groups (the cultural restorationists and the industrial trainers) essentially against the third group (new progressives), has three facets. The first facet is the use of these opposing views (on who should determine educational policy, the provision of schooling, and accountability) as a basis for public discourse without making recourse to available research on the evidence for, and functional and dysfunctional consequences of, the policies being debated. The second facet is the often successful attempt to deny a voice in policy formation to any individual or group judged, on whatever grounds, to be likely to hold the disfavoured view. Comments such as 'oh, yes, you would say that, for you have a vested interest in the old system' are examples of this facet of the public discourse of derision. The epistemological commitment implied in such statements, is to a belief which is not open to counter-argument and which allows for the worth of a non-believer either as an individual or a member of a group, to be denied. The third facet of the public discourse of derision is the projection onto the disfavoured group of the causes of apparent policy failure, because, at an earlier time, educationalists were said to have opposed it. Thus Lawlor (1994), in talking about the use of the United Kingdom National Curriculum as a way of undermining the influence of educationalists, writes:

> . . . the very consensus it was designed to challenge has shaped and been absorbed into it, so it has become acceptable to education's moral majority. Instead of the minimum curriculum originally envisaged, which would ensure basic standards in the most important subjects, there sprouted an ever-ramifying 'entitlement curriculum', designed to lay down what every child should learn, and how he or she should learn it. (Lawlor, 1994)

The discourse of derision is now, through a variety of tactics, used in attempts to influence educational policy throughout the world. One tactic is to compare indexes of educational achievement in the home country unfavourably with those in another, more economically successful, country. Berliner (1992) suggests that the unfavourable perspective is often attained by overlooking the social price attending that apparent success; for example, the distortion to adolescence caused by excessive study and the incidence of corruption concerning assessment grades, in Japan.

Another tactic is to misuse existing statistics, to extrapolate unjustifiably beyond existing data, while again being ignorant of, or overlooking, relevant social factors. For example, Berliner (1992) has demonstrated that it is entirely justified to make a range of assertions for the United States which are contrary to New Right statements. Thus, there is strong evidence to suggest that today's young people in the United States are cleverer than their predecessors, both in terms of their rate and breadth of learning and in terms of their overall achievement. Whilst raw average Scholastic Aptitude Test scores have declined by about 3 per cent since 1965, there has also been a rapid increase in participation in education by those from rural areas and the ethnic minorities — groups which historically returned lower scores than urban groups in the ethnic majority. Overall, the performance of the United States students in standardized attainment tests is probably not declining. In general, the schools of the USA are not expensive, when viewed against a background of prevailing social conditions, and support high levels of achievement by many students.

It would seem from Berliner's (1992) analysis that some of the criticisms of today's educational systems arise from a series of identifiable errors in the evidence on which the criticisms are based. One such error is the general failure of those systems to collect a database that is sufficiently broad, standardized and long-term, to show real trends. For the research that has been done, analysis has not allowed for changed social circumstances within an education system; for example, changing rates and compositions of participation, which stem from changes in such social circumstances as housing, family composition and health. There have also been substantial technical changes in achievement testing which have not been identified and allowed for in the production of apparently comparable statistics. Worst of all, by no means all testing has been conducted in a technically competent manner.

The New Right's use of research in these ways can be identified in respect of particular government documents. Hammersley and Scarth (1993), in reviewing a major British report on primary schooling, conclude that the authors selectively interpreted evidence, engaged in over-interpretation of evidence to support an apparently pre-formed conclusion — that is, they drew false links between effects and causes — and progressed unjustifiably from conclusions to remedies. When properly conducted, research can show the inadequacies of governmental statements. Thus Raban, Clark and McIntyre (1993) have shown that an oft-repeated claim, that British primary teachers are not using the phonics approach to teach reading and have abandoned the use of reading schemes, is quite untrue.

The New Right's growth in influence over educational policy formation has very significant implications for teacher development. First, the lines of communication from teachers to policy makers have been severely weakened in the attempt to prevent bureaucratic capture. Secondly, governments are much less willing to support teacher-development activities that encourage the skills of critical inquiry, which would themselves be applied to existing and anticipated policies. Thirdly, and allied to the second, is the emphasis given to teacher development focused on compliance with regulations and with the implementation of official policy in the classroom. For example, in New Zealand, the current teacher development in science education which is directly government funded, is on the implementation of new curricula and the new New Zealand Qualifications Framework. The funding given to schools for professional development (and which is not captured to implement new policy) is often spent on topics in science education, such as getting students thinking, accelerated learning and mixed ability classes. Direct government teacher development activities have not focused on how to reply to the increasingly prevalent use of the discourse of derision, how to be included in education policy-making or how to undertake action-research and critical inquiry. Teacher development programmes have largely been seen as moulding the teacher as a technician to implement government policies rather than as empowering teachers as professionals and contributors to the reconstruction of what it means to be a teacher of science and critical inquirers. Whilst the educators involved in running the programmes have done the most they can to base the programmes on educational principles, our criticism remains.

The Cultural Landscape of Teaching and Learning

The tensions within and between the different social contexts are played out within the different aspects of schooling. These different aspects may be referred to collectively as the cultural landscape of teaching and learning. Teachers working in schools necessarily work amidst these tensions, which in turn, influence teachers' learning in teacher development situations. In this section, the tensions in each of the key aspects of schooling are considered.

The Structure of the State Educational System

In New Zealand and the United Kingdom, state schools — that is, those for the great majority of the population — are now expected to act as isolated units. The notion of a network of educational provision, in which individual schools act to some extent in concert and which is under the guidance of a locally accountable coordinating authority, has been abandoned. Rather, schools are now expected to act separately, in competition with each other for students. The dominant relationship is to be with the central Government, which allocates resources, largely on the basis of the number of students of a given age that a school has. For schools, the notion of networking between agencies and roles is difficult. Informed observers (for example, Smythe, 1992; Pryke, 1994) are noting a common pattern of emerging problems: the central Government agencies are unable to deal efficiently with the myriad of individual institutions; the quality of individuals who have become trustees or governors varies greatly; schools vary in their capacity to make up shortfalls in central funding; and attention is drawn away from education to matters of finance.

The Management of Schools

The focus of school management is moving from professional matters to administrative ones. It is also becoming an increasingly specialized activity. This is a consequence of, simultaneously, a greater allocation of legally binding tasks to schools and an ever more frugal allocation of finance with which to carry out those tasks. Making the money go round is a concern for each individual school, with serious consequences for failure. There is a risk that school management, in its growing concern with finance, is becoming separated, in terms of both career track and priorities, from the traditionally dominant concerns of schools — that is, with the welfare and progress, in the broadest sense, of students. Mitchell, McGee, Moltzen and Oliver (1993), in a research report on the effects of restructuring on schools in New Zealand, indicate that increased workloads for teachers, principals and trustees have occurred. For principals, these workloads were often seen to be excessive and were largely the result of increased management responsibilities at the expense of professional leadership.

The Expectations of Students

Students have, of course, always kept a close eye on the relationship between how much time and energy they expend in formal school learning and the reward for that effort in terms of public recognition through examination results and/or personal satisfaction. A simple response by students to the New Right curriculum prescriptions that exist in the United Kingdom, for example, might be to memorize the knowledge required to pass an examination. On the other hand, post-industrial and post-modern influences in students' lives are towards being knowledge creators, with highly developed skills of problem-solving, innovation and entrepreneurship, communication, negotiation, information location and usage, and learning-to-learn. Few of these are assessed in examinations and, therefore, few are given formal status in the education system.

The Nature of the Curriculum

A revision of the school curriculum has been a feature of recently restructured education systems. In the United Kingdom, a national curriculum has been developed for the first time. In New Zealand, the existing syllabuses have been revised to form a curriculum framework and curriculum statements for each 'subject' or learning area, over the range of schooling (ages 5–17 years).

A major issue in the curriculum developments has been what view of knowledge should inform education. One tension is between the views of the cultural restorationists, who favour the academic curriculum (knowing what, or the ability to reproduce knowledge), and the industrial trainers, who favour the 'pre-vocational' curriculum (knowing how, or the ability to use knowledge in unfamiliar contexts) (Ball, 1990). In the United Kingdom, 'knowing what' (the ability to reproduce knowledge) seems to have triumphed over 'knowing how', leaving creativity (the ability to invent knowledge) by the wayside. A second tension surrounds whether pre-vocational education is of value for all students and whether it can co-exist with academic education, as is argued in New South Wales:

> The commonsense recognition that schooling must provide our young
> people with knowledge, skills, and attitudes that are relevant to the world

of work ... in no way conflicts with the Government's commitment to a broad general education for personal growth and community responsibility. (Metherell, 1989, p. 10)

This view is also currently being adopted in New Zealand, with the Government's imposition of the vocational New Zealand Qualifications Framework into the years of general schooling for 15- to 17-year-olds. In addition, vocationalism is evident in the national curriculum. On the other hand (in 1994 at least), the United Kingdom seems to be moving towards a curriculum with a fairly clearly defined branching into the academic and the pre-vocational at age 14 (Dearing, 1994). It does seem highly likely that the rigid specification of content in the United Kingdom's academic curriculum will be superseded or joined by an equally rigidly defined pre-vocational curriculum. A third tension regarding views of knowledge concerns ontological commitments. In science education, this has been evident in the debates as to whether scientists and learners of science can come to know the world as it truly is or whether knowledge is a construction that models reality.

Another tension in the curriculum has been created with the requirement set by governments that the curriculum be specified in terms of levels of achievement over the range years of schooling. These levels are used for measuring learning outcomes and are based on a belief in the need for accountability and on behaviourist views of learning. The notion of levels is at odds with constructivist views of learning. The tension that this creates is evident in the English language version of the New Zealand science curriculum (Ministry of Education, 1993), in which the knowledge to be learnt is categorized into eight levels, while the learning outcomes relating to skills are categorized into four only. Separating the scientific knowledge to be learnt from the skills of scientific investigation to be learnt, conflicts with a view of science as an activity for knowledge creation. Separating knowledge to be learnt from the cognitive skills of constructing knowledge by learners is also problematic.

Curriculum Development

Until recently, the curricula in many countries underwent slow, even imperceptible, change as a result of the initiatives of the many parties to educational provision. Some initiatives came from individual teachers, some from the staff of a school working in concert, some through the corporate activities of professional associations, some from public examination bodies, and some from government-funded national curriculum development initiatives, with considerable overlap between the categories. Those new ideas which were successful in a range of classrooms were disseminated through the informal networks which linked educationalists. In New Zealand, there has been a national curriculum in science for many years and new ideas became part of the national curriculum in the next review and revision. Whether informally or formally, the new ideas gradually gained acceptance among teachers, although commonly that acceptance was far from universal, and the adoption of the ideas was far from uniform. Implementation of new ideas and the development of the next curriculum statement often occurred concurrently. New content gradually evolved into a form in which it could be taught by unsupported, individual teachers, new teaching methods were devised, new approaches to assessment were incorporated. The emphasis was on curriculum evolution: the individual teacher had the last word on what happened in the classroom. National curricula, where they existed, legitimized broadly accepted new content, teaching technique, and assessment methods.

The new tighter curriculum statements — which are subject to arbitrary, or at least sudden, change at the behest of central government — are leading to a new dynamic of change, as illustrated in the contexts of New Zealand and the United Kingdom. New Zealand has had a national science curriculum for over 45 years, but since 1989 the process of developing the national curriculum in science and other subject areas has changed. First, the curriculum is no longer developed over many years by central government staff members in consultation with teachers. Instead, the development is contracted out to a non-ministerial person, for example, a teacher educator in a college of education. Secondly, the contract signed by both the Government and the developer has rigid specifications as to the format and scope of the curriculum. These parameters are not open to negotiation by the developers and writers. Thirdly, the contracted curriculum developer is not involved in the initial policy development with respect to science education but is seen as implementing the policy decision of writing a new curriculum within the parameters set. Hence, dialogue between the different stakeholders in the science curriculum at the time of developing new policy is severely limited. The contracted curriculum developer may involve teachers (primary, secondary and tertiary) as writers or as consultants, but the debates about the aims of science education and the ontological and epistemological beliefs about teaching and learning are largely excluded from the formal curriculum development process. The debates are more visible in the consultation over draft curricula. An implementation process has been funded by the Government to take place after the development is done, not concurrently as previously (Bell, 1990).

In the United Kingdom, the draft curriculum statements in science have been written by groups comprised of teachers, academic scientists and bureaucrats, with the voices of the bureaucrats being most dominant. The publication of draft curricula has usually been followed by a very short period of 'consultation' with teachers. The post-consultation documents, usually very close in content and structure to their predecessors, often then have to be implemented at very short notice, a process which is usually accompanied by frantic efforts to achieve implementation within individual schools. As there is a lack of even short-term additional funding, although compliance must be demonstrated, the emphasis is inevitably on making the minimum changes to existing practice (Bowe, Ball, and Gold, 1992). The locus of control for initiating change has moved outside the classroom and the school. Change in actual curriculum and classroom practice is episodic; is relatively unconsidered or considered by groups containing a substantial number of individuals who have agendas other than the welfare of schools, teachers, and students;

takes different forms in different schools; and is probably more apparent than real. The historic complaint of 'innovation without change' has been superseded by 'change without innovation'. Teacher development tends, under these circumstances, to be simplistic in the extreme, with a focus on becoming familiar with the new requirements in detail and turning them into schemes of work, making as few changes to existing practice as possible. Critical review of the new prescription is discounted.

The tension between teacher development for imposed, rapid change, on the one hand, and teacher development for the ongoing, sustained development of curricula and teacher for the growth of science education, on the other hand, is obvious for those involved. The notion of teacher development for the critical, inquiring teachers existing within a New Right policy and funding context is difficult, to put it mildly. The previous traditions of teacher-collective curriculum development, as the basis for teacher development activities are in abeyance. The model being proposed in this book would, in contrast to present practice, place greater, rather than lesser emphasis on curriculum development as teacher development.

The Nature of Teaching

The way that teaching takes place in a given classroom — the mix of particular techniques used and the role of the teacher and students in an activity — is governed by the teacher's beliefs about the nature of knowledge and the nature of learning. Two extreme positions, at either end of a continuum, can be characterized as follows. The first position is governed by a set of beliefs that knowledge is real and exists independently of people; that students are passive potential recipients of that knowledge; and that the teacher is an expert whose task is to present knowledge directly, in a logical sequence, to the students. The second position is governed by the contrasting set of beliefs that particular knowledge is the construction of people; that students learn by reconstructing their own ideas in the light of their experiences and socially agreed knowledge; and that the teacher, whilst having a thorough grasp of the particular knowledge, has the task of facilitating the reconstruction, extension or replacement of students' existing knowledge, using whatever teaching techniques seem appropriate.

It is probably broadly true to say that the first of these two sets of beliefs has underpinned the teaching in most classrooms since systematic formal education was established for all young citizens in the mid-1800s or so. However, the second of these two sets, whilst it has always been present in the practice of some actual classrooms and in many theoretical views of classrooms, has gradually gained credibility with teachers over approximately the last fifteen years. If they were given freedom to choose how they teach, and relief from the burden of an overloaded curriculum content, a significant minority of teachers would be heavily influenced in their decisions by the second set of beliefs, the constructivist perspective.

However, the New Right-inspired educational policies are in tension with those of many educationalists with regard to views of knowledge and learning, as is evident in government documents. For example, in the United Kingdom, the new curricula are couched in terms of content to be learned and the amount of content is high. Teachers are required to 'deliver' that content, a term which implies a process of passing over something tangible. This trend is against the professional judgment of teachers, fails to recognize the active agency of students in their own learning, and is in favour of a commodity-production view of knowledge. Assessment policies of New Right governments — for example, the policies of the New Zealand Qualifications Authority — are often in tension with constructivist views of learning and may act as a barrier to teachers developing their teaching in accordance with their professional judgment.

The Nature and Management of Student Assessment

The three interlocking issues in respect of assessment are always why it is being conducted, by whom, and how. Teachers would agree that all students need a publicly validated statement of their achievements when they leave compulsory schooling. Most would feel that assessment, when conducted on a regular basis during the period of schooling, should directly produce information that can be used to improve an individual's achievement. The corollary to this is that such assessment is best carried out by the teacher within the framework of normal teaching and includes the use of the techniques of observation and informal interview, spread over a period of time such that a student can realistically demonstrate learning achievements.

However, the recent requiements set by New Right governments, that schools should be accountable for learning outcomes have created tensions with the views of many teachers. For example, in the United Kingdom, the new curriculum developments are driven by a belief that schools are not causing students to learn enough — by which is meant that students are not learning a large enough quantity of the 'facts' valued by the curriculum policy makers. The distinction between formative and summative assessment is confused. The New Right remedy in Britain (and in modified forms in other countries) has been the introduction of large-scale, nationwide tests for students, to be carried out largely in a paper-and-pencil format at regular intervals, at ages 7, 11, 14, 16 (Dearing, 1994). The information to be yielded by these tests seems incapable of direct use for improving students' learning. Its main purpose seems to be as publishable data to be presented to parents as indicating the worth of, and effort made by, individual schools in respect of the inculcation of factual information. The fact that the improvement in any student's learning is substantially governed by the base line of prior achievement and by the student's home circumstances is overlooked in this approach. In New Zealand, the audit and accountability activities of the Education Review Office (ERO), mean that schools must collect assessment data to indicate learning outcomes for the regular reviews. The collection of data for the review and audit places excessive demands on teachers and administrators in schools, and there is a danger that it will be at odds with assessment required for the learning prescribed in the curriculum, external examinations, and the Unit Standards for the New Zealand Qualifications Framework.

The introduction of pre-vocational, or even vocational, elements into the curriculum for the compulsory school years seems likely to make the management of assessment still more problematic for teachers. For example, in New Zealand, the vocationally based New Zealand Qualifications Framework extends down into the senior secondary school and creates a tension with the learning outcomes prescribed by the science curriculum. At first glance, the New Zealand Qualifications Framework appears to resolve the problem of two separate sets of assessment for academic and vocational requirements:

> All national qualifications are to be built of the same basic blocks-unit standards — each carrying a number of credits assigned to one of eight levels . . . Unit standards will be introduced in schools at age 15 and will be the main school-based qualifications . . . It is intended that all existing national qualifications, including trade certificates and degrees, will be converted to the unit standard system and placed within the framework. (Irwin, 1994)

But the academic and vocational curricula are based on differing views of knowledge and learning, such that combining them is highly problematic for teachers. The systems approach to the framework results in the people being assessed and moulded to fit the system, rather than the reverse.

Staff Appraisal and School Inspection

The appraisal of schoolteachers by school principals and inspectors, like that of students by the teachers themselves, has always occurred. In most cases this has been informal, without ongoing, direct observation of the teaching conducted in classrooms. It has been dependent, perhaps unduly, on the casual reactions of other staff, observation at semi-public events, for example, during staff meetings, short visits by inspectors to classrooms, and the evaluation of the public-examination results of students (where applicable) against unstated norms already established in the school.

The recent introduction of techniques into education, many derived from industry, has included the establishment of formal appraisal. In many countries, the system is still evolving, with concerns being expressed by trade unions as to the degree of linkage between performance, assessed by perhaps artificial or irrelevant criteria and pay. However, the system generally includes the production of formal statements of personal professional goals mainly by the teacher; the observation of classes by more senior staff; and a formal interview. In a proportion of cases, the outcomes of appraisal are linked to the provision of in-service education and training opportunities. Hickcox and Musella (1992) have produced a summary of ideas which could make appraisal a more positive experience for the appraised. In their view, there should be a separation of supervision intended to direct teachers' improvement from that for judgment of performance; relevant skill training for those making judgments; an expansion of concerns in appraisal beyond those focused on the classroom to include career development; a shift towards procedures which reduce the use of a linear sequence of events in appraisal; and increased procedures which emphasize more negotiation between appraiser and appraisee in the formation of judgments.

Whilst in-school procedures for appraising teachers are, in many cases, moving in the direction of the proposals summarized by Hickcox and Musella (1992), they are being off-set by the introduction of external procedures set up to monitor nation- or province-wide standards of the schools. The approaches used vary. In British Columbia (Canada), Ministry of Education staff regularly monitor the work (including Grade 12 exam results), and public reception, of individual schools, with formal inspections being carried out every six years, and augmented by province-wide assessment of reading and writing in Grades 4, 7, and 10 (Charbonneau, 1993). In the United Kingdom, the Office for Standards in Education (Ofsted) carries out highly structured snapshot evaluations of the work of individual schools at four-yearly intervals. However conducted, these evaluations must have a major impact on the patterns of work of, and priorities assigned by individual teachers. It is not clear whether teachers actually participate in any teacher development designed to support them in respect of their personal appraisals. In many schools, great collective effort is made to prepare teachers to participate in the whole-school, externally conducted appraisals.

Teacher Development

In recent restructuring by the New Zealand Government, responsibility for teacher development was devolved from the centre to schools. The State is no longer the provider of teacher in-service but is still the funder. The funding is distributed directly to schools and to some providers for the implementation of new policy initiatives through contracts for services. Mitchell, McGee, Moltzen and Oliver (1993) report that since the restructuring, there is a perception that more in-service work is occurring, with teachers undertaking a wide and intense range of staff-development activities, sometimes to the point of overloading themselves. The in-service work is more school-based. However, teachers report that there is not enough time for in-service work and the current level of in-service work is not enough to implement the rapid and extensive changes being sought. The demands for in-service work to implement new government policy, leave little money, time and energy for teachers to address their own professional concerns.

Educational Research

Another tension in schools is whether and how to address the nature and outcomes of educational research. Educational research has always had a chequered history, largely because education has not yet unequivocally emerged as a distinct and separate subject for academic study. Rather than centring on education *per se*, discussion has been about the history of education, educational psychology, the sociology of education, the philosophy of education. A noticeable omission highlighted by recent developments has been substantive attention to the economics of education. This is probably a chicken-and-egg situation; because there has been no distinctive subject of education, researchers have come from established traditions. Historians have, naturally enough, wanted to focus on the history of education, scientists have wanted to focus on the provision and outcomes of science education, and so on. Perhaps most significantly, these researchers have set the research agenda in terms of the kinds of problems that would be of interest in their parent disciplines, rather than in terms of problems which lie at the heart of everyday classroom practice and which would be of interest to teachers. As a consequence, the outcomes of a substantial portion of the research, on which scarce resources have been used, have been of little significance to the classroom teacher. The chalkboard evaluation of educational research, in general, has been negative; it has been largely ignored.

The situation of research in science education, which lies at the interface of the politically indistinct area of research in education and the politically distinct area of research in science, is somewhat clearer and more positive. Nevertheless, a range of criticisms of the focus of science education research has been put forward by Hurd (1991) and Rutherford (1993). Such criticisms can be turned into the form of challenges. If research into science education is to have more impact on practice — that is, if teachers are to pay more attention to it — it must directly address perceived and anticipated problems of practice. It must address a wider range of problems than is currently the case. It must relax the customary tight methodological constraints on studies so that they correspond to the full parameters of the context within which a problem is set. Studies of similar problems in different contexts must be brought together into a cohesive whole, such that the public debate of issues is facilitated. Studies must not be done by science educators in isolation, but by drawing on expertise in the social, behavioural and policy sciences. Lastly, a continuing review of the philosophy and methodology of much science education research is called for. As Hurd (1991) puts it:

> The physical science model, so widely used in educational research, with its emphasis on the experimental control of variables and statistical analysis, has limited value for investigating issues raised by the reform movement. The whole idea of trying to pinpoint answers to questions that are raised in advance of a study produces results of little consequence. Better would be a model derived from ecology that recognises complexities and assumes broad patterns of interactive behaviour such as would be characteristic of a teacher and students in learning situations. (Hurd, 1991, p. 727)

The qualitative–quantitative debate has been going on for more than twenty years. Many journals report studies that use both paradigms or transcend them.

In Shavelson's (1988) view, it is a fallacy, for educational research in general, to assume that the direct applicability of research to practice can be achieved. For direct application to be possible:

> Research would have to be relevant to a particular issue and be available before a decision needed to be made; research would address the issue within the parameters of feasible action and provide clear, simple, and unambiguous results; research would be known and understood by the policy-maker or practitioner and not cross entrenched interests; recommendations from research would be implemented within existing resources; and research findings would lead to choices different from those that decision makers would otherwise have made. (Shavelson, 1988, p. 5)

Frequently, the scope of science education research is unlikely to match exactly the particular problems of practice, and research does not produce timeless truths because the context of practice is continually changing under the influence of continual governmental changes in education, so there is a 'sell by' date for all research. For teachers, the implications of research may seem outside of their scope of agency or validity.

Educational research has always received low levels of funding in most countries, perhaps because the complexity of the subject under study has rarely produced knowledge which can be used, either directly or by metaphorical transfer, to predict future events successfully. However, matters have recently taken a decided turn for the worse. The newly introduced curricula do suggest agendas for relevant, practice-oriented research (McNamara, 1990). However, governments in the United Kingdom and elsewhere, adhering to a discourse of belief and evidently wishing to deny substantiated grounds for opposition to their policies, have both sharply reduced even the already deficient funding and sought to control the publication of any results of inquiry which might prejudice support for their policies. Teacher development focused on an appreciation of existing research and on the acquisition of the skills needed to conduct research is rarely encountered outside university courses.

Summary

The differing social contexts for education in which teachers work are creating tensions in schooling and education in New Zealand and the United Kingdom. These tensions are evident in the different cultural aspects of schooling, the work of teachers and teacher development. These tensions create challenges for teacher development and for the model presented in this book. This and other challenges are addressed in the final chapter.

9 Challenges

Summary of the Model

In this book, we have presented and argued for a model of teacher development that has been successful for teachers wanting to use new teaching activities in the classroom; to think about teaching, learning and other aspects of science education in new ways; and to improve the learning of science by their students. The main aspects of the model are now summarized.

Social, Personal and Professional Development

In the model, teacher development is seen as social, personal and professional development. Social development as part of teacher development involves the renegotiation and reconstruction of the rules and norms of what it means to be a teacher (of science, for example). Teachers need to be the central contributors to this. It also involves the development of ways of working with others that enable the kinds of social interaction necessary for renegotiating and reconstructing of what it means to be a teacher of science.

Personal development as part of teacher development involves each individual teacher constructing, evaluating and accepting or rejecting for herself or himself the new socially constructed knowledge about what it means to be a teacher (of science, for example), and managing the feelings associated with changing their activities and beliefs about science education, particularly when they go 'against the grain' (Cochran-Smith, 1991) of the current or proposed socially constructed and accepted knowledge.

Professional development as a part of teacher development involves not only the use of new teaching activities in the classroom but also the development of the beliefs and conceptions underlying the actions. The clarification of core values and commitments is important for the development of moral frameworks in education (Shotter, 1984; Hargreaves, 1994). It also involves learning science as well as science education.

The social-personal-professional model promotes development in all three areas. To focus on one alone will not promote the desired learning and development. In the past, professional development was focused on to the exclusion of the other two aspects. In recent times, personal development — self-development and self-understanding — has been emphasized. But as Hargreaves (1994, pp. 71–4) comments, an over-emphasis on the personal, with a lack of attention to social and political awareness, can be damaging. An over-emphasis on the personal, can lead to political naivety, excessive feelings of guilt at not being able to effect change, and a sense of hopelessness.

Learning

In the social-personal-professional model, teacher development is viewed as learning by teachers. Learning as teacher development is conceptualized in the model from a social constructivist perspective. Learning is seen as occurring within the social contexts of the classroom and the wider social, political, economic and historical contexts of our societies. Knowledge is seen as constructed and reconstructed by people, both personally and socially. Learning involves the interaction of personal and social constructions; change in one is mediated by the other. The socially constructed knowledge is the context, the outcome and an integral part of the learning. Learning is part of human development, which includes the development of self-identity (as a teacher of science). Learners have partial agency to change both the socially constructed knowledge and their own construction of what it means to be a teacher of science. Social interaction is part of learning. Learners are seen as able to reconstruct their knowledge through reflection and learning is seen as involving metacognition — that is, teachers as learners knowing about and monitoring their own learning and thinking. It involves their knowing about and monitoring the change process and reconceptualizing their conceptions of teacher development.

Empowerment

The teacher-development process in the social-personal-professional model is viewed as one of empowerment for ongoing development, rather than one of continued dependency on a facilitator's or others' suggestions for change. Teacher development is promoted when teachers are able to: contribute to the teacher development process and programme; feel that their contributions are valued, for example, that their opinions, ideas, teaching activities, suggestions in decision-making, and initiatives are worthwhile; experience competency in teaching; have a sense of ownership towards and control over the nature of their own development; address their concerns and needs; volunteer for the programme or an aspect of the programme; negotiate the content and form of the programme; determine the pace and nature of the changes; reconceptualize their view of teacher development; view themselves as learners; become innovative and creative, rather than only implement given strategies; and feel that the changes are possible and beneficial in the current school and political situation.

Empowerment also includes the teachers being supported to critically inquire into the ideologies, values and theoretical commitments of innovations and imposed change. In doing so, they may be better able to unravel the confusion created by competing ideologies. It includes teachers taking action to change their world based on their beliefs (O'Loughlin, 1992b). Empowerment is not achieved through contrived collegiality, forced reflection or ownership through compliance with policy (Hargreaves, 1994, p. 69).

What it Means to be a Teacher of Science

Teacher development involves the renegotiation and the reconstruction of what it means to be a teacher of science. As teachers bear the ultimate responsibility for teaching, their centrality in the social construction of knowledge about teaching must be recognized. Whilst others, for example, parents and scientists, may also contribute to this social construction of what it means to be a teacher of science, the centrality of the teachers in the process is being emphasised. Teacher development involves learning new ways to work and talk with other teachers (and other stakeholders in science education) to renegotiate and reconstruct what it means to be a teacher of science. Anecdoting is one such way for teachers to share with each other what they are doing in the classroom, to give support and feedback and to engage in reflection and critical inquiry. This interaction and reconstruction of what it means to be a teacher of science is important, not just in terms of individual teachers working in classrooms, but in terms of teachers' awareness and action with respect to the wider social and political contexts in which they work.

The Focus of Teacher Development

Teacher development involves addressing the concerns of teachers with respect to improving learning in the classroom, as well as the concerns of parents, employers and politicians. Most teachers seeking teacher development wish to be better teachers and to achieve 'better learning' for their students. Feedback is an integral part of changing and developing, and feedback to indicate that they are feeling better about themselves as teachers and that better learning conditions and outcomes are occurring, supports teachers during the process of change.

Teacher development often includes the implementation of new curricula, new research findings and the new teaching ideas of others. But it also includes addressing the concerns of teachers, who must deal with the tensions of competing ideologies in education today. In addressing the concerns of teachers, the reconstruction of what it means to be a teacher of science includes taking into account their voices. Currently, the concerns of teachers include continuity, progression, differentiation, the inclusive curriculum and subject knowledge.

Challenges of the Model

The social-personal-professional model of teacher development raises challenges for teachers, teacher educators, school managers and policy makers. In turn, the social contexts in which teacher development occurs raises challenges for the model. The challenges of the model are now outlined and discussed.

Social Development

A major challenge of the social-personal-professional model is for teachers, teacher educators, school managers and policy makers to promote the renegotiation and reconstruction of what it means to be a teacher of science as a key part of teacher development. Anecdoting was used by the teachers in the research project as a way to reconstruct within the group what it means to be a teacher of science; for example, with respect to listening to students, getting students thinking, re-thinking noisy classrooms, covering the curriculum and assessment procedures. But reconstruction of the socially constructed knowledge also includes teachers using the skills of renegotiating and reconstructing in other groups, for example, school-based groupings such as the science department or the meetings of the entire school staff; locally based groups such as the local science-teachers' association; national education groups, such as a national curriculum writing group; and groups of other stakeholders in science education, for example, the Royal Society, the Institute of Physics, and teacher unions. At present, few, if any, teacher-development programmes focus on helping teachers acquire and practise the skills the renegotiating and reconstructing of what it means to be a teacher of science. Most science educators pick up the skills by trial and error in meetings and conferences. Funding is required for the provision of this aspect of teacher development; funding is particularly important for teachers to have quality time with other teachers.

Being a contributor to the social construction and reconstruction of what it means to be a teacher of science, necessitates clarifying one's beliefs, values and knowledge. Forums for teachers to clarify, reflect on and develop these are important. A part of this is learning about the values, beliefs and ideologies of others — for example, the neo-conservative politicians — and evaluating them. It may also involve reflecting critically on aspects of post-modernity; for example, clarifying one's own position regarding bicultural and multi-cultural educational situations, because teachers are not only required to teach from a basis of their own values, beliefs and experiences but also to teach with cultural sensitivity and cultural safety towards students of other cultures. Critical inquiry will assist teachers in these tasks. Few, if any, teacher-development programmes being funded by government provide for this aspect of teacher development as they are being funded for the express purpose of implementing new policy.

The forums for teachers of science to communicate their ideas, wishes and concerns with themselves and others need to be re-established, given the minimal networking that is possible under the funding and conditions of working established by current New Right governments in New Zealand and the United Kingdom. For example, in New Zealand until the late 1980s, Department of Education national and local curriculum development and teacher development courses provided a forum for teachers to reconstruct what it means to be a teacher of science and for government policy makers to be present to hear and discuss this socially constructed knowledge. Since the restructuring of education administration, the contract method of curriculum development and teacher development limits rather than promotes discussion amongst teachers and other science educators during policy formation. The teacher unions were key contributors to these debates but their energy has had to be directed to industrial rather than professional matters in recent years. Other forums are evolving; for example, the meetings and conferences of the national and regional Association of Science Educators, the Royal Society and its subgroups of the professional associations of scientists, and the meetings of the Australasian Science Education Research Association are increasingly becoming places to hear what others are thinking and doing, and in addition to reconstruct the collective social knowledge about science education. The problem still remains of a shortage of teacher development programmes that provide the space for teachers to discuss their notions of, and concerns about, science education, and for communicating this to a government with little commitment to real consultation.

Forums for all the stakeholders in science education to negotiate and reconstruct aspects of science education during new policy development need to be maintained or re-established after the restructuring of education systems. Without them, newspapers and other media may become the only forum for teachers as well as the general public.

Science educators need to create their own spaces for their voices to be heard in terms of their professional knowledge, values and theoretical commitments. Relying on others' meetings as forums to be a contributor can marginalize science teachers' voices. Given that teachers are ultimately responsible for teaching, their voices need to be central (but not sole) to the social construction of what it means to be a teacher of science.

The challenge of the model is for these forums to be supported and funded, and for them to enable empowerment of teachers, rather than being used manipulatively, for example, by governments. The model also challenges educators to consider new ways of communicating with each other and with other stakeholders in the education enterprise. Communicating through anecdoting has been focused on in this book. There are other ways; for example, using e-mail or Internet facilities, classroom visits for feedback, new ideas or joint problem-solving, watching videos of classroom action, and case studies.

Professional Development

Another aspect of the social-personal-professional model is professional development — including the development of classroom teaching activities and the theoretical notions underlying them. Professional development is the main outcome sought by teachers, although social and personal development are crucial to achieving it. Most teachers come to teacher development courses seeking new teaching ideas and new ways to think about science education and to learn some new science. Without the professional-development aspects, teacher development programmes become hollow. The challenge of the model is to keep a focus on professional development, whilst ensuring that social and personal development occur as well.

Under the restructured education systems, as exist in New Zealand and the United Kingdom, the funding for continued innovations in science education is insecure. In the past, innovations in classroom teaching have arisen from sustained research programmes — for example, the Learning in Science Projects at the University of Waikato and the Children's Learning in Science Projects at Leeds University — and from ongoing curriculum development projects — for example, the Curriculum Review in Science in New Zealand in the 1980s (Bell, 1990) and the Secondary Science Curriculum Review in the United Kingdom (Michell, 1987). The changed nature of research funding and of the ways of changing official curriculum documents means that opportunities for teachers to innovate, and develop professionally whilst doing so, are much reduced. The challenge of the model to policy makers and funding agencies is to provide funding for sustained, ongoing innovation.

The other side of professional development is the reconceptualizing of the thinking that underlies practices in science education. Critical and reflective thinking on a range of theoretical perspectives and classroom activities is required for this. The challenge of the model is for opportunities to be provided for this reconceptualizing through a range of teacher development activities; for example, in university-based credit courses for higher qualifications, in professional association meetings, and curriculum writing tasks.

Personal Development

Providing the support for the personal development aspect of teacher development is a challenge given by the model. Few schools provide support for innovative teachers, in the way that they do for beginning teachers or teachers facing deregistration and dismissal. Such support requires funding of staff time to provide that support and allow the innovations to be tried out. Time and funding for support are needed if sustained teacher development is to occur. For example, in New Zealand, teacher development facilitators on some Ministry of Education contracts to implement the new curriculum are funded to make visits to schools in between the three meetings of the programme. These school visits are costly on facilitator time and travel but their value is acknowledged by teachers (Gilmore, 1994).

The stressful side of changing classroom activities while maintaining classroom control, maintaining learning outcomes, covering the curriculum and explaining the changes to students, parents and school management, is known to many in science education. The challenge of the model is for more provision in teacher development programmes (that is, more time and funding) for workshops on stress management, the change process and communication skills.

Curriculum Development as Teacher Development

The social-personal-professional model challenges the notion of curriculum development as a distinct process occurring prior to teacher development or implementation, which is the notion underlying the research, development, dissemination (RDD model). In the social-personal-professional model, curriculum development is seen as a part of teacher development and teacher development is seen as a part of curriculum development — the two are concurrent and reciprocal. Changes to one aspect of the classroom teaching by a teacher requires changes to other aspects of teaching, schooling and education. For example, using a new teaching activity may require changing the assessment procedures in the classroom and school or rewriting the school curriculum (within the guidelines of a national curriculum). Whilst the literature acknowledges the role of teacher development in the implementation of new curricula, the role of curriculum development as a part of teacher development is not so well acknowledged. The model then challenges the notion of curriculum development explicit in neo-conservative government policies, which separate out policy making from policy implementation, and which contract out curriculum development tasks to be done over a short time frame.

A reciprocal and interdependent view of curriculum development and teacher-development needs to consider four levels at which curriculum and teacher development occurs. First, there is the national level, which involves curriculum and teacher development in the process of the development of a national curriculum in science. The discussions to reach a negotiated and agreed to document require the professional development of all stakeholders involved, including teachers, teacher educators, politicians, parents, scientists, employers and bureaucrats.

Secondly, there is the school level of curriculum and teacher development. For example, this may involve teachers undertaking teacher development for school change; for example, developing the ability to write a school-policy statement on equity or assessment. It may involve rewriting the school programme for science in the light of new national curricula.

Thirdly, there is the level of change to a teacher's curriculum in the classroom. Individual teachers may change their activities to implement a new school policy, new national curriculum policy or new innovations arising from research. This entails an appraisal of personal commitments to the school, the subject, their colleagues and students, to the proposed change, and a consideration of what the changes would mean within the (probably unchanged!) physical resources available.

Lastly, there is the level of curriculum change as students experience it. Every student builds up a view of what the curriculum being experienced in a given subject is about. This is constructed from a personal overview of the whole-school curriculum and the inter-relationship between its parts, from personal experience of the subject in previous years, from the opinions of peers, older siblings, parents or guardians, and from textbooks. In our view, no new teacher-intended curriculum should be introduced without an evaluation of the existing student-experienced curriculum because curriculum development and teacher development are only effective if the students' experienced-curriculum changes in a way that improves learning.

In a review covering the 1970s onward, Fullan and Hargreaves (1992) point out that, in all reported cases of successful curriculum development (curriculum innovation), teacher development was a contributing factor. However, they do point out the limitations to those (relatively few) sustained successes. They all involved sustained input from highly trained and experienced facilitators, who are in very short supply. The reports said little about the impact of the innovations on the students or the teachers as individuals or on the school as an organization. The scope of their apparent success would seem to have been very limited. The success of the individual projects reported has an uncertain predictive power when considered in the context of conditions in many schools today, where multiple, and perhaps interacting, innovations are being introduced simultaneously.

Fullan and Hargreaves (1992) suggest, from their historical analysis, a number of factors to explain both failure to introduce an innovation, and initial success followed by a gradual decline in effectiveness towards failure and abandonment. A lack of funding with which to introduce the innovation was a major contributing factor, particularly when accompanied by attempts to manage the innovation from outside an individual school. A lack of appreciation, on the part of the sponsors of the innovation, of how it related to existing practices in the school was also evident. Many innovations were built around an inadequate model for their introduction. A lack of time for teachers to take on the additional work involved, teacher turnover, and a lack of appropriate, and appropriately timed, teacher development, also contributed to cases of failure.

In the light of this evidence and the need to undertake multiple innovations in a school at the same time, Fullan and Hargreaves (1992) suggest that a comprehensive model of teacher development, the key to successful curriculum innovation, must take into account the following four elements: firstly, the teacher's purpose, that is, what the teacher is trying to achieve; secondly, the teacher as a person; thirdly, the social contexts within which a teacher actually works, both in terms of the neighbourhood and within the school itself; and fourthly, the culture of teaching within the school. The model of teacher development proposed in Chapter 2 subsumes these elements within an articulated whole.

Empowerment

Another challenge issued by the social-personal-professional model is that to empower teachers to be key contributors in the reconstruction of what it means to be a teacher of science. This includes being a contributor to the writing of national, school and classroom curricula; having a say in the nature and focus of teacher development programmes; and being in a position to change inter-related aspects of schooling, rather than just one aspect in isolation. However, there is a need to be alerted to the danger of organizations and governments being manipulative rather than empowering of teachers if schools and teachers have the responsibility without power, as the centre retains or increases control over essentials of curriculum and testing (Hargreaves, 1994, p. 69).

Time

The social-personal-professional model challenges the current short length of time given for teacher development. For example, some teacher-development programmes contracted to the New Zealand Ministry of Education to implement the new science curriculum, consist of three one-day meetings, along with school visits by the facilitator between the meetings. From their experiences of the programme within this time frame, most teachers felt they understood the philosophy of the new curriculum but wanted more time and support to put the new ideas into practice (Gilmore, 1994). With respect to the social-personal-professional model, many teachers were at situation 1 (confirmation and desiring change: see Chapter 2) only at the end of the funded programme. On one hand, we acknowledge that educational funds are a finite resource. On the other hand, we maintain that changing teaching is not the same as changing a factory production line. In changing their teaching, teachers are changing not only actions, but beliefs as well. Furthermore, that change will be slower (and rightly so) if the changes go against their professional commitments. In addition, teachers have to manage the response of students, parents, school management and others to that change. In managing the responses to their changes, teachers are not merely keeping classroom control or telling others about why they are changing. They are having to work over a period of time with others to renegotiate what it means to be a teacher of science. Changing beliefs and views about education and teaching does not happen instantly for teachers, parents, managers or politicians.

Challenges for the Model

The social-personal-professional model of teacher development raises challenges for teachers, teacher educators, school managers and policy makers. In turn, the social and political contexts in which teacher development occurs, raise challenges for the model.

The model of teacher development, as outlined in Chapters 2–7, has the potential to support sustained, and self-directed, change. However, as discussed in Chapter 8, the current social and political contexts within which teacher development is framed seem antipathetic to a realization of that potential. The following are some challenges to be addressed if the model is to be useful to teachers.

The Need for a Definite Response

For the model to be used in teacher development, educationalists must respond to the New Right political policies that are counter to the use of the model. The educational establishment cannot:

... act as if today would be better if it were more like yesterday, but as if in any case tomorrow will be broadly similar to both. To support this belief, it has a formal sequence of responses, at both trivial and serious levels. These are: (a) it is not a problem (b) it may well be a problem but it is being exaggerated (c) it is indeed a problem but it is being badly expressed (d) it is certainly a problem but it is being grossly/obsessionally/ hysterically formulated (e) it is of course a problem but it is already well known and everything likely to solve it has already been tried (f) it is a problem but it is (has become) boring. (Williams, 1983)

The central task of educationalists, through the teacher development that they undertake, is to respond appropriately to the demands now made of them and to the opportunities that they can discern, within the climate of beliefs and actions in which teaching is now set. This response must be positive where there is evidence that there are justified criticisms made of the curriculum, of teaching, and of the quality and quantity of learning, or where opportunities have hitherto been lost: it is crucial that students' learning (however assessed) be improved. The response must be neutral where the changes proposed or possible are cosmetic, having no substantial implications for teaching and learning, and merely represent fashions in government: many new prescriptions represent 'valued old wine, presented in new bottles'. The response must be negative where, in the considered opinion of educationalists, the proposed changes have destructive implications for the long-term capacities of students to respond to the demands of their lives. Thus, the inclusion within the curriculum of a critical evaluation of the status of knowledge must be defended.

Educationalists need to acquire the skills that will enable them to establish a genuine public space for the discussion of education — including the ability to carry forward ideas that have broad support into widespread effective practice, and the ability to defend their views and actions against destructive argument, where that is encountered. These skills respectively suggest that they must sustain the notion of teaching as a profession and be able to respond to the discourse of derision.

Retaining a Commitment to Teaching as a Profession

The issue of whether education has been, is, or can ever be, a profession, has been widely debated. Indeed, taking Perkin's (1985) definition that: 'professions, like all conscious groupings, are best thought of as teams for the mobilisation of resources in the pursuit of status and income', it may be that many educationalists would not want to be a member of one, on ethical and moral grounds. However, other views of the worth of being in such a group are available. In a profession, a corpus of theoretical knowledge, related both inductively and deductively to practical knowledge, is held by practitioners who are a relative minority. The function of this theoretical knowledge is to provide justification to link practice across widely differing contexts. In addition, a corpus of practical knowledge, consisting of protocols on the proper relation to clients, and on what should be done, when, and how, is held by all practitioners within a profession. These constitute the ethical and moral dimensions of professional behaviour. Professionals do engage in a closely defined, heavily circumscribed activity of self-advertising, manifest through collective, centralized organizations. They are proactive as well as responsive, and are involved in discretionary judgments in the practising of their profession.

Perkin (1985) advocates that education is not a true profession, for three reasons. It is perceived to lack a distinctive body of theoretical or practical knowledge necessary for teaching. For example, in New Zealand teachers employed in state schools teaching children do not have to be registered (although vets have to be registered to care for the family cat). Anyone deemed suitable by a school Board of Trustees is eligible for employment, whether or not they are registered teachers, and whether or not they have a science or teaching qualification. Educationalists have no ultimate control over the selection, training and qualification of members. Teachers and educators in the United Kingdom have an organization which is divided into several trades unions and many subject associations and which can therefore be perceived as ineffectual politically when compared to other professional groups, such as medical practitioners. Returning to Perkin's (1985) definition above, the interplay or causes and consequences of this ineffectuality are a lack of bargaining power, relatively low remuneration and low status.

We assert that educationalists must take active and sustained measures to establish education as a profession (Hargreaves, 1994). This assertion is a goal to work towards as we acknowledge that the present positioning of educators, as directed by neo-conservative governments, does not make this an easy task. The need to establish education as a profession is most pressing in a time of imposed change, and the reaction of experienced teachers, who constitute the great majority in most educational services, to imposed change is of key importance here. Sikes (1992) has summarized the likely responses of teachers to imposed change, which is what is being mandated in many countries. These responses are divided into three categories. First, in terms of teachers as people, imposed change could mean that:

a teacher's initial reasons for being a teacher no longer apply, that their expectations cannot be met, and that their commitment comes to seem misplaced;

the initial grounding teachers receive and the ideas which underlie their educational ideologies and philosophies go out of fashion and are viewed unfavourably, meaning that teachers are faced with the idea that they have been wrong and may even have disadvantaged their pupils;

professional and personal life-cycle needs and expectations are not met. (Sikes, 1992, p. 41)

A second response to imposed change is in terms of the professional aims and purposes, in which teachers vary widely. For some, the imposed changes will lead to a gap between what they value in schools and the expectations and conditions prevailing there. A third response to imposed change is in terms of the context and conditions in which teachers work. Imposed change under conditions of fiscal austerity could mean that many teachers will lack the time and physical resources with which to meet the new, and usually expanded, requirements. Lastly, a response to imposed change may be in terms of the cultural values within which teachers work. As Sikes (1992) points out:

> Within educational institutions, teacher cultures develop. These cultures are the product of the beliefs, values and characteristics of the staff, students and community which combine to make up the shared understandings, the rules and norms which are 'the way we do things here'. Changes which are imposed from outside threaten . . . teacher cultures. The result is that people lose their sense of meaning and direction, their 'framework of reality', their confidence that they know what to do, and consequently they experience confusion and a kind of alienation. (Sikes, 1992, p. 43)

The responses of teachers under these circumstances may vary. Some will carry on as before, perhaps introducing the required changes in a cosmetic manner. Some will form or join cliques and factions within the staff to support particular views on the changes. Others will simply leave teaching. Some will take advantage of the change for career enhancement. Others will adopt a general attitude of resistance and sabotage.

If education were a profession, then teachers would have a collective mechanism through which to have the maximum influence on the nature and extent of changes that a government sought to bring about. They could deploy skills to ensure that the implementation of required changes was built on elements of teacher culture that were central to its philosophy and clearly defendable. They could ensure that all teachers had the opportunity to participate actively in the process of implementing change. For such a profession to be established, or re-established, core theories of education must be clearly set out, their relation to good practice in a wide variety of contexts established, and skills of advocacy built up. In addition, the development of education as a profession will in some way help to ensure that innovative and successful teachers keep contributing to teaching and learning in schools.

The Capacity to Respond Appropriately to the Discourse of Derision

As we discussed earlier, the tactics used by the New Right to drive educationalists from the arena of influence over educational policy-making have several elements: the use of the rhetoric of political argument, the misuse of educational research to support preformed conclusions, and the blaming of educationalists for former and current policy failure. Teacher development needs to focus on skills to make appropriate responses to these tactics.

Economics

Another challenge to the model is the cost of its provision. The model in advocating social, personal and professional development is advocating many meetings of teachers over one to three years. In the current political climates of tighter financial management and provision, and increased government controls on curriculum, assessment and evaluation, the financing of the model by governments is unlikely.

Conclusion

In this book, we have presented a model of teacher development as social, personal and professional development based on research findings in science education. We discussed this model with respect to the social, political and economic contexts in which schooling and education are occurring. We have theorised the model in terms of views of learning and human development. In concluding this book, we wish to acknowledge that we have not given a recipe that will automatically lead to better learning for teachers. Knowing what to do differently will of itself not necessarily result in the changes occurring, as the teachers in the research project appreciated. The wider political and social contexts at the moment are making it very difficult for educators to effect the changes that they would want. However, teachers, in wanting to help their students develop and grow in a post-modern world, are persistent in seeking changes based on their concerns. We hope that there is something in this book — its analysis and theorizing — that enables those change to be made.

References

ADLER, S. (1990) 'The reflective practitioner and the curriculum of teacher education', Paper presented to the Annual Meeting of Teacher Educators, Las Vegas, February.

ANDERSON, C. (1989) 'The role of education in the academic disciplines in teacher preparation', in WOOLFOLK, A. (Ed) *Research Perspectives on the Graduate Preparation of Teachers*, Englewood Cliffs, NJ, Prentice Hall, pp. 88–107.

APPLE, M. (1993) *Official Knowledge*, New York, Routledge.

ATWATER, M. and RILEY, J. (1993) 'Multicultural science education: Perspectives, definitions, and research agenda', *Science Education*, **77**, 6, pp. 661–8.

BALL, S. (1990) *Politics and Policy Making in Education*, London, Routledge.

BATES, R. (1990) 'Educational policy and the new cult of efficiency', in MIDDLETON, S., CODD, J. and JONES, A. (Eds) *New Zealand Education Policy Today: Critical Perspectives*, Wellington, Allen and Unwin.

BEGG, A.J.C. (1994) 'Professional development of high school mathematics teachers', Unpublished DPhil thesis, University of Waikato, Hamilton, New Zealand.

BELENKY, F.M., CLINCHY, M.B., GOLDBERGER, R. and TARULE, M.J. (1986) *Women's Ways of Knowing: The Development of Self, Voice and Mind*, USA, Basic Books.

BELL, B. (1981) 'When is an animal not an animal?', *Journal of Biological Education*, **15**, 3, pp. 213–18.

BELL, B.F. (1988) 'Girls and science', in MIDDLETON, S. (Ed) *Women and Education in Aotearoa*, Wellington, Allen and Unwin, Port Nicholson press, pp. 153–160.

BELL, B. (1990) 'Science curriculum development: A recent New Zealand example', in *SAME papers 1990*, Hamilton, Centre for Science and Mathematics Education Research, University of Waikato, pp. 1–31.

BELL, B. (1993a) (Ed) *I Know about LISP But How do I Put it into Practice?*, Final Report of the Learning in Science Project (Teacher Development), Hamilton, Centre for Science and Mathematics Education Research, University of Waikato.

BELL, B. (1993b) *Taking into Account Students' Thinking: A Teacher Development Guide*, Hamilton, Centre for Science and Mathematics Education Research, University of Waikato.

BELL, B. (1993c) 'Teaching that takes into account students' thinking: 1 Planning', *New Zealand Science Teacher*, **74**, pp. 4–7.

BELL, B. (1993d) *Children's Science, Constructivism and Learning in Science*, Geelong, Deakin University Press.

BELL, B. (1994a) 'Teaching that takes into account students' thinking: 2 Responding to and interacting with students' thinking', *New Zealand Science Teacher*, **75**, pp. 21–5.

BELL, B. (1994b) 'Using anecdotes in teacher development', *International Journal of Science Education*, **16**, 5, pp. 575–84.

BELL, B. and GILBERT, J. (1994) 'Teacher development as personal, professional and social development', *Teaching and Teacher Education*, **10**, 5, pp. 483–97.

BELL, B. and PEARSON, J. (1992) ' "Better" learning', *International Journal of Science Education*, **14**, 3, pp. 349–61.

BELL, B. and PEARSON, J. (1993a) 'Feeling better about myself as a teacher', in BELL, B. (1993a) op. cit., pp. 84–128.

BELL, B. and PEARSON, J. (1993b) 'Feedback on learning', in BELL, B. (1993a) op. cit., pp. 129–46.

BELL, B. and PEARSON, J. (1993c) 'Feedback, support, reflection', in BELL, B. (1993a) op. cit., pp. 154–61, 184–215.

BELL, B. and PEARSON, J. (1993d) 'The change process', in BELL, B. (1993a) op. cit., pp. 162–83.

BELL, B.F., PEARSON, J.D. and KIRKWOOD, V.M. (1991) 'Course components', Working paper 408. Learning in Science Project (Teacher Development), Centre for Science and Mathematics Education Research, University of Waikato.

BERGER, P. and LUCKMANN, T. (1966) *The Social Construction of Reality: A Treatise in the Sociology of Knowledge*, New York, Penguin Books.

BERLINER, D. (1992) 'Educational reform in an era of disinformation', Paper given to the American Association of Colleges of Teacher Education, San Antonio, Texas, February.

BIDDULPH, F. (1991) *Burning: A Science Unit for 10–13-year-old Students*, Hamilton, Centre for Science and Mathematics Education Research, University of Waikato.

BIDDULPH, F. and OSBORNE, R. (1984) *Making Sense of Our World: An Interactive Approach*, Hamilton, Centre for Science and Mathematics Education Research, University of Waikato.

BOSTON, J. (1991) 'The theoretical underpinnings of public sector restructuring in New Zealand', in BOSTON, J., MARTIN, J., PALLOT, J. and WALSH, P. (Eds) *Reshaping the State: New Zealand's Bureaucratic Revolution*, Auckland, Oxford University Press.

BOWE, R., BALL, S. and GOLD, A. (1992) *Reforming Education and Changing Schools*, London, Routledge.

BRISCOE, C. (1991) 'The dynamic interactions among beliefs, role metaphors, and teaching practices: A case study of teacher change', *Science Education*, **75**, 2, pp. 185–99.

BRUNER, J. (1990) *Acts of Meaning*, Cambridge, MA, Harvard University Press.

BULLOCK, A., STALLYBRASS, O. and TROMBLEY, S. (Eds) (1988) *The Fontana Dictionary of Modern Thought*, 2nd ed., London, Fontana Press.

BURDEN, P. (1990) 'Teacher development', in HOUSTON, W. (Ed) *Handbook of Research on Teacher Education*, New York, MacMillan, pp. 311–28.

BUTEFISH, W.L. (1990) 'Science teachers' perceptions of their interactive decisions', *Journal of Educational Research*, **84**, 2, pp. 107–14.

CARRÉ, C. (1993) 'Performance in subject-matter knowledge in science', in BENNETT, N. and CARRÉ, C. (Eds) *Learning to Teach*, London, Routledge, pp. 18–35.

CHAPMAN, M. (1986) 'The structure of exchange: Piaget's sociological theory', *Human Development*, **29**, pp. 181–194.

CHARBONNEAU, A. (1993) *Improving the Quality of Education in British Columbia*, British Columbia, Ministry of Education.

CLANDININ, D.J. and CONNELLY, F.M. (1991) 'Narrative and story in practice and research', in SCHÖN, D. (Ed) *The Reflective Turn*, New York, Teachers' College Press, pp. 258–81.

CLAXTON, G. (1989) *Being a Teacher: A Positive Approach to Change and Stress*, London, Cassell.

CLAXTON, G. and CARR, M.C. (1991) 'Understanding the change: The personal perspective', in *SAME papers 1991*, Hamilton, Centre for Science and Mathematics Education Research, University of Waikato, pp. 1–14.

COBB, P. (1994) 'Where is the mind? Constructivist and sociocultural perspectives on mathematical development', *Educational Researcher*, **20**, 7, pp. 13–20.

COCHRAN-SMITH, M. (1991) 'Learning to teach against the grain', *Harvard Educational Review*, **61**, 3, pp. 279–310.

COLE, A.L. (1988) 'Personal signals in spontaneous teaching practice', *Qualitative Studies in Education*, **2**, 2, pp. 25–39.

CONFREY, J. (1993) 'Forging a revised theory of intellectual development: Piaget, Vygotsky and Beyond', Paper presented to the Canadian Mathematics Education Study Group, May 28–31.

CORTAZZI, M. (1993) *Narrative Analysis*, London, Falmer Press.

COSGROVE, M. and OSBORNE, R. (1985) 'Lesson frameworks for changing children's ideas', in OSBORNE, R. and FREYBERG, P. (Eds) *Learning in Science: The Implications of Children's Science*, Auckland, Heinemann, pp. 101–11.

COSGROVE, M., OSBORNE, R. and FORRET, M. (1989) *Electric Current: Developing Learner's Views: Teachers' Guide*, 3rd ed., Waikato Education Centre, Hamilton.

DALE, R. (1989) *The State and Educational Policy*, Milton Keynes, Open University.

DANIEL, J. (1975) 'Learning styles and strategies: The work of Gordon Pask', in ENTWISTLE, N. and HOUNSELL, D. (Eds) *How Students Learn*, Lancaster, University of Lancaster, Institute for Research and Development in Post-Compulsory Education, pp. 83–92.

DAVIES, B. (1991) 'The concept of agency: A feminist poststructuralist analysis', *Social Analysis: Special Issue on Postmodern Critical Theorising*, **30**, pp. 42–53.

DAVIES, B. (1993) *Shards of Glass*, Sydney, Allen and Unwin.

DAWKINS, J. (1988) *Strengthening Australia's Schools: A Consideration of the Focus and Content of Schooling*, Canberra, Parliament House, DEET.

DEARING, R. (1994) (chair) *Final Report of the Review of the National Curriculum*, London, Department for Education.

DEPARTMENT OF EDUCATION AND SCIENCE (1985) *Science 5–16: A Statement of Policy*, London, HMSO.

DRIVER, R. (1978) 'When is a stage not a stage? A critique of Piaget's theory of cognitive development and its implication to science education', in *Educational Research*, **21**, 1, pp. 54–61.

DRIVER, R. (1983) *Pupil as Scientist?*, Milton Keynes, Open University Press.

DRIVER, R. (1988) 'Theory into practice II: A constructivist approach to curriculum development', in FENSHAM, P. (Ed) *Development and Dilemmas in Science Education*, London, Falmer Press, pp. 133–49.

DRIVER, R. (1989) 'Students' conceptions and the learning of science', *International Journal of Science Education*, **11**, pp. 481–90.

DRIVER, R., ASOKO, H., LEACH, J., MORTIMER, E. and SCOTT, P. (1994) 'Constructing scientific knowledge in the classroom', in *Educational Researcher*, **23**, 7, pp. 5–12.

DRIVER, R., GUESNE, E. and TIBERGHIEN, A. (1985) *Children's Ideas in Science*, Milton Keynes, Open University Press.

DUIT, R. (1994) 'Research on students' conceptions — developments and trends', in PFUNDT, H. and DUIT, R. *Bibliography: Students' Alternative Frameworks and Science Education*, 4th Edition, Kiel, Germany, IPN at the University of Kiel.

ELLERTON, N. and CLEMENTS, M. (1992) 'Some pluses and minuses of radical constructivism in mathematics education', *Mathematics Education Research Journal*, **4**, 2, pp. 1–22.

ENTWISTLE, N. (1988) 'Motivational factors in approaches to learning', in SCHMECK, R. (Ed) *Learning Strategies and Learning Styles*, New York, Plenum, pp. 26–64.

EPSTEIN, D. (1993) 'Defining accountability in education', *British Educational Research Journal*, **19**, 3, pp. 243–58.

ERICKSON, G. and MACKINNON, A. (1991) 'Exploring children's and teachers' understandings', in SCHÖN, D. (Ed) *The Reflective Turn*, New York, Teachers College Press, pp. 15–36.

FENSHAM, P. (1986) 'Science for all', *Educational Leadership*, **44**, pp. 18–23.

FENSHAM, P. (1994) 'Progressing in school science curriculum: A rational prospect or a chimera', Paper presented to the 1994 Conference of the Australasian Science Education Research Association, Hobart, July.

FENSHAM, P., GUNSTONE, R. and WHITE, R. (1994) *The Content of Science: A Constructivist Approach to its Teaching and Learning*, London, Falmer Press.

FINLAYSON, D. (1987) 'School climate: An outmoded metaphor?', *Journal of Curriculum Studies*, **19**, 2, pp. 163–73.

FORGAS, J. (1981) *Social Cognition: Perspectives on Everyday Understanding*, London, Academic Press.

FULLAN, M. and HARGREAVES, A. (1992) 'Teacher development and educational change', in FULLAN, M. and HARGREAVES, A. (Eds) *Teacher Development and Educational Change*, London, Falmer Press, pp. 1–9.

GAULD, C. (1987) 'Students' beliefs and cognitive structure', *Research in Science Education*, **17**, pp. 87–93.

GERGEN, K. (1985) 'The social constructionist movement in modern psychology', *American Psychologist*, pp. 26–275.

GERGEN, K. (1991) *The Saturated Self: Dilemmas of Identity in Contemporary Life*, USA, Basic Books.

GILBERT, JANE (1993) 'Teacher development: A literature review', in BELL, B. (Ed) *I Know about LISP, but How Do I Put it into Practice?*, Hamilton, Centre for Science and Mathematics Education Research, University of Waikato, pp. 15–38.

GILBERT, JANE (1994a) 'The construction, reconstruction, and deconstruction of statements on gender equity in two science curriculum documents: Work in progress', in GILBERT, J. (Ed) *Feminism/Science Education*, Hamilton, Centre for Science and Mathematics Education Research, University of Waikato, pp. 16–38.

GILBERT, JANE (1994b) 'The construction and re-construction of the concept of the reflective practitioner in the discourses of teacher development', *International Journal of Science Education*, **16**, 5, pp. 511–22.

GILBERT, J., OSBORNE, R. and FENSHAM, P. (1982) 'Children's science and its consequences for teaching', *Science Education*, **66**, 4, pp. 623–33.

GILBERT, J.K. and WATTS, M. (1983) 'Conceptions, misconceptions and alternative conceptions: Changing perspectives in science education', *Studies in Science Education*, **10**, pp. 61–98.

GILLISS, G. (1988) 'Schön's reflective practitioner: A model for teachers?', in GRIMMETT, P. and ERICKSON, G. (Eds) *Reflection in Teacher Education*, New York, Teachers College Press.

GILMORE, A. (1994) *Evaluation of the Teacher Development Programmes: Mathematics and Science in the National Curriculum*, Christchurch, The University of Canterbury.

GRACE, G. (1990) 'The New Zealand Treasury and the commodification of education', in MIDDLETON, S., CODD, J. and JONES, A. (Eds) *New Zealand Education Policy Today: Critical Perspectives*, Wellington, Allen and Unwin.

GREENWOOD, J.D. (1994) *Realism, Identity and Emotion*, London, Sage Publications.

GRIMMETT, P. (1988) 'The nature of reflection and Schön's conception in perspective', in GRIMMETT, P. and ERICKSON, G. (Eds) *Reflection in Teacher Education*, New York, Teachers College Press, pp. 5–15.

GUNSTONE, R. and NORTHFIELD, J. (1994) 'Metacognition and learning to teach', *International Journal of Science Education*, **16**, 5, pp. 523–38.

HABERMAS, J. (1976) *Legitimation Crisis*, London, Heinemann.

HAMMERSLEY, M. and SCARTH, J. (1993) 'Beware of wise men bearing gifts: A case study of the misuse of educational research', *British Educational Research Journal*, **19**, 5, pp. 489–98.

HARDING, J. (1983) *Switched off: The Science Education of Girls*, York, Longman for Schools Council.

HARGREAVES, A. (1992) 'Cultures of teaching: A focus for change', in HARGREAVES,

A. and FULLAN, M. (Eds) *Understanding Teacher Development*, New York, Teachers College Press, pp. 216–40.

HARGREAVES, A. (1994) *Changing Teachers, Changing Times*, London, Cassell.

HARRÉ, R. (1981) 'Rituals, rhetoric and social cognition', in FORGAS, J. (Ed) *Social Cognition: Perspectives on Everyday Understanding*, London, Academic Press.

HARRÉ, R. and GILLETT, G. (1994) *The Discursive Mind*, London, Sage Publications.

HARRI-AUGSTEIN, S. and THOMAS, L. (1991) *Learning Conversations*, London, Routledge.

HENNESSY, S. (1993) 'Situated cognition and cognitive apprenticeship: Implications for classroom learning', *Studies in Science Education*, **22**, pp. 1–41.

HEWSON, P.W. and HEWSON, M.G. (1988) 'An appropriate conception of teaching science: A view from studies of science learning', *Science Education*, **72**, 5, pp. 597–614.

HICKCOX, E. and MUSELLA, D. (1992) 'Teacher performance appraisal and staff development', in FULLAN, M. and HARGREAVES, A. (Eds) *Teacher Development and Educational Change*, London, Falmer Press, pp. 31–60.

HODSON, D. (1993) 'In search of a rationale for multicultural science education', *Science Education*, **77**, 6, pp. 685–711.

HURD, D. (1991) 'Issues in linking research to science teaching', *Science Education*, **75**, 6, pp. 723–32.

IRWIN, M. (1994) 'Curriculum cartwheel', *The Times Higher Educational Supplement*, 1 July, p. 16.

JACQUES, D. (1991) *Learning in Groups*, London, Kogan Page.

KELLY, A. (1981) *The Missing Half: Girl and Science Education*, Manchester, Manchester University Press.

KELLY, G. (1969) 'Ontological acceleration', in MAHER, B. (Ed) *Clinical Psychology and Personality: the Selected Papers of George Kelly*, New York, Wiley, pp. 15–24.

KIRKWOOD, V. and CARR, M.C. (1988) *Final Report: Learning in Science Project (Energy)*, Hamilton, Centre for Science and Mathematics Education Research, University of Waikato.

KNOWLES, M. (1989) *The Adult Learner: A Neglected Species*, Houston, Gulf.

KOHLBERG, L. (1970) *Moral Development*, New York, Holt, Reinhart and Winston.

KRUGER, C., SUMMERS, M. and PALACIO, D. (1990) 'An investigation of some English primary school teachers' understanding of the concepts force and gravity', *British Educational Research Journal*, **16**, 4, pp. 383–97.

LAUDER, H. (1990) 'The New Right revolution and education in New Zealand', in MIDDLETON, S., CODD, J. and JONES, A. (Eds) *New Zealand Educational Policy Today: Critical Perspectives*, Wellington, Allen and Unwin, pp. 27–39.

LAVE, J. (1995) *What's the situation with learning (after two decades of practice)?* Address of the 1994 recipient of the Scribner award, American Education Research Association Conference, San Francisco, 18–22 April.

LAWLOR, S. (1994) 'The crazy National Curriculum', *The Observer*, (Education Section), 20 February, p. 24.

LEITHWOOD, K. (1992) 'The principal's role in teacher development', in FULLAN, M. and HARGREAVES, A. (Eds) *Teacher Development and Educational Change*, London, Falmer Press, pp. 86–103.

LEMKE, J. (1990) *Talking Science: Language, Learning and Values*, Norwood, New Jersey, Ablex Publishing Corporation.

LOUDEN, W. (1992) 'Understanding reflection through collaborative research', in HARGREAVES, A. and FULLAN, M. (Eds) *Understanding Teacher Development*, New York, Teachers College Press, pp. 178–215.

MARKS, M.B. (1989) 'Practice into theory: The teacher authenticates research findings', *Educational Research Quarterly*, **13**, 3, pp. 17–25.

MARSHALL, H.H. (1988) 'Work or learning: Implications of classroom metaphors', *Educational Researcher*, **17**, 9, pp. 9–16.

MARTON, F. (1988) 'Describing and improving learning', in SCHMECK, R. (Ed) *Learning Strategies and Learning Styles*, New York, Plenum, pp. 53–82.

MATTINGLY, C. (1991) 'Narrative reflections on practical actions: Two learning experiments in reflective storytelling', in SCHÖN, D. (Ed) *The Reflective Turn*, New York, Teachers' College Press, pp. 235–57.

MAYS, W. (1982) 'Piaget's sociological theory', in MOGDILL, S. and C. (Eds) *Jean Piaget: Consensus and Controversy*, London, Holt, Rinehart and Winston, pp. 31–50.

MCCARTY, H. (1993) 'From deadwood to greenwood: Working with burned out staff', *Journal of Staff Development*, **14**, 1, pp. 42–6.

MCCOMISH, J. (1994) 'What has constructivism got to do with feminism?', in GILBERT, J. (Ed) *Feminism/Science Education*, Hamilton, Centre for Science and Mathematics Education Research, University of Waikato, pp. 16–38.

MCKINLEY, E., MCPHERSON WAITI, P. and BELL, B. (1992) 'Language, culture and science education', *International Journal of Science Education*, **14**, 5, pp. 579–95.

MCNAMARA, D. (1990) 'The National Curriculum: An agenda for research', *British Educational Research Journal*, **16**, 3, pp. 225–35.

METHERELL, T. (1989) *Excellence and Equity: New South Wales Curriculum Reform*, Sydney, NSW Ministry of Education and Youth Affairs.

MICHELL, M. (1987) *Better Science: Key Proposals, Secondary Science Curriculum Review*, London, Heinneman Education Books, Association for Science Education.

MIDDLETON, S., CODD, J. and JONES, A. (1990) (Eds) *New Zealand Education Policy Today: Critical Perspectives*, Wellington, Allen and Unwin.

MILLAR, R. (1989) 'Constructive criticisms', *International Journal of Science Education*, **11**, pp. 587–96.

MINISTRY OF EDUCATION (1993) *Science in the New Zealand Curriculum*, Wellington, Learning Media.

MITCHELL, D., MCGEE, C., MOLTZEN, R. and OLIVER, D. (1993) *Hear Our Voices: Final Report of the Monitoring Today's Schools Research Project*, Hamilton, University of Waikato.

MOLI, S. (1993) 'Some Samoan science teachers' views of teaching and learning', in *SAME papers 1993*, Hamilton, Centre for Science and Mathematics Education Research, University of Waikato, pp. 84–103.

NORTHFIELD, J. and SYMINGTON, D. (1991) *Learning in Science Viewed as Personal Construction: An Australian Perspective*, Perth, National Key Centre for Science and Mathematics, Curtin University of Technology.

NUSSBAUM, J. and NOVICK, S. (1982) 'Alternative frameworks, conceptual conflict and accommodation: Toward a principled teaching strategy', *Instructional Science*, **11**, pp. 183–200.

NUTHALL, G. and ALTON-LEE, A. (1990) 'Research on teaching and learning: Thirty years of change', *The Elementary School Journal*, **90**, 5, pp. 547–70.

NUTHALL, G. and ALTON-LEE, A. (1993) 'Predicting learning from student experience of teaching: A theory of student knowledge construction in classrooms', *American Educational Research Journal*, **30**, 4, pp. 799–840.

OGBORN, J. (1993) 'A view of "understanding"', in BLACK, P. and LUCAS, A. (Eds) *Children's Informal Ideas in Science*, London, Routledge, pp. 102–19.

O'LOUGHLIN, M. (1992a) 'Rethinking science education: Beyond Piagetian constructivism towards a socio-cultural model of teaching and learning', *Journal of Research in Science Teaching*, **29**, 8, pp. 791–820.

O'LOUGHLIN, M. (1992b) 'Engaging teachers in emanicipatory knowledge construction', *Journal of Teacher Education*, **43**, 5, pp. 336–46.

OLSSEN, M. (1991) 'Producing the truth about people: Science and the cult of the individual in educational psychology', in MORSS, J. and LINZEY, T. (Eds) *Growing Up: The Politics of Human Learning*, London, Longman, pp. 188–209.

OSBORNE, J. (1993) 'Beyond constructivism', Paper given at the Third International Seminar on Misconceptions and Learning Strategies in Science and Mathematics Education, Cornell University, August.

OSBORNE, R. (1985) 'Theories of learning: Wittrock', in OSBORNE, R. and GILBERT, J. (Eds) 'Some Issue of Theory in Science Education', Papers based on seminars at the Science Education Research Unit, University of Waikato, Hamilton, New Zealand, July, pp. 6–18.

OSBORNE, R.J., BELL, B. and GILBERT, J. (1983) 'Science teaching and children's views of the world', *European Journal of Science Education*, **5**, 1, pp. 1–5.

OSBORNE, R.J. and BIDDULPH, F. (1985) *Final report: Learning in Science Project (Primary)*, Hamilton, Centre for Science and Mathematics Education Research, University of Waikato.

OSBORNE, R.J. and FREYBERG, P.S. (1985) *Learning in Science: The Implications of Children's Science*, Auckland, Heinemann.

OSBORNE, R.J. and WITTROCK, M. (1985) 'The generative learning model and its implications for learning in science', *Studies in Science Education*, **12**, pp. 59–87.

PEARSON, J. and BELL, B. (1993) *The Teacher Development that Occurred*, Report of the Learning in Science Project (Teacher Development). Hamilton, Centre for Science and Mathematics Education Research, University of Waikato.

PERKIN, H. (1985) 'The teaching profession and the game of life', in GORDON, P., PERKIN, H., SOCKETT, H. and HOYLE, E. (Eds) *Is Teaching a Profession?*, London, University of London, Institute of Education, pp. 12–25.

PERRY, G. (1970) *Forms of Intellectual and Ethical Development in the College Years*, New York, Holt, Rinehart, and Winston.

PFUNDT, H. and DUIT, R. (1994) *Bibliography of Students' Alternative Frameworks and Science Education*, 4th ed. Kiel, IPN.

PHILLIPS, D. (1995) *The Many Faces of Constructivism.* Invited address to the 1995 National Association for Research in Science Teaching Annual Meeting, San Francisco, April 22–25.

PIAGET, J. (1970) 'Piaget's theory', in MUSSEN, P. (Ed) *Carmichael's Manual of Child Psychology*, New York, Wiley, pp. 61–84.

POPE, M. and GILBERT, J. (1983) 'Personal experience and the construction of knowledge in science', *Science Education*, **67**, 2, pp. 193–203.

POPE, M. and KEEN, T. (1981) *Personal Construct Psychology and Education*, London, Academic.

POSNER, G.J., STRIKE, K.A., HEWSON, P.W. and GERTZOG, W.A. (1982) 'Accommodation of a scientific conception: Towards a theory of conceptual change', *Science Education*, **66**, 2, pp. 211–27.

POSTLETHWAITE, K. (1993) *Differentiated Science Teaching*, Buckingham, Open University.

PRYKE, R. (1994) 'Week by week', *Education*, 24 June, p. 498.

RABAN, B., CLARK, U. and MCINTYRE, J. (1993) *Evaluation of the Implementation of English in the National Curriculum at Key Stages 1, 2 and 3 (1991–3)*, London, Schools Curriculum and Assessment Authority.

RAKOW, S. and BERMUDEZ, A. (1993) 'Science is "ciencia": Meeting the needs of Hispanic American students', *Science Education*, **77**, 6, pp. 669–84.

REISS, M. (1993) *Science Education for a Pluralistic Society*, Buckingham, Open University.

RESNICK, L. (1991) 'Shared cognition: Thinking as social practice', in RESNICK, L., LEVINE, J. and TEASLEY, S. (Eds) *Perspectives on Socially Shared Cognition*, Washington, American Psychological Association.

ROBERTSON, H. (1992) 'Teacher development and gender equity', in HARGREAVES, A. and FULLAN, M. (Eds) *Understanding Teacher Development*, New York, Cassell and Teachers College Press, pp. 43–61.

RUTHERFORD, F. (1993) 'Project 2061 draws on research', *2061 Today*, **3**, 1, pp. 1–5.

SCHÖN, D. (1983) *The Reflective Practitioner*, London, Temple Smith.

SCHÖN, D. (1987) *Educating the Reflective Practitioner*, San Francisco, Jossey Bass.

SCHÖN, D. (1991) (Ed) *The Reflective Turn*, New York, Teachers College Press.

SCHUTZ, A. and LUCKMANN, T. (1973) *Structures of the Life World*, London, Heinemann.

SCOTT, P., ASOKO, H. and DRIVER, R. (1991) 'Teaching for conceptual change: A review of strategies', in DUIT, R., GOLDBERG, F. and NIEDDERER, H. (Eds) *Research in Physics Learning: Theoretical Issues and Empirical Studies*, Kiel, University of Kiel.

SEDDON, T. (1991) 'Rethinking teachers and teaching in science', *Studies in Science Education*, **19**, pp. 95–117.

SHAVELSON, R. (1988) 'Contributions of educational research to policy and practice:

Constructing, challenging, changing cognition', *Educational Researcher*, **17**, 7, pp. 4–22.

SHEPPARD, C. and GILBERT, J. (1991) 'Course design, teaching method, and student epistemology', *Higher Education*, **22**, pp. 229–49.

SHOTTER, J. (1984) *Social Accountability and Selfhood*, Oxford, Basil Blackwell.

SHULMAN, L. (1987) 'Knowledge and teaching: Foundations of the new reforms', *Harvard Educational Review*, **57**, pp. 1–22.

SIKES, P. (1985) 'The life cycle of the teacher', in BALL, S. and GOODSON, I. (Eds) *Teachers' Lives and Careers*, London, Falmer Press, pp. 27–60.

SIKES, P. (1992) 'Imposed change and the experienced teacher', in FULLAN, M. and HARGREAVES, D. (Eds) *Teacher Development and Educational Change*, London, Falmer Press, pp. 36–55.

SIKULA, J. (1990) 'National Commission reports of the 1980s', in HOSTON, W. (Ed) *Handbook of Research on Teacher Education*, New York, MacMillan, pp. 72–82.

SIMON, S., BLACK, P., BROWN, M. and BLONDEL, E. (1994) 'Progression in learning: The equilibrium of forces', Paper given to the American Education Research Association Annual Meeting, New Orleans, April.

SMAIL, B. (1984) *Girl-friendly Science: Avoiding Sex Bias in the Curriculum*, York, Longman for the Schools Council.

SMYTHE, J. (1992) 'Teachers' work and the politics of reflection', *American Education Research Journal*, **29**, 2, pp. 267–300.

SOLOMON, J. (1983) 'Teaching about energy: How pupils think in two domains', *European Journal of Science Education*, **5**, 1, pp. 49–59.

SOLOMON, J. (1987) 'Social influences on the construction of pupils' understanding in science', *Studies in Science Education*, **14**, pp. 63–82.

SOLOMON, J. (1994) 'The rise and fall of constructivism', *Studies in Science Education*, **23**, pp. 1–19.

STAVY, R. and BERKOVITZ, B. (1980) 'Cognitive conflict as a basis for teaching quantitative aspects of the concept of temperature', *Science Education*, **64**, 5, pp. 679–92.

SUCHTING, W. (1992) 'Constructivism deconstructed', *Science and Education*, **1**, pp. 223–54.

SUTHERLAND, S. (1992) *Irrationality: The Enemy Within*, London, Constable.

TASKER, R., FREYBERG, P.S. and OSBORNE, R.J. (1982) *Final Report: Learning in Science Project (Form 1–4)*, Hamilton, Centre for Science and Mathematics Education Research, University of Waikato.

TAYLOR, P. (1991) 'Collaborating to reconstruct teaching: The influence of researcher beliefs', Paper presented at the annual meeting of the American Educational Research Association, Chicago, April 3–7.

THE MATHEMATICAL ASSOCIATION (1991) *Develop Your Teaching: A Professional Development Pack for Mathematics and other Teachers*, Cheltenham, Stanley Thornes.

THIESSEN, D. (1992) 'Classroom-based teacher development', in HARGREAVES, A. and FULLAN, M. (1992) (Ed) *Understanding Teacher Development*, New York, Teachers College Press, pp. 85–109.

THORP, S., DESHPANDE, P. and EDWARDS, C. (1994) *Race, Equality, and Science Education*, Hatfield, Association for Science Education.

TICKLE, L. (1989) 'New teachers and the development of professionalism', in HOLLY, M. and MCLOUGHLIN, C. (Eds) *Perspectives on Teacher Professional Development*, London, Falmer Press, pp. 93–118.

TOBIN, K. (1990) 'Social constructivist perspectives on the reform of science education', *Australasian Science Teacher Journal*, **36**, 4, pp. 29–35.

TOBIN, K. (1993) 'Referents for making sense of science teaching', *International Journal of Science Education*, **15**, 3, pp. 241–54.

VON GLASERSFELD, E. (1984) 'An introduction to radical constructivism', in WATZLAWICK, P. (Ed) *The Invented Reality*, New York, Norton, pp. 18–40.

VON GLASERSFELD, E. (1991) 'Knowing without metaphysics: Aspects of the radical constructivist position', in STEIER, F. (Ed) *Research and Reflexivity*, London, Sage, pp. 12–29.

VON GLASERSFELD, E. (1992a) 'A constructivist view of learning and teaching', in DUIT, R., GOLDBERG, F. and NIEDDERER, H. (Eds) *Research in Physics Learning: Theoretical Issues and Empirical Studies*, Kiel, Germany, IPN at the University of Kiel.

VON GLASERSFELD, E. (1992b) 'Constructivism deconstructed: A reply to Suchting', *Science and Education*, **1**, pp. 378–84.

VYGOTSKY, L. (1978) *Mind in Society: The Development of Higher Psychological Processes*, Cambridge, MA, Harvard University Press.

WEISSGLASS, J. (1994) 'Reflections on educational change support groups', *People and Education*, **2**, 2, pp. 225–48.

WHEATLEY, G.H. (1991) 'Constructivist perspectives on science and mathematics learning', *Science Education*, **75**, 1, pp. 9–21.

WHITE, R. (1988) *Learning Science*, Oxford, Basil Blackwell.

WHITE, R. (1991) 'An overview of the Australasian perspective', in NORTHFIELD, J. and SYMINGTON, D. (Eds) *Learning in Science Viewed as Personal Construction: An Australasian perspective*, Perth, Science and Mathematics Education Centre, Curtin University, pp. 1–13.

WHYTE, J. (1985) *Gender, Science and Technology: In-service Handbook*, York, Longman.

WILLIAMS, R. (1983) 'Intellectuals behind the screens', *Times Educational Supplement*, 21 January, p. 11.

WYLIE, C. (1992) *The Impact of Tomorrow's Schools in Primary Schools and Intermediates: 1991 Survey Report*, Wellington, Council for Educational Research.

ZEICHNER, K. and TABACHNICK, R. (1991) 'Reflections on reflective teaching', in TABACHNICK R. and ZEICHNER, K. (Ed) *Issues and Practice in Inquiry-oriented Teacher Education*, London, Falmer Press, pp. 1–21.

ZEICHNER, K., TABACHNICK, R. and DENSMORE, K. (1987) 'Individual, institutional, and cultural, influences on the development of teachers' craft knowledge', in CALDERHEAD, J. (Ed) *Exploring Teachers' Thinking*, London, Cassell, pp. 21–59.

Index